Mobile App Development for Businesses

Create a Product Roadmap and Digitize Your Operations

Maja Dakić

Apress®

Mobile App Development for Businesses: Create a Product Roadmap and Digitize Your Operations

Maja Dakić
Novi Sad, Serbia

ISBN-13 (pbk): 978-1-4842-9475-8   ISBN-13 (electronic): 978-1-4842-9476-5
https://doi.org/10.1007/978-1-4842-9476-5

Managing Director, Apress Media LLC: Welmoed Spahr
Acquisitions Editor: Miriam Haidara
Development Editor: James Markham
Coordinating Editor: Jessica Vakili

Distributed to the book trade worldwide by Springer Science+Business Media New York, 233 Spring Street, 6th Floor, New York, NY 10013. Phone 1-800-SPRINGER, fax (201) 348-4505, e-mail orders-ny@springer-sbm.com, or visit www.springeronline.com. Apress Media, LLC is a California LLC and the sole member (owner) is Springer Science + Business Media Finance Inc (SSBM Finance Inc). SSBM Finance Inc is a **Delaware** corporation.

For information on translations, please e-mail booktranslations@springernature.com; for reprint, paperback, or audio rights, please e-mail bookpermissions@springernature.com.

Apress titles may be purchased in bulk for academic, corporate, or promotional use. eBook versions and licenses are also available for most titles. For more information, reference our Print and eBook Bulk Sales web page at http://www.apress.com/bulk-sales.

Any source code or other supplementary material referenced by the author in this book is available to readers on the Github repository: https://github.com/Apress/Mobile-App-Development-for-Businesses. For more detailed information, please visit http://www.apress.com/source-code.

Printed on acid-free paper

To my family—my husband Danijel and children Dorotea and David Dakić

Thank you for your support, patience and laughter which mean everything to me. You always believed in me and encouraged me to follow my dreams.
To my husband Danijel - your support has made me reach these heights, you are my ROCK!
To my beloved daughter Dorotea and son David who fill our life with happiness and fun - I love you to the Moon and back... and again!

This book is dedicated to you with all my love - you are my entire world!

To my Zesium company and CEO Darko Milić

Without your support, this book would not have been possible

You encouraged me to create our Zesium blog that inspired this book - your support has been invaluable to me over the years. You have guided me where there is no path and together, we have paved the way for our future victories!

To my friend and colleague, Branislav Manojlović

My dear friend, thank you for being there when I needed assistance - you were never too busy to extend a helping hand to me with your insights and feedback. I am truly grateful for your wisdom and friendship.

This book is for you!

Table of Contents

About the Author

Maja Dakić has logged nearly 15 years in business writing, translation, and sales. She earned a Master of Arts in English from the University of Novi Sad, Serbia. Following her sales and business writing years at different companies, Maja transitioned to the IT sector, where she helped promote companies across the world—landing media placements in local and national platforms. During that time, she gained a unique perspective on what it takes to develop, launch, and sustain successful software solutions and products. Today, she works at Zesium, where she has founded the Zesium blog and serves as Editor in Chief. She's a regular contributor to DataDrivenInvestor and DataSeries publications, where she has more than 40 published articles covering various technical topics.

About the Technical Reviewer

Branislav Manojlović is a mobile developer professional with several years of experience in mobile application development, focusing on iOS mobile application development. He has a background in research and mobile application testing and is familiar with phases of the software development life cycle (SDLC), Agile methodology, and Quality Assurance (QA) methodologies. Branislav graduated from the Faculty of Technical Sciences in Novi Sad, Serbia, with a degree in Computer Engineering and Telecommunications.

Acknowledgments

I thank my family for their support, patience, and laughter, which mean everything to me. You always believed in me and encouraged me to follow my dreams.

To my husband, Danijel—your support has made me reach these heights. You are my ROCK!

To my beloved daughter, Dorotea, and son, David, who fill our lives with happiness and fun—*I love you to the Moon and back... and again!*

This book is dedicated to you with all my love—you are my entire world!

Without the support of my company, Zesium, and CEO Darko Milić, this book would not have been possible. You encouraged me to create our Zesium blog that inspired this book—your support has been invaluable to me over the years. You have guided me where there was no path, and together, we have paved the way for our future victories!

My dear friend Branislav Manojlović, thank you for being there when I needed assistance—you were never too busy to extend a helping hand to me with your insights and feedback. I am truly grateful for your wisdom and friendship.

CHAPTER 1

Why Does Your Business Need a Mobile App?

In our first chapter, we will explain why your business needs a mobile application—we will list the reasons and the benefits along with crucial characteristics of a good mobile app and examples of some off-the-shelf solutions, which can help you until you develop your own mobile app.

1.1. Why Are Mobile Apps the Future of Business?

MOBILE is the new battleground!

Although the statement may seem a bit exaggerated to you, being digitally present is the life breath for any business today!

The recent statistical reports confirm that mobile apps dominate today—they outnumbered desktop users, and as in May 2023, 56.86% of all web traffic came through mobile devices as per Oberlo (Figure 1-1).

© Maja Dakić 2023
M. Dakić, *Mobile App Development for Businesses*,
https://doi.org/10.1007/978-1-4842-9476-5_1

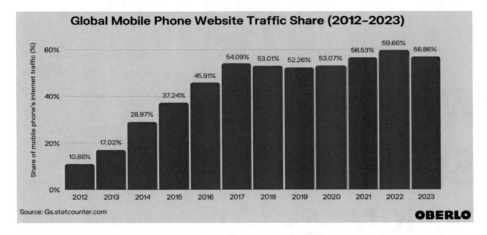

Figure 1-1. *Mobile Internet traffic from 2012 to 2023 (Oberlo, www.oberlo.com/statistics/mobile-internet-traffic)*

Leave aside the statistical details, and think about your own habits—how much time do you spend on your smartphone?

Since the majority of smartphone users, including yourself, spend their time surfing the Net, you should use this trend to your advantage regardless if you're an established business or a startup.

No matter if you listen to music, use social networks, or just chat with your friends, you went **MOBILE**.

Considering the **"mobile"** scene, company owners face the situation where websites are not enough anymore for business, since online activities have not only increased but moved to **MOBILE** (Figure 1-2).

Mobile applications have become **THE** most common tool—almost any business wishing to improve their ROI (*Return on Investment*) should think about investing in a mobile app as these have become a *"survival kit"* in an already clogged market.

Mobile apps are versatile, and you can use them not only for communication but also for informing, payment, socializing, **AND** running your business.

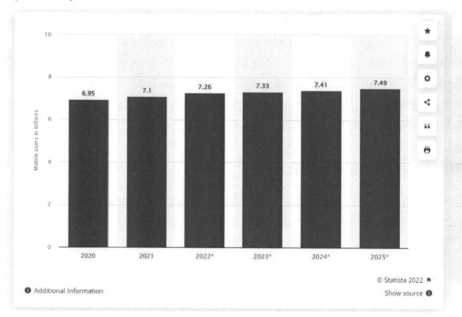

Figure 1-2. *Number of mobile Internet users in the world (Statista,*
www.statista.com/forecasts/1146312/mobile-internet-users-
in-the-world)

Improving your business means investing in new trends to gain a
competitive edge. However, most small- and medium-sized enterprises
(SMEs) and startups do not have enough budget. Hence, focus first on
building an MVP (*Minimum Viable Product*) and make a strong online
presence.

However you decide to take on, there's no better way than having a
mobile app.

What Is Mobile Commerce and Why Is It Crucial for Mobile Adoption?

Mobile commerce is highly important for mobile adoption in business.

Mobile commerce or mCommerce is browsing, buying, and selling products/services on mobile devices like smartphones—in common words, it is "*a retail outlet in your customer's pocket*."

As per a statistical report, more than 10% of all retail sales in the United States is expected to be generated via mobile commerce by 2025.

Types of mCommerce

Mobile commerce is not just buying a product online—it includes the entire purchase behavior made using a mobile device.

There are different variations of mCommerce:

- Browsing products via mobile devices

- Searching for specific products via mobile

- Reading product reviews or comparisons via mobile

- Purchasing app services (*food delivery apps* or *car sharing apps*)

- Purchasing digital content (*paid apps, music, videos,* etc.) via mobile

- Interacting with branded apps (like *the Amazon Shopping app*) via mobile

- Mobile banking

- Mobile retail payments (*Apple Pay* or *Samsung Pay*)

- Mobile person-to-person payments (*Venmo* or *Cash App*)

Mobile commerce is important because the number of mobile users is increasing—such growing numbers represent a huge increase in mCommerce activities in the future.

As per Statista, 72.8% of all retail ecommerce was generated via mobile commerce in 2021, which is a huge increase in comparison with 58.9% in 2017 (Figure 1-3).

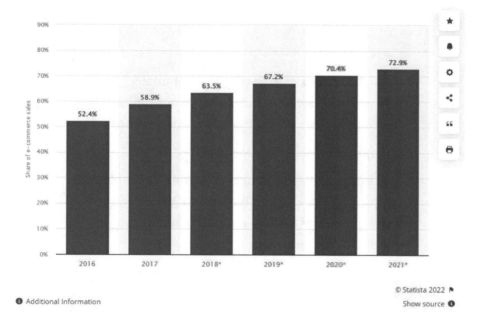

Figure 1-3. *Global mobile retail commerce share from 2016 to 2021 (Statista, statista.com/global-mobile-retail-commerce-share-2021)*

With the advances in technology, shopping habits have also evolved.

Modern customers want more information before spending their money—they usually check more details online like specifications, reviews, prices, etc., and they usually do it via their mobile devices.

Considering that mCommerce significantly influences customers' habits, it will only grow in popularity as more and more people own smartphone devices.

1.2. Reasons to Develop a Mobile App for Your Business

When thinking about mobile applications, one thing you surely ask yourself is

"Why would my business need any kind of mobile app?"
Before making a decision, think about several points:

- *How about similar apps?*

  Find similar apps like the one you're thinking about—check the reviews and comments as these can give you valuable insights if your app idea is viable.

- *Will my app solve users' problems?*

  Always **keep your customers in mind**—think about their pain points and add features that can resolve those issues and facilitate communication. Target that "*WOW*" unique feature if you decide to build your own app.

- *Will my target audience actually use the app?*

  Think about your users: How old are they? What do they like?

  Consider age, gender, habits, preferences, and similar. Track some metrics (e.g., *Google Analytics, Leadfeeder, Smartlook*, etc.) and find out how many users access your website via mobile.

- *Will the collected data simplify the process?*

  Simplifying data input for your customers, such as shipping address or billing, will offer a huge benefit; thus, they will be more prone to return and

do business with you. In case you depend on the
return customers (*food delivery services* and others),
removing the burdensome data input/entry may
increase sales.

- *Do you have a customer loyalty program or other
  incentives?*

  Mobile apps are effective tools **for loyalty programs**
  (*coupons, discounts,* or *other incentives*). Let your
  customers share content and promote your business
  on social media platforms. Try to exploit phone
  functionalities like the camera or accelerometer
  sensor and include them to your app if necessary
  (e.g., *wearables*), since these features offer
  experience that a website cannot compete with.

- *How about branding?*

  When your business offers a mobile app, your
  mobile users make your brand visible. Taking into
  account the "*effective frequency*" in advertising, the
  more people are exposed to your brand, the more
  they will recognize it and recommend it.

After you've thought about why your business would need a mobile
app, let's explore the reasons building a mobile application can grow your
business.

Allows Offline Access

One of the most important reasons to have your own mobile app is
to enable your customers to **access your business even without the
Internet**. Web applications cannot offer this feature because they function
only in an HTML environment, which requires the Internet connection.

Giving people access to your business wherever they are can be a valuable asset where any updates can be uploaded once the user goes back online.

For example, syncing cloud-based services and app data will smoothly occur between offline and online mobile apps.

Finally, mobile websites usually run on JavaScript, which may be buggy. Mobile apps are built using faster code and hold more of their data within the device's main processor.

Increases Brand Visibility

Your brand is what makes your business unique—your logo, colors, design, products, services, and other elements.

Developing a mobile app for your business is a good way to **increase your brand awareness**—additionally, you will have the edge over your competitors who do not have a mobile app.

Mobile apps enable you to add content and promotions and consistently keep your customers updated and engaged, contributing to your brand's credibility.

When customers can access your brand easily, it shows that you are there for them.

Improves Customer Ratings

Do not be fooled that web apps (like *Gmail, Figma,* etc.) are the same as mobile apps. Although they appear similar, mobile apps are more user-friendly and efficient to complete tasks.

Mobile apps exploit features like *GPS, Wi-Fi, touchscreen, camera,* and *connectivity tools* like Bluetooth and others. All these features seamlessly integrate with mobile apps, bringing more to satisfied customers.

Mobile apps can also integrate with other apps (*like social share features*) and automatically bring users to their favorite mobile app. You can also integrate popular messaging apps if your customers want to join chat groups and share their experience about your app or services.

In short, mobile apps **enable more personalization for users than desktop apps**.

Improves Customer Retention

If you want to retain your customers, you must provide top-notch features that match their needs.

Security is one of the reasons most users prefer mobile payment options—the data is stored on their personal devices, giving them more confidence to provide their personal information. You can offer your customers payment options like PayPal and similar tools to make the payments more secure.

Let's look at Starbucks, for example—26% of their total order transactions in U.S. had been through mobile payments as per their fiscal second quarter report from 2021 due to convenient features such as order-ahead. Try to implement incentive programs for your loyal customers within the app, which can increase customer retention even more.

When customers are happy with your service and **trust your mobile app**, they are most likely to come back and purchase again from you.

Provides Personalization

Personalization is one of the biggest assets you may provide to your customers.

Mobile apps are great for **personalization, contributing to greater engagement and conversions**. When a customer can customize any product/service per their own preferences, it shows that you care about their needs.

9

With personalization, you can gather important data on how customers modify your mobile app—with their consent, it allows you to personalize your services further and provide features they actually need.

Such insights will help you tweak your App Store Optimization (ASO) in a way more likely to generate more successful rates (Figure 1-4).

Figure 1-4. *Difference between SEO (Search Engine Optimization) and ASO (App Radar, appradar.com/academy)*

Serves On-Demand More Effectively

Mobile apps enable on-demand businesses to serve their customers more effectively.

If you are a small or medium business (SME), a mobile app can help maintain contact with your consumers even during uncertain times. For instance, during the pandemic, there was a huge increase in logistics and food delivery apps due to social distancing regulations. This situation gave a chance for SMEs to compete with bigger brands and meet consumers' needs amid the crisis.

Provide a mobile app to your customers and **deliver the best on-demand service despite the circumstances**.

Improves Digital Marketing

Mobile apps can easily be **integrated with various social media platforms** to strengthen your brand position.

Your customers can become your brand advocates as they recommend or share your app with their friends and family. When app users connect with other users, it increases promotion for your business.

While generating leads from your mobile app, it also improves your SEO within the digital marketing strategies.

You can also exploit features like push notifications to send localized promotions to your app users, thus connecting other marketing campaigns to your app.

Builds Customer Loyalty

Customer loyalty is crucial for long-term success.

As businesses cannot survive without customers, you should **build loyalty by consistently improving customer experience** to turn them into loyal brand ambassadors.

11

For instance, push notifications within mobile are more likely to get a response from users that convert rather than via your website. Mobile push notifications get a staggering 27.6% retention rate (90 days) as opposed to apps without notifications—it is worthwhile to think about this additional strategy once developing your mobile app (Figure 1-5).

The customer is the heartbeat of every business.

30, 60, 90 days retention, all industries

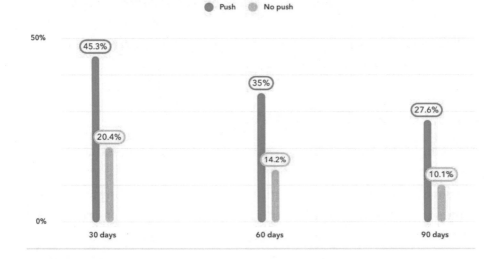

Figure 1-5. *Retention of users with push notifications over a period of time (30, 60, 90 days; GetVero/Digital Trends)*

Generates More Income

Since smartphones dominate the global market, it's not surprising that Google Play and Apple Store generate billions in combined sales through mobile and gaming apps.

The recent pandemic caused a massive increase in app development, user engagement, and app dwell-time rates.

With a mobile app, **you can earn in different ways** like *in-app ads*, *purchases*, *subscriptions*, *affiliate programs*, or *sponsorships*. (For more on app monetization, see Section "The Best Mobile App Monetization Methods".)

Bring your business to the digital marketing era by driving your business mobile.

1.3. Key Benefits of Mobile for Your Business

After you've realized that your business should "*app up*," let's list some key benefits of having a mobile app helping you grow your business.

Payment Convenience

Mobile payment is one of the most valuable benefits—this type of payments provides greater convenience to customers, being faster and more secure. Mobile payment is less complicated, allowing customers to pay without physically handing over cash or a credit card.

Check within your target market which payment services your customers prefer (*PayPal, Apple Pay, Visa, Samsung Pay,* or any other local solution) and share them with your development team.

No matter if you offer customers to purchase online or in a brick-and-mortar store, mobile payments are getting increasingly common to streamline the purchase process.

Payment convenience can greatly aid your business as customers today are more prone to quick and personalized shopping experiences.

Customer Loyalty

The value you can provide to your customers with a mobile app is unparalleled—it increases interaction with your customers to provide them with value they cannot get anywhere else.

A common approach is to create the loyalty program or upgrade the existing, if you already have one. Instead of "*vintage*" point collection, you can possibly facilitate the program by collecting the same points but converting them to discounts or other incentives. Another idea can be to offer additional rewards exclusively to your mobile app subscribers, thus encouraging them to go mobile.

If you provide easy access to your loyalty programs to your users, they will be more prone to follow up on their purchase in the future, resulting in more return customers and more sales.

Direct Marketing

Mobile apps provide ample information to users (*general*, *pricing*, *discounts*, etc.), and this can be a huge benefit for your business.

With a mobile app, you can provide such information directly to your customers—users can access info on discounts, promotions, or new products with just a tap. Direct communication is the best through push notifications, reminding them of your products whenever it is appropriate.

Be careful not to bother your customers—if you overuse push notifications, it can trigger counter-effects, and you may lose them. (For more on push notifications, see Section 4.3.)

Recognized Brand

No matter if you've just started your business or you've been operating for some time, the first thing you should always strive for is to be "***recognized***." Build your brand consistently since the market is overcrowded with mobile apps.

If you want your business to be recognized, don't JUST develop a mobile app—more important is to **PROVIDE VALUE** to your customers. That means having the necessary features to attract targeted users while appealing in design to contribute to your brand awareness.

It's all about trust—if you foster trust in your mutual relationship, the more likely your customers will engage with your business.

Remember, your mobile app can strengthen your brand and help educate your customers WHY they should trust you.

Always stay in touch with your customers.

Interaction and Engagement

What really matters for your business is to **enable customers to contact you easily**.

Many people prefer to communicate via a message rather than a phone call. Your users need an effective way to reach you—having a mobile app with the messaging feature can make a big difference.

Make sure to develop a mobile app that is able to **connect with your customers and save their sales records** for further insights.

A mobile app is a great way **to engage your users**—increase user acquisition and retention with features like push notifications, rewards, and loyalty programs. Many users respond positively to loyalty programs as they see them as a way to save money and earn rewards/points, special discount codes, or more.

All these features allow you to establish direct communication with your users.

Improved Social Media Presence

The trend of social media sync in mobile apps has proven itself as a game-changing tool.

Some studies have shown that most small- and medium-sized enterprises (SMEs) turn to social media as their marketing channel—social media shows **the success rate of your marketing efforts** and the entire growth process. That way, you will know if any stage of your marketing strategy falls behind and which part exactly so you **can improve or change the approach**.

Integrating your mobile app with social media provides features like *keyword monitoring, all-in-views of social media accounts, various ways to engage with customers, deep analysis and recommendation,* and more—all of these are beneficial for your business.

If you want to engage with your users, facilitate a registration/login process or enable your users to reach you at all times and sync up your mobile app with social media sites like Facebook, Instagram, LinkedIn, or other social media platforms.

Facilitate the entire process for your customers through social media.

Enabled Geo-targeting

If you have trouble with targeting your key users, a mobile app can save your effort with its location-specific and time-sensitive features.

Incorporating geolocation into your mobile app **enables you to send special offers to your users** who are close to your brick-and-mortar store.

Geo-targeting can help you cut your overhead costs, narrow your focus, and deliver ads specifically tailored (*deliver targeted ads to users at the right time and in the right place*) for your preferred user group. You can also display coupons and deals to potential users nearby or just help them find your business directly on a map.

Geo-targeting enables you to send personalized messages to your customers.

Directed Customer Feedback

Mobile apps provide various mechanisms for capturing user feedback.

Let's take a quick look at some of these customer feedback mechanisms:

- *Widgets*: Great for generating open-ended responses about a specific element of your brand.

- *Surveys*: To boost your response rates, it's important to ensure that the survey matches the context of your app and show them only when convenient.

- *"Rate my app" prompts*: App ratings not only inform you about customer satisfaction but also boost your app's reputation in the app store.

In a nutshell, mobile feedback mechanisms often have higher response rates, are available around the clock, and require low maintenance.

There are many things we can list as important when building a mobile app, but what to pay attention to if you wish your app to actively serve your customers?

In the next section, take a look at some **crucial characteristics of a successful mobile app** to cover when creating a mobile application.

Crucial Characteristics Your Mobile App Should Have

If you want to grow your business going mobile, your mobile app has to be the following.

Problem Solver

The most important for mobile apps is **to solve a problem for users**.

Ask yourself what your users' pain points are and add functionalities that resolve them, facilitating interaction.

Your app needs to meet the users' needs—clarify what you intend to achieve with your app, conduct a research, and once you identify users' problems, it will help you design your mobile app.

Simple and User-Friendly

When I say simple, I mean **UNCLUTTERED**. Include only a few basic features since the app needs to do one thing well—to solve a problem for users.

Start with your core focus, and only then shift focus to additional features—especially after your users supply valuable feedback.

Provide users with onboarding on how to navigate your app—if they cannot understand your app process, they will surely abandon it.

Focusing on details can help separate your app from other apps— include gamification, animations, sound effects, or other little quirks and bring life back to your app to make it a bit more impressive.

Your app must be **easy to navigate, user-friendly, and visually appealing** in order to retain users in the future.

Top Performer

A poor app performance will surely lead to negative user experience (UX) and losing valuable downloads, revenue, or brand recognition.

Think about some of the best apps you've tried—they **don't crash, they aren't slow**, and they do exactly what you expect them to do. Great apps offer fast response time, and their users can handle the app in just a couple of taps or seconds.

Your mobile app has to **launch quickly** the first time so not to keep users waiting for too long—**test your app regularly** to fix bugs or slow performance.

Available Offline and Personalized

Most mobile apps need an Internet connection to work—offering your users an app that functions even **offline** is a great advantage.

Offline access to features continues promoting a positive user experience, which makes a difference when ranking the top apps.

It is highly important for your app to create **a unique value**—the app users want personalization in a way where interactions are tailored to their preferences, location, and usage behavior.

Very important: **Leverage profile information insights from the user history** and deliver such personalized content to users, and you will surely get a positive experience and higher user engagement.

Freemium

With all the apps today in the stores, **offering your app for free will increase the possibility for your app's success**. Everyone likes to download apps for free and test them out prior to deciding if they're worth the price.

People like to see first-hand what you offer without any risks—offering a free basic app is key to grab the users' attention and increase traction. If they are satisfied with your app, they'll be happy to pay for in-app purchases or try premium features.

This approach cannot guarantee success, but it will definitely increase the number of people who will give your app a chance.

Updated Regularly

It is very important to **create a channel for communication**, allowing users to connect, get help, or simply provide feedback. **Feedback is essential**—gathering insights from users will ensure having the most effective user interface for your app. Create an easy-to-use feedback channel to encourage communication with users and prevent public negative reviews.

Another important process is to **create regular updates** to provide a mobile app with lasting popularity. Maintain ongoing updates—release continuous app updates and keep users coming back for more.

Built-In Metrics

Mobile app analytics serve to understand users' behavior—**tracking the data** can be used to measure the success of your app, provide further insights, and identify the points where you can make improvements.

Built-in app analytics allow you to track downloads, user engagement, and retention, and these numbers can be a life savior for your app. You can get full insights into how to boost user experience and optimize marketing strategy, which can make or break your app's success.

Early Marketed

No matter how good, flawless, or streamlined your app is, if no person uses it, it will not be successful.

You need to **start with your marketing strategy much before the launch** of your app since it gives a push to your users to try out your app the moment it hits the stores.

Great apps are promoted long before they are released for public purchase in the stores.

Marketing and app launch strategy should contain three phases: *prelaunch, launch*, and *post launch*. This way you provide the best strategy possible for an app to become visible and ensure that your plan promotes your app through various channels and techniques.

Nothing can guarantee the popularity of your app, but sticking by these simple features can greatly contribute to your app's visibility and provide a more solid chance for success.

1.4. BONUS: The Best Apps for Small and Medium Businesses

If you do not have time to wait until your own mobile application is developed, a business "*off-the-shelf*" app may be the right transitory solution for you.

I provide you with the list of some apps suitable for small and medium businesses, but make sure to do your own research and check which one would match your needs.

Cloud-Based Apps

G Suite

G Suite is great as it lets you share files among PCs, tablets, and smartphones. You have 30 GB online storage free, and you can upgrade if you need more storage space. You also get access to different Google apps to create docs, spreadsheets, presentations, charts, and more.

Dropbox Business

Dropbox Business is a cloud-based app enabling you to sync files and folders through various platforms on the go. Its plans are the best for the small businesses that count fewer than ten people.

Microsoft OneDrive

Microsoft OneDrive is similar to other cloud-based apps, allowing its users to store and share files through synced folders. Additional services like settings backup or an automatic photo upload work only on Windows 8 or Windows Phone users.

Microsoft Azure

Microsoft Azure is a platform designed to provide companies with built-in migration tools. It supports almost all the popular platforms like iPhone, Android, and Windows Phone apps along with its web service.

It is suitable for all business types from small- to medium-sized companies. It provides customer support online and has multilayer security with data backup, keeping your files safe even when giving access to employees.

Inventory Management

Inventory Now (iOS)

The Inventory Now app is designed only for iOS and includes functions of a sophisticated point-of-sale (POS).

This app allows you to keep track of your inventory throughout the product cycle—the barcode scanner function allows easy addition of new products, and data can be imported/exported as a spreadsheet while automatically backed up to your Dropbox account.

Veeqo

Veeqo syncs with popular ecommerce platforms like Magento, Shopify, Etsy, Amazon, eBay, etc. Many functionalities are available through the mobile app, enabling you to run your business remotely.

Sortly

The Sortly app allows you to manage your inventory remotely—you can maintain your catalogue with custom tags, look up barcodes, or use the built-in scanner. All of this is a part of its free version.

On Shelf

The On Shelf app tracks your inventory providing you with customers' purchase history, email-specific product offers to customers, the Import contacts option, and more. It comes in two apps each for iPad and iPhone, and the cloud backup is an additional cost.

Accounting/Finance

QuickBooks

QuickBooks is simple accounting software enabling you to track your business's sales and expenses, view financial statements, pay your employees and vendors, maximize your tax deduction, and much more.

QuickBooks connects to many accounts like business bank accounts, credit card accounts, PayPal, and Square, simplifying your accounting processes.

FreshBooks

The FreshBooks app provides insights into your cash flow, expenses, invoices, etc.—high-quality customer service is included in all plans at no additional cost.

You can create personal invoices to match your business, track and organize your expenses from anywhere, and create customizable reports.

Wave

Wave is the only **REALLY** free accounting software system, enabling you to use their online-based platform or mobile invoicing without payment for a subscription.

It is great for small businesses, independent contractors, or sole proprietors with fewer employees—it lets you track sales and expenses, manage invoices or customer payments, scan receipts, and generate accounting reports.

Gusto

The Gusto app makes your company's payroll, tax, and benefit processes more efficient as it manages all those plus online employee onboarding.

Gusto handles all local, state, and federal tax filings and automates deductions for benefits and workers' payments, as well as emailing digital pay slips to the employees.

POS/Payments

Square

Square enables its users to get a small, portable card reader that is attached to the mobile device to perform payments quickly and is said to be the best for businesses that perform in-person sales.

Square also offers a POS system under the name of Square Register for businesses, which is compatible with both iOS and Android devices.

PayPal Here

PayPal Here processes credit cards, checks, and invoices via your phone. The features include fund transfers, inventory management, and sales reporting along with a credit card and chip reader.

The important thing is that PayPal Here works through your PayPal account, so make sure you're synced up properly to use it.

QuickBooks GoPayment

QuickBooks GoPayment enables you to review analytics data, swipe or scan your credit card, monitor your best-selling items, as well as review keyed-in details to accept payments from customers.

It directly integrates with QuickBooks, TurboTax, or Mint.

Project Management/Organization

Trello

Trello is a good choice if you manage more than just a few employees—it is a card-based system that allows you to easily create, assign, monitor, and complete various tasks.

It can be used online or via your mobile device, and it integrates with apps like Evernote, Slack, and more.

Asana

Asana is similar to Trello, yet it uses a highly customizable list format that you can design as you wish.

You can share notes, upload files, and communicate without emails. Asana integrates with Google Drive, Dropbox, and Slack.

Basecamp

Basecamp allows you to organize your projects into six categories—your team can access a chatroom, a message board or any documents, task lists, or a calendar.

It offers integrations with various third-party tools and provides extensive reports, so you can have an overview of the work process in one place.

Evernote

Evernote is an app that enables you to keep your notes organized—you can store and share your personal or business to-do lists, reminders, and notes across mobile or desktop devices.

Communication

Slack

Slack is an instant messaging app with a simple and clear user interface (UI). You can send a message to your relevant team members, create different channels per different projects, and include only the relevant members. You also have voice and video call options as well as the option to send files via the app.

It also integrates with Google Drive, Asana, Salesforce, and more.

Zoom

Zoom is a video conferencing tool, and it is perfect if you like live communication rather than a chatroom. You can arrange for individual or group calls, record your conversations, and store them on the cloud. Unless you pay, you will be limited to 40-minute meetings, so it can be tricky if you need more time with your team members.

It also enables screen sharing, which enables smooth and quick communication.

Skype

Although Skype has been referred to as outdated, it is still a widespread common tool for internal communication. Its features cover most necessary things like group chats, file and screen sharing, free audio and video calls, and more. It is simple to use, which makes it the most popular tool.

However, Skype offers a more serious version being Skype Business, which provides similar services with an addition of integration with Office apps, online meetings, and few more add-ons.

Other
Expensify

Expensify is an app that keeps track of your expenses and makes the process less stressful for you. You can link your credit or debit card to your Expensify account, or you can take pictures of your receipts, and the app will automatically extract the relevant details. You can also make an expense report, which takes only a few minutes.

Mailchimp

Mailchimp allows you to build and manage your emailing lists and easily create and send newsletters, offers, etc. You can customize your email templates and track the performance reports on your email campaigns. Such insight enables you to send your customers more relevant offers. It may be referred to as a tool for bigger business, but it can make your business process much easier, so it's worth a try. It's freemium, but if you want an upgrade, it starts from $9.99/month.

Some alternatives to Mailchimp are SalesLoft, MixMax, Mailshake, and others.

Polaris Office

Polaris Office is an alternative to Apple's iWork allowing you to edit, create, and sync files from your phone or another device. You can create spreadsheets and docs and much more. Monthly subscription starts at $6.99.

Today, we have more tools than ever to help business owners like you—from accounting software to business management apps. All of them serve solely one purpose: **to enable small or medium business owners to remain agile and efficient**.

This is a suggested list of apps that can help you streamline your business operation, but keep in mind that there are many more apps depending on your business needs.

As a small business owner, the more you can automate tasks, stay organized, and streamline your operations, the more efficient and productive your business will become.

Key Takeaways

- Most people have already shifted to mobile devices, so it would be wise to think about going **MOBILE**—mobile apps are diverse, and you can use them for running your business. That is the very reason small and medium business (SME) owners need to catch on quickly.

- Mobile commerce is on the rise, and it includes all purchase decision behavior made by customers via a mobile device. Pay attention to this trend as mCommerce does not show any signs of slowing down since more people own a smartphone and decide to perform online actions via mobile.

- When considering whether to develop your mobile app, think about how your app will solve a certain problem, whether your target audience will use it, how will you gather users' data, etc. Then, consider what mobile apps can provide to your business like offline access, personalization, better customer ratings and retention, better brand visibility, and more.

- The benefits of the mobile app for your business are endless—from payment convenience, improved customer engagement, and loyalty to direct marketing and improved brand presence on the Web and social media networks.

- If you decide to develop your mobile app, keep in mind a few important characteristics—it has to resolve some issues for your users, it has to be simple and easy to navigate with top performance (*quick loading* and others), and it should provide offline and personalized services. Additionally, think about offering your basic app version for free to attract your target audience, and to do so, always start your marketing early.

- Until you develop your app, check my list of the most common "off-the-shelf" apps that can help any of your business departments. From accounting and payments up to communication, there is an app for everything. Always remember that generic apps have limited features and not the exact ones you specifically need.

CHAPTER 2

How to Choose the Platform for Your Mobile App?

In the previous chapter, I've explained why your business needs a mobile app—in this chapter, I will help you better understand different platforms for developing a mobile app and provide reasons a custom app can be a better choice for your business. Additionally, I bring you guidelines on how to choose a reliable development partner and what time it will take for your mobile app to be delivered.

2.1. Pros and Cons of Different Types of Apps

Which type of a mobile app should you build?

Unfortunately, there is no definitive answer.

The debate between *native* apps and *hybrid* apps and *web* apps is still ongoing, with no clear winner—all three choices have their own benefits.

I'll list them all along with their advantages and disadvantages for you to better understand and reach your own decision.

© Maja Dakić 2023
M. Dakić, *Mobile App Development for Businesses*,
https://doi.org/10.1007/978-1-4842-9476-5_2

Web Apps

According to TechTarget, a web app *"is an application that is accessed via a web browser over a network such as the Internet."*

So how is a web app different from a website?

The difference is subjective, but most would agree that a website is *"generally just informational while a web app provides additional functionality and interactivity"* (geeksforgeeks.org, Difference Between Web Application and Website, updated January 27, 2022).

For example, Wikipedia is a website as it provides information, while Facebook is a web app since it is more interactive.

Advantages

You do not need to download web apps as they load in browsers like Chrome, Safari, or Firefox (*or others*) and do not take up any memory or storage on users' devices. It is more cost-effective to develop web apps as they are responsive and easy to set up. With the availability of the cloud, storage is almost infinite. There are no frequent updates required, and it is easy to change the interface.

Recent web apps can also harness some features of native apps, and these are worth checking—progressive web apps (PWAs).

Disadvantages

Web apps lack some benefits like working offline, so users will have to be online to access the app. Web apps can also operate at a slightly slower speed than the one hosted on a server locally, and since dependent on the website, it may fail if the website experiences failure. During the development, make sure that your app is supported across a variety of browsers. Also keep in mind that web apps lack the feature of a quality control system.

Native Apps

A native app, or native application, is a software application built in a specific programming language, for the specific device platform, either iOS or Android.

Native iOS apps are written in Swift or Objective-C, and native Android apps are written in Java and Kotlin.

Advantages

Native apps are fast and responsive, providing the best experience to users through features like push notifications, which web apps lack. iOS (Apple) mobile devices currently do not support mobile web push notifications although Apple has announced the support will come in 2023. For Android, their mobile devices support mobile web push notifications for users running Chrome, Firefox, and Opera. User value is another advantage since the app icons have value that web apps lack—making your app act like the rest of the user experience is a great asset. This is noticeable when dark mode became available on both platforms.

Native apps can exploit the device features like camera, compass, accelerometer, and more to make the experience even better. All in all, by building native, you do not have to compromise with UI/UX for your app.

Disadvantages

Android and iOS are native apps, so you would have to work with two teams and develop two applications for every platform. It takes longer to build, and the cost can be higher due to the fact that you build two apps instead of only one.

Cross-Platform Apps

Cross-platform apps are compatible with multiple mobile operating systems (OSs). They are usually written in React Native, Cordova, Google's Flutter, etc.

Advantages

Cross-platform apps are built with just one set of code, reducing time and cost of development as you employ only one team. However, the entire process timeline depends on your app's complexity, features, and integration, so take this into account. Since you can launch these apps on multiple platforms, it provides you with an opportunity to reach a larger audience at the same time.

Disadvantages

Cross-platform apps have integration challenges due to inconsistent communication between the device and non-native components—as a result, they may appear slow at times. However, performance greatly varies depending on the technology, so check the available apps on the market to get the feel of such apps' performance.

Cross-apps can have a delayed access to the latest updates of the certain platform and cannot fully utilize the advantage of native-only features to deliver excellent user experience.

Hybrid Apps

You install it like a native app, but it's actually a web app on the inside.

Hybrid apps, like web apps, are built with JavaScript, HTML, and CSS and run in something called a web view, a simplified browser within your app.

Advantages

Instead of building two apps, you're building one app, and by tweaking it a bit, it works on both platforms. Considering this, you'll probably require fewer developers, thus reducing the time of development. Hybrid apps are also easier to scale to another platform, and similar to native apps, hybrid apps let you retain the same ability to access device features.

Disadvantages

Performance is probably the biggest disadvantage of hybrid apps. They load in a browser-like component called a web view; they are only as good as the web view, which is responsible for displaying the UI and for running JavaScript code. By building a hybrid app, you won't be able to please both camps—if you try too hard to customize the app based on the platform, it may end up costing the same as two native apps.

There are some ways you can do this, which we will discuss shortly.

2.2. Reasons to Consider When Deciding on a Mobile App Platform

When it comes to choosing the right development platform for the mobile app you have in mind, there's no easy way to decide.

As we already listed pros and cons of each variation of the apps, try to consider the following:

- When it comes to choosing your mobile platform, the **target audience** is one of the biggest determining factors. If you want your app to target the mass market, you should prioritize the most popular Android and iOS platforms. Try to check other alternative OS apart from these main ones, to be sure you target the right market.

35

- When choosing the right platform, you have to know **where the most users will be** so that you can capture them at the right place and at the right time. Would you target a market in which a particular operating system (OS) is more readily accepted and is used by a big percentage of the demographics? If this is the case, a native solution is a better option than a cross-platform one. In the event of a divided market and if you want a user base that's more extensive, then it would be wise to opt for a hybrid or a cross-platform app (see Section 2.1).

- An app with an **engaging UI** delivering a **streamlined user experience** has a better chance of success when compared with those with a shabby outlook.

- The best platform should be able to provide **integration standards** with third-party services. The platform should also support relevant features, which include scalability, store deployments, access control, and synchronization of data.

- A mobile application development platform should also have **middleware and extensible back-end services** so it could offer features like push notifications, authentication, and storage of data.

- Don't forget that app development may involve many **hidden costs**. Mobile application platforms entail development upgrades, efforts, and app maintenance that greatly vary, from one development company to another.

- The final decision also depends on the **budget** you're willing to allocate. This is because building numerous native apps could significantly cost more compared with single cross-platform app development.

There is no absolute winner as it all depends on your company needs. When weighing pros and cons, native development sounds like the right choice. However, keep in mind that what works for one app may not apply to another—it all depends on what type of app you are trying to build.

Do your own research when deciding on the best platform for your mobile app, and it will help you reach the right decision.

How a Custom-Built Mobile App Benefits Your Business

If you wish to streamline your business operations and increase efficiency, a custom mobile app might be the answer to your problem instead of "*off-the-shelf*" products.

Prior to anything, consider the pros and cons of developing a customized app vs. web-based applications that users can access from their desktops (see Section 2.1).

As per Statista, people are more prone to spend time on smartphones—around 50% of the Internet traffic comes from mobile phones (Figure 2-1).

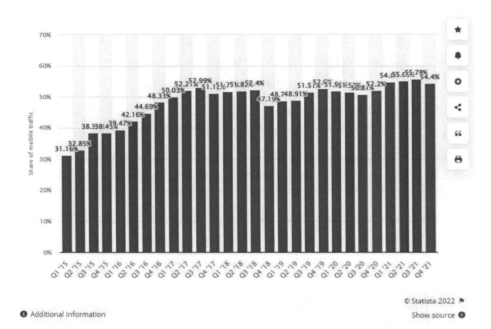

Figure 2-1. *Percentage of mobile traffic worldwide in 2015–2022 (Statista, January 2022,* www.statista.com/statistics/277125/ share-of-website-traffic-coming-from-mobile-devices/)

Once you've decided your business needs a custom-built app, explore the ways how such an app can help improve productivity and boost revenue in your company.

Take a look at how a custom mobile app can become your biggest asset for your business.

Follows YOUR Needs

When people want to have clothes sewn specifically for their body measurements, they go to the tailor. The same goes for your business needs as well.

If you wish your business to offer a complete experience to its users, you should make a customized app. It serves your specific needs the best as opposed to a generic app that may not match all your requirements.

The customized app has features (*admin back end, communication framework*, etc.) streamlined to make a positive impact on your business.

Provides Better Personalization

Having a customized mobile app is perhaps the only way to ensure the best user experience.

Custom apps are built with a specific target audience in mind; thus, it can help you attract new and retain the existing customers.

Features and functionalities vary, depending on your business needs, but as long as it improves customer engagement, you can hope for a higher ROI.

Improves Productivity

No matter the size of your business, a custom app can facilitate smooth workplace collaboration by integrating various functionalities—improved efficiency will trigger increase in productivity.

In the case of generic apps, it is a rare case that those apps and your existing software package can interact with each other seamlessly, and this can lead to a decline of your employees' productivity—they could experience errors continually, thus failing to complete their work effectively.

Increases Profit

A custom app adds value to your revenue outcome. With all features at hand, you can offer better service to your customers and also motivate them to spend.

The custom app allows you to take advantage of such revenue options. Since a custom app always keeps your business requirements in mind, it actually acts as a far-reaching app with multiple functions so you won't need multiple apps.

Also, as these apps are tailored for your specific work process, you will get business ROI increased in turn.

Scalable

Ready-made apps are as they are—if the company that built it shuts down or simply decides not to maintain the app anymore, you will be in a fuss searching for another supported software.

When your business starts growing, mobile apps allow you to cast more power to the mix. Of course, this may sometimes depend on your development partner, so choose wisely (see Section 2.3).

Scalability of your custom app follows the scope of your business—if you plan to expand, you can notify your development team so that all features are built at the right time.

This way, you ensure your app serves your purpose and can scale up easily if the need arises.

More Secure

Security is the foundation of a successful online business.

The success of your app depends highly on its security. There are many threats but also solutions to how your app developers can handle those threats (*obfuscating code, protecting local storage*, etc.).

"Off-the-shelf" apps may or may not have specific security features, and it can put your business data at risk. Using a multi-vendor app means you have less control over how secure your business transactions are.

Having a custom app made solely for your business can fortify your data security system.

You can choose on-premises storage or the cloud for your custom application, or if you're a large business, you can determine different levels of authentication to control the accessibility of employees—this level of security is impossible with generic apps.

Easier for CUSTOMers

Custom apps allow you to send personalized updates related to your products/services to your customers in real time.

If given consent, you can access customer details and receive valuable feedback, which can be a great asset when you strive to improve customer retention.

The custom app can always help you gather required client information; it can save time for your clients and employees especially that they don't need to submit any hard-copy documents.

Simple Access

With a custom app, you are able to access all your documents (*files, invoices, tasks, calendars,* etc.) at any time internally with your employees or with your clients quickly—you can easily synchronize your phone with your desktop.

Custom apps enable you to keep a real-time check on your project progress and deadlines. The updates can be sent upon completion of each phase of the project, thus managing the work process for each stage of the project effectively.

"Off-the-shelf" apps, from a business perspective, don't treat your customers in a special way.

A custom app is actually the thing that preserves your customers as well as converts any possible prospects into real customers. Evaluate your business strategy and think about building a more powerful tool that can put your company ahead of the pack.

In the next part, we will list the reasons native mobile applications can be better for your business.

Why Do Native Apps Outperform?

In this section, let's examine why native mobile apps offer considerable advantages over mobile websites or hybrid apps.

Better Performance

When a B2B customer places an order on a mobile device, it **HAS** to work.

Native apps are quick and responsive with quick page loads, which is highly important for flawless user experience. For example, if there are interruptions in the connectivity of an ecommerce mobile app, you cannot ensure an accurately placed order. This can be the key difference between getting and losing a customer.

Mobile users reported that a mobile browser gave more challenges (e.g., *pinch and zoom screens* or *the lack of push notifications to provide quick updates*), adding that mobile sites can be slower than apps.

Works Offline

The ability to search for products and enter orders, even offline, is another crucial reason mobile users prefer B2B mobile apps over mobile-optimized sites.

As mobile devices are made to use on the go and it frequently happens that connectivity is lost while traveling, being able to continue working, even offline, is an important advantage of B2B mobile apps over an optimized site.

A native mobile commerce app can exploit the mobile device's camera as a barcode scanner, letting your buyer to quickly place an order whenever the need arises.

Better Personalization

For business users that have multiple accounts on multiple sites, the ability to quickly and easily log in, search for products, review past history, and complete their transaction is a real benefit.

Such features can greatly aid your users, personalizing their experience and simplifying the entire process for them.

Better Customer Loyalty

Native apps avoid elements that don't work well on the small screen yet provide the ones that are easy to see and use on the small screen along with simple and consistent navigation.

Although the initial expenses may be higher with native apps, your end result will save you time and money in the long run. By offering better performance and leveraging the device features, you're able to offer your users better and more personalized experiences.

The combination of native mobile app benefits will result in higher conversion rates and will eventually increase your customers' loyalty.

More Interactive

Native apps are more interactive and intuitive and run much smoother considering user input and output. They have better user experience as the flow is more natural (*due to specific UI standards for each platform*).

Native apps bring a different approach on how to deal with content, discarding visual clutter and displaying content in the most intuitive way possible for the mobile users, even offline.

These apps outrun the others because they are built in accordance with both technical and user experience guidelines—they can also quickly access the built-in capabilities of the user's device (e.g., *contacts*, *GPS*, *camera*, etc.).

The decision to build either a native, web, or hybrid mobile app should depend on your business objectives. It's important to work with an excellent app development company that specializes in platform-specific design and development.

I would usually recommend native app development as it is best to stay with native and not sacrifice on the design elements that are unique to each platform.

2.3. How to Choose the Best Development Partner for Your Mobile App

Today, mobile apps have become the survival kit for every online business and the best way to reach out to your target customers.

Choosing a proper mobile app company is a crucial decision, yet with so many app development companies on the market, it makes it difficult to reach a definite decision.

If you're thinking how to start your search, check these simple steps that may help you reach a smarter decision.

1. Define Your Requirements

List your own precise specifications and clearly outline exact things you want in your mobile app. Remember, it all depends on your industry and the type of products/services you offer, but the core remains the same.

Before you reach out to any app company with your request, make sure you have the clear picture of

- The goals of your app

- Features and functions necessary

- Whether it fits your business model

- Interaction with other software (*payment, accounting, CMS*, etc.)

Even if you don't have precise answers to each of these points, don't worry—a skillful mobile app team should suggest ideas that can help your app be more efficient.

At Zesium , for example, our first step of development is discussing all the details thoroughly with our partners—only then our team creates a feature list and a mind map that outline both the purpose of the app and the way users will use it.

2. Analyze Existing Developers

Check the reputation of the existing companies by a short online research.

Collect the details via the published reviews for app development, number of years of experience, product portfolio, different types of services offered, background, previous client records, etc.

To stay on the right track, consider a reputable company that has a demonstrated track record of high-quality work.

This research can help you shortlist the right kind of mobile app development companies.

3. Define Your Budget

Once you define the requirements of your app, you need to define the budget to complete your business goal.

The best approach would be to contact mobile app development experts since there are no exact guidelines for the costs—it all depends on the complexity of your app.

There are some app development calculators online like App Development Cost Calculator or Digitalya App Cost Calculator so you can try to get a rough estimation for your mobile app idea.

Working with small development companies may end up costing you more in the long run—if they have less expertise, they can make mistakes, which you will need to pay someone else to fix, and sometimes an inexperienced team can run over budget.

On the other hand, the general rule says the larger the firm, the larger the price. Larger companies are better equipped to guarantee high quality and stick to the initial budget, but many of them have a lot of overhead, which increases the cost.

Since each project demands a specific kind of development, make sure you choose the most suitable developer for the job at hand.

4. Use Your Social Media

In your search for a trustworthy developer, don't forget your professional network like LinkedIn —all you have to do is to inform your connections about your needs. You can do it by personal posts or social ads, but using both options would be the best choice. Your post should be visual, relevant, and with a strong call to action (CTA).

Social media like Facebook, Twitter, or Instagram can also be great tools for finding the right mobile company—you can describe your project, post the requirements, and wait.

Generally, it works the same way like with LinkedIn; you just need to be persistent. The more motivated you are, the better the chances are to find the right company.

5. Visit Dedicated Websites

Websites like Clutch, GoodFirms, Toptal, App Futura, or DesignRush are excellent choices since they contain app development companies' profiles, along with their portfolios and reviews of their past work.

You can also visit the sites that host freelance profiles such as Upwork.

The best approach would be to reach out to companies that were mentioned on tech-related news sites and have the proper experience within mobile app development.

All the above-mentioned sites have a reputation system where you can review a prospect's past work and read their reviews.

6. Check for Support

Some online companies focus solely on selling their applications instead of making them beneficial for customers.

If a company doesn't offer solid support, it could be a big setback for your business especially if you have spent a significant amount of money to develop the same app.

However, long-established companies know the value of their customers and will gladly assist on issues related to the maintenance of their mobile applications.

7. Check for an Innovative Approach

Mobile app development companies that develop innovative solutions and practice the latest methodologies (*Kanban/Scrum/Agile*) would be a great choice for your business app.

Your company can win a huge business momentum online if you hire innovative mobile development companies because they develop mobile apps for forward-looking businesses.

Always try to reach out to such companies who can improve your business standards.

8. Check for Cost-Effectiveness

Consumers usually want to buy high-quality products at affordable pricing. Since developing a successful app is not an easy task, there is always a fight between cost and quality. That is usually because top-quality applications cost a lot and vice versa.

However, if a company has a longtime existence across the world, then the cost of their products sold will be relatively less. Only such companies can provide their services at efficient costs.

Companies in the United States and Western Europe are regarded as the most expensive, while SE Asia offers the lowest prices.

Finding a good compromise between price and quality lies in the middle.

9. Check for a Technically Efficient Company

It is important to check if the mobile app development companies consist of technically efficient developers prior to handing over your mobile app development project to them.

It's also necessary to know which technologies the company works with and whether they are capable of putting up well with the application development idea and the platform you chose to go with.

Mobile app companies that work exclusively on mobile app development technologies are a good choice.

Keep in mind that a top-quality mobile app development company should understand your exact requirements and should never compromise on the quality of the interface.

So don't rush when you are making a choice, but carefully consider all pros and cons and figure which one works the best for YOU.

2.4. BONUS: How Long Does It Take to Develop a Mobile App?

Once you decide that you will develop a mobile app for your business, you will face the most common question for all business owners and startup founders: *How much time and effort does it take to create an app*?

The answer is not as simple as the question, but let's try to do some rough estimation.

Data from different studies says that it takes 4–5 months to create a mobile app.

For example, take a look at what a study by GoodFirms says (Figure 2-2).

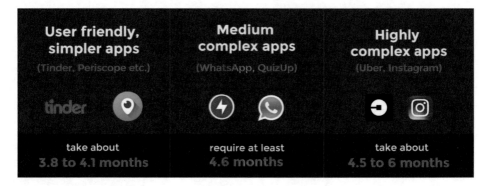

Figure 2-2. *Division of mobile app development complexity and timeline (GoodFirms)*

These studies suggest that app development is roughly from 4 to 6 months to complete; however, keep in mind that there are variations and they'll depend on additional features you'd like to include, besides the basic ones.

Small apps would have features such as *login, newsfeed,* and a possibility to *connect and interact with friends.*

A medium-sized app would have all mentioned plus *sharing settings* (sharing with external platforms), *geo-localization, video support,* and *some sort of integration.*

The most complex apps would additionally feature *multiple languages, robust settings, photo/video editing,* and *algorithms allowing to receive tailor-made content.*

The more complex the app, the longer it takes to be developed.

Start with a V1.0 MVP

Although an app takes roughly 4–6 months to develop, the first version of an app (**v1.0 app**) may be built in less than 4 months, but it depends on many factors.

Some of these factors are as follows:

- *Apps range from a few weeks' simple apps to years-long work since quality takes time.*

- *Apps that target many features require more time to build than simpler ones.*

- *The timeline is somewhat determined by budget.*

- *A team of cross-technology experts can speed up the building process.*

- *A more efficient timeline can be achieved with the team with the right skills and experience.*

Too many features for v1.0 apps can cause problems since apps that are more focused will perform better, so keep it simple.

The following figure is my favorite when it comes to understanding the MVP and how it should be built (Figure 2-3).

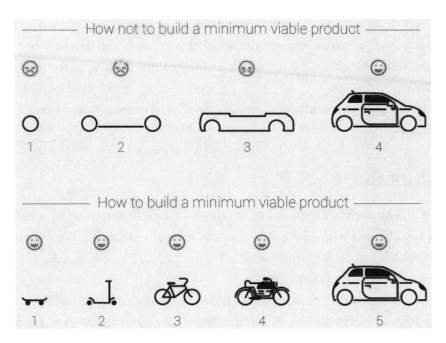

Figure 2-3. *How much does it cost to develop the MVP (Business of Apps)*

Key Stages in App Development

Since an app development is a repetitive process with different stages of researching, building, testing, tweaking, and releasing your app, let's list them.

Idea!

The first stage is researching your "**app idea**."

List the reasons you want to create an app, how it will contribute to your customers, whether there is an existing similar app on the market, how will it be different, and what will it do for your consumers and similar.

You will have to do extensive research on the target market demand and establish customer pain points, market size, and validation of your product idea. You should also research your competitors' apps for further insights.

This stage will usually take several weeks of research and idea validation.

Feature Set

Now think about your app's functionalities—*what do you want your app to do, which tasks will it perform, how will it handle data, etc.* For example, *will it deliver products? Track your fleet in real time? Provide quick communication and payment?*

Some features are more general like *login*, and most apps have them, while other features like *geolocation* will be found only in relevant apps like car sharing apps or delivery apps.

To help you, here are some features you can include: *sign-up/login, social login (Facebook, Instagram, Twitter, etc.), profile management, the search option, call and chat options, geolocation, group chat feature, voice and video calls, real-time tracking of drivers/vehicles/cargo, journey history, map view, payment method, real-time traffic updates,* and many more.

You should also establish "*use cases*," tailored to function as templates on how your ideal users will interact with the app. You also have to decide whether your app will be available for iOS, Android, and/or Windows.

Although it is said that developing an app for more than one OS takes longer to finish, it is not always the case. If Android and iOS teams work side by side, they can both finish approximately at the same time. However, the pricing for creating an app for both platforms will certainly be higher.

Expect for this stage to take 3–5 weeks figuring out core functions and features.

Wireframing

Now it's time for you to create a "storyboard" and test your idea against reality.

You (or your development team) should create wireframes—the visual architecture of the app—as they represent each screen of your app and the way how those screens are linked.

Today, it's easy to do wireframes since there are numerous software tools (InVision, Adobe XD, Balsamiq) that allow you (or developers) to quickly create prototypes.

After wireframing is done, you should test the prototype work. You let users or friends "play" with your app and provide you with valuable feedback.

For example, some people choose to develop wireframes early during the features stage, which greatly helps with basic visual representation.

This stage requires from a few days to a few weeks depending on the complexity.

App Development

The app development consists of multiple activities like back end, front end, design of specific screens, creating UI resources, and QA testing during the development. However, the two biggest parts are back end and front end.

Front end consists of interactive elements visible to users. Front-end developers are responsible for the look, feel, and final design of the interface.

Back end is composed of the logistics that goes behind making the front end functional. Back-end development focuses on how the app works. It consists of a server, database, and application—it's what communicates the information to the users. It includes all activities happening "*behind the curtain*" such as *database management, server-side logistics, data integration*, and more.

It takes approximately 18+ weeks to complete. (*It is said 10 weeks for back end and 8 weeks for front end, but it usually differs depending on the complexity of the app.*)

Beta Testing

Prior to beta testing, detailed testing should always be performed during all phases of the software development life cycle (SDLC).

In the beta testing stage, the app is examined under various conditions to ensure it's bug-free and that users are comfortable with the interface.

You should only launch beta testing once you've thoroughly completed alpha testing with your own coding team. You should test the app for usability, compatibility, security, interface checks, stress, and performance.

In user acceptance testing, you'll discover if the mobile app works for your end users or not.

Don't forget it's a good idea to test early and often—it will keep your final costs low. There are websites exclusively dedicated to beta testing like Beta Family, BetaList, Erli Bird, etc.

Beta testing can take 3–4 weeks to collect all relevant details for further improvement.

The Launch!

Your app is finally finished, tested, and ready to launch—by now your app has a name, a logo, a short description, and promotional images.

The policies for launching an app are different for different application stores, so keep in mind that this may take a couple of days.

So your app is launched?

Yes! Congrats! You can celebrate, but your work isn't done yet.

Maintenance

As your app will be in the hands of the users, you will get a lot of feedback—you need to incorporate the feedback into the future versions of an app so to improve the usability and functionality.

It is also important to utilize analytics to track app performance like downloads, user engagement, and retention.

This usage behavior will give you insight into how to improve the app and enhance the user experience.

Key Takeaways

- When deciding on the right platform for your mobile app, always think of your target audience. Although cross- and hybrid versions have their own benefits like reduced cost, timeframe, and wider reach, some downfalls follow like poor performance and limited customer experience. Native apps may take longer to develop, but they are faster and responsive with a wider range of functionalities. Additionally, the levels of service you can provide with native versions are irreplaceable for your business growth.

- When thinking of going down the custom app path, remember that "off-the-shelf" apps, from a business perspective, don't treat your customers in a special way. A custom app is actually the thing that retains your customers as well as converts any possible prospects into real customers.

55

- When choosing your app development partner, do your own research—start with an online search (local or wider), define your app scope and budget, visit dedicated sites that provide company reviews, check the portfolio for tech efficiency, and always double-check for support and maintenance services.

- Roughly speaking, estimates per each of the stages in app development would result in the final timeframe of approximately **4–6 months** to build a mobile app. Building a mobile app can be a long and complex process that requires lots of preparation to do it properly. You should remain flexible in your timeline expectations and make sure to have access to your mobile development team in the post-launch stage.

- Always strive for the MVP version first—this way you can reduce the time of the development and provide your customers basic features that work smoothly. User feedback will help you tweak your product development roadmap and possibly upgrade your app further to correspond to your customers' needs. No matter if you develop an MVP or a full product, stages are the same for all: put down your idea into visual representation or wireframes, find a good development partner, and once all details are confirmed, you can hope for your first app release.

CHAPTER 3

Create a Mobile App Product Roadmap

The previous chapter brought some light on different platforms for mobile apps and how to better understand the time necessary for a mobile app to be developed as well as short guidelines on how to choose a reliable mobile app development partner. In this chapter, we move to more concrete aspects like how to turn your idea into a roadmap and how to write one along with some specific examples of the best roadmap tools to use. Additionally, I bring you a list of mistakes you should be aware of when developing your business mobile app.

3.1. Turn Your Idea into Actionable Milestones

In order to start developing your product, you need to write your mobile app specification.

You can do it on your own or ask professionals to help, but it is an important step in a successful product development.

An **app specification** is a detailed document about the app requirements that will align a development team with your idea—it helps to clearly understand what needs to be done.

© Maja Dakić 2023
M. Dakić, *Mobile App Development for Businesses*,
https://doi.org/10.1007/978-1-4842-9476-5_3

A mobile app specification should be clear, understandable, and straight to the point. Bear in mind that you can always modify the requirements along the way, and if you do it properly, you'll prevent any unpleasant surprises at the end.

Let's dive first into what types of milestones a specification should contain.

1. Short Company Description

The first section should include a **short description of your company**— your vision, your nature of business, how long you've been operating, and if you possess (*or released*) any prior software solutions or apps.

Such information provides a picture about your company, principles you want your solution to be based on (*in case you have any previous solutions*), and the nature of your business processes.

A development partner can then gain more insight into your way of doing business and your idea—as a result, they can match the desired solution to your actual business strategy more easily.

2. Your App Idea

In this section, write down **the basic purpose of your app and what problem it should solve**.

Prior to any work, conduct market research—evaluate your current customers, review your competitors, define target audience, and similar.

Ask yourself: *What is your app intended to achieve? What central pain point does it need to resolve?*

Table 3-1 can help you organize your research.

Table 3-1. *How to Organize Market Research (ChromeInfotech by Medium)*

Primary Research		Secondary Research	
What does it include?	**How to do research?**	**What does it include?**	**How to do research?**
Helps with determining the need for your mobile app idea in the market	Through various online forums, focus groups, social media platforms, personal visits, using landing pages, Facebook ads	Helps with strengthening the mobile app's core	Do a SWOT (Strength, Weaknesses, Opportunities, and Threats) analysis
Helps with framing the business plan (model)	Research on sales and marketing strategy; define the company and business model, and analysis of present market conditions	Assists with developing a practical social media strategy	Research target audience, optimize social media accounts, know what is trending, use both—paid and organic strategy
Helps with creating an effective marketing strategy	Define how you want to market your app, decide between—organic and paid marketing, identify pre-launch and post-launch pitfalls	—	—

Source: https://medium.com/@ChromeInfotech

Another way to analyze your product development can be setting SMART objectives:

> *Specific*: Set realistic numbers. For example, *"I want to generate more than 100 downloads within a week after the app is released in the app store."*
>
> *Measurable*: Make sure your goal is trackable. For example, *"I want new users to log into my app at least once daily."*

Attainable: Give yourself a challenging goal but not impossible. For example, "*I want to reach a million downloads in a year.*"

Realistic: Be honest with yourself and don't forget about the hurdles you need to overcome. For example, "*I want my MVP to be finalized in 2 months.*"

Timely: Give yourself a deadline, but don't set an unspecific goal like "*I'll finalize my app some day next year.*"

Since the document will be used by your development partner to create more technical records, try to be as specific as possible.

Try to include market research results, any analytics you may have, previous user feedback if any, etc. as it will only help your product to be developed exactly as you wish.

3. Your Target Audience

The next step is to **define your target audience**—try to determine who will use your app and who are the people most likely to buy it: end users or businesses.

This will help you get a better idea of the functional requirements of the app to be delivered.

The target audience defines the user experience (UX) and a feature set to a great extent. For example, a social app would have a sharing option as a core feature for an app aimed at teenagers, while an app for children would be simpler with large screen elements. If you want to develop an app for tourists, you will definitely need a geolocation feature and possibly offer in-app payment options.

Try to outline a general description of your "***user persona***," describing it in as many details as possible—*age, occupation, app experience, hobbies, preferences (sports, music,* etc.).

Once you do that, it will be much easier to outline the app features.

4. Preferred Technology Stack

This section is more a part of technical documentation—you should think about whether you want to target Android/iOS users or both platforms (see Section 2.1) as it greatly influences budget scope and delivery time.

If you decide to move forward with native apps, it instantly means developing two applications.

You do not have to develop both versions at the beginning—check your research on platform users (Android/iOS) and develop firstly the one that the majority of your target audience uses.

In case you need to specify which device will support your app—whether it will be responsive, cross-platform, etc.—check a list of reference devices:

- Desktop browsers

- Mobile website (browser)

- *Native mobile apps*: Android, iOS, Windows

- Tablet

- *Smart TV*: Android TV, Tizen OS (Samsung), Firefox OS (Panasonic), webOS (LG)

- Facebook applications

- *Virtual Reality*: HTC Vive, Oculus Rift, Samsung Gear VR, PlayStation VR

- Kiosks

Always pay attention to screen orientation—for mobile and tablets, designs can appear different in portrait and landscape modes. If you have any doubts about it, conduct a usability test. In Figure 3-1 below, check the safe design resolutions per different screens.

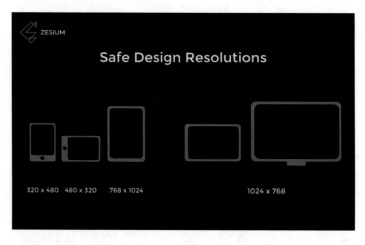

Figure 3-1. *Safe design resolutions (Zesium)*

When considering technologies, if you have any certain preferences, share them with your development partner so they can arrange for the **necessary software capacities**. This part is important if you wish to upgrade an existing product—it's a must to inform your developers as they need to use the same technology to ensure smooth integration.

In case you don't have any idea on technologies you want to use, consult your development partner, and they will surely advise you on the best possible solution for your app to function flawlessly. Always seek for more than one proposal on the technology stack, to avoid development within the technologies that suit the development company and not your own app.

5. List of Features

In this section, try to describe the features you'd like to have in your app.

Try to imagine how the users will use your app and break it into individual steps. Take notes for a start—imagine you open your app, a splash screen appears, and then try to list the actions you take as a user.

For example, some basic features may be as follows:

- *Login*: The most used feature—it can be login via email, or you can choose a social login through social networks to help users log in without too much hassle.

- *Payment system*: If you're building an app with any kind of paid services, you will need secure payment gateways like Stripe, Braintree, or others.

- *Geolocation*: This feature uses your location, and it's essential with apps for taxi or car sharing apps, rental platforms, social apps, etc.

- *Push notifications*: You'd need to let your developers know if you want this feature in your app—push notifications must fit with the app goals, so be careful with this feature.

- *Chat*: This is very useful but only in the apps where chat is necessary like social apps, dating apps, etc. You can have live chat or a comment-based chat depending on the app requirements.

- *Monetization*: If you plan to include some type of paid content or in-app ads, you would need this feature.

You can also prioritize the features and make clear which ones are more important than others with the MoSCoW method, marking them with **M**ust, **S**hould, **C**ould, and **W**on't levels of priority (Figure 3-2).

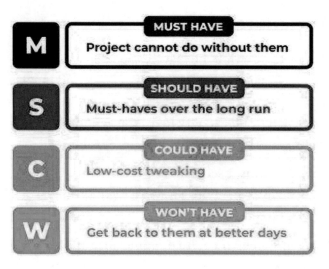

Figure 3-2. *MoSCoW method for feature prioritization (Railsware)*

What's been given is just a short list of features that you may wish to implement in your app—with your own feature list, your development team can determine which integrations, APIs, and other third-party elements will be needed.

6. List of Admin Features

Most apps usually have an administrator to manage the application— you should outline how you would like to control it: which options and permissions should be available.

Based on your outline, the development team will create an admin panel featuring the specified options as you prefer:

- Managing all users

- Multi-level access system

- Remote support and maintenance

- Access to various app analytics

7. Visual Design

"An image is worth a thousand words."

No matter how well you describe your idea in words, a simple sketch will give a much better idea of the style, layout, user flow, and position of elements on the screen.

When you create wireframes, you can better see the relationship between the features and outline the functionalities necessary for implementation. Your development team will create wireframes, but make sure to provide them with enough details.

If you want your developers to understand the main points of UI, you must be clear on your definitions of fidelity as it can represent different things to different people.

Figure 3-3 lists the most common wireframe fidelity.

Figure 3-3. *The most common wireframe fidelity (Zesium)*

8. Timeline and Budget

Time necessary for building a mobile app is harder to estimate (see Section 2.4).

With money, it is mainly the same—if you have a limited budget, it means that you will have to build an MVP first and later use it for the basis for upgrades or building a full product.

There are some rough calculations as per the complexity of the app; see Table 3-1.

9. Acceptance Criteria

Acceptance criteria are the conditions that a mobile app must meet in order to be accepted by the owner. It should be done in cooperation with a QA team and the technical development team.

Outline the mandatory requirements for an app performance that you want to see in the final release. For example, you can put "*mobile app page should load under 3 seconds*" and others.

You should create some test cases where the acceptance criteria can be measured as you will be able to see the conditions in which your app will be used and the performance level that should be achieved.

10. Contact Persons

An effective communication between you and your development partner is the key element for a successful cooperation. Having all contact details at the start of the project ensures a healthy beginning of a relationship.

It would be helpful if you can identify the key people in charge of the project besides the CEO or CTO role, such as

- *Project manager*: In case you're outsourcing only a part of the project

- *Product owner*: A coordinator of the development process so that the product delivers the intended business value

- *Marketing manager*: Responsible for promotion of a product or an MVP

There are many ways to write a mobile app specification, and **ALL** of them can be correct, depending on your needs.

You can use one of many templates online, or you can create your own specification template to fit your own projects.

Provide as many details as possible about your project—the more comprehensive the specification, the smoother the start of the project.

Bear in mind that there are no two projects alike, so each specification will have some differences along the way, but the core is the same—explaining the idea in detail.

3.2. How to Write a Mobile App Product Roadmap

Before you start, keep in mind that the development process is risky and requires following a lot of steps—that's why you should use product roadmaps.

Roadmapping is all about prioritizing and organizing—it allows you to analyze feature ideas and to decide which features should be released and which features to remove or restructure to make more sense for your app purpose.

How to use your roadmap to overview your product's long-term development?

Firstly, you need to understand your product vision and define a clear product development strategy. The roadmap, as the name says, leads your team to the goal and plans what needs to be done to reach the same goal.

Let's break down the process of **HOW to create a successful roadmap** to achieve your goal into steps for you to follow when writing a mobile app roadmap.

Define Your Strategy

Firstly, you come up with a plan—you don't have to go into many details, but instead, focus on how the roadmap will fit a strategic direction for your business.

It'll help you to articulate your product's mission, the problem it will resolve, its target users, and its Unique Value Proposition (UVP).

Define your user persona(s), do a research of your market and your competitors, listen to your customers, and talk to your stakeholders.

Once you've presented your vision to everyone who will be involved, you have the necessary info to start working on your roadmap.

Define Your Readers

One of the most important things today is to know whom you're writing the roadmap for. Do not worry too much about this part as your development partner can help you with writing.

The roadmap is not unisize for everyone—you should pay attention to format, its type, and content as it must be suitable for your specific team.

For example, a roadmap listing only technical features will suit your engineering team.

The selected format will propose necessary information to be emphasized and the goals to be prioritized.

Measure and Update

Consistently measure data to gain insight on the actual progress or possible barriers. If you define your KPIs (*key performance indicators*) on time, you'll understand what areas to focus on with your first release or what to improve when tweaking for your product's later releases.

If you're building a Minimum Viable Product (MVP), focus only on a limited number of metrics.

You should create a master list of **ALL** features you want to include and then start organizing and prioritizing them to keep your product development lean.

The best known method is the **MoSCoW** method—I've already mentioned it in Section 3.1, yet it's no harm to repeat. It is an acronym that stands for **M**ust, **S**hould, **C**ould, and **W**on't. The method helps you define which features to implement first and which can come later and if any of the features need to be removed completely. It will keep your project on track.

Your particular metrics will help you measure the progress, leaving you enough space to tweak your actions toward the best results possible. Some relevant metrics can be *analyzing the market and/or competition, sprint burndown, flow efficiency, velocity, cycle time,* and more.

Be aware of **feature creep**—always keep in mind that users like it simple.

Once you gather the necessary information, you can revise your goals and determine which features need urgent attention and which can be added later in the next release.

Use Roadmapping Tools

Today, there are many cloud-based roadmapping tools that enable you to speed up the process and update it easily along the way.

Some of the tools you can use for roadmapping are OpenProject, Roadmap Planner, ProductPlan, Aha!, Productfolio, Roadmunk, and more.

You can choose the best software as per your specific needs and budget.

Analyze Feedback

User feedback is a goldmine—it can help pinpoint segments in your product that can be improved. The details given will help you decide if you are on a good track or need to change the direction entirely.

Analyze user feedback and try to mix approaches and review all existing feedback, including direct channels like surveys, interviews, chatbots, etc.

It can also be a good idea to engage voice of the customer (VoC) tools like Mopinion or Apptentive —they can help you gather feedback and monitor trends for your product.

Understanding your users will help determine not only which segments to improve but also which technology to use—for example, if your users mainly use iOS, you'll know which technology to go with, or if you have a feedback on the most important features your users value, you will have a solid start for features to include or cut out.

All these insights will be greatly valuable when it comes to prioritizing future product development areas.

UnderSWOT

Many companies apply SWOT analysis for determining the state of their business, and it is possible to do the same for your product development.

You should bring all your findings together into a comprehensive SWOT analysis for your mobile app idea as well.

SWOT is an analytical framework that helps you create a big picture, analyze the situation, and find the best solution. It identifies both the internal and external factors that make an impact on your development process.

The SWOT analysis will give you an overview of potential opportunities and risks along the development process (Figure 3-4).

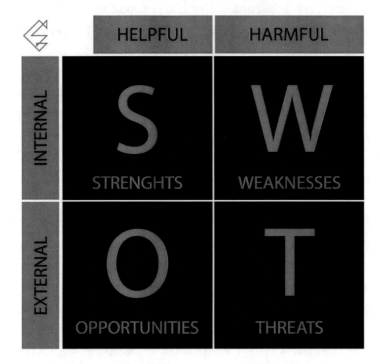

Figure 3-4. *SWOT analytical framework (Zesium)*

A product roadmap is useful when it conveys the development strategy, prioritizes high-level features, evolves along with the product requirements, and acts as a communication tool between the teams.

Not only is a product roadmap essential for communicating **the strategic purpose of your mobile app** but it also shows the **exact goals** and matches them to **your business objectives**.

Roadmap Template Tools

If you don't have time or don't know how to create your own roadmap template, don't worry. There are many valuable tools to help you out.

Here are the most popular ones:

Roadmunk: One of the most popular tools for roadmapping with different "*views*" of your roadmap. Thus, it is suitable for different teams involved (*developers, marketing team*, etc.). They give **14 days of trial period** as well as a batch of free templates.

Aha!: A roadmapping software with a really impressive integration list with various applications such as Jira, Slack, Zendesk, Confluence, Trello, and the list goes on. They also give a free **trial of 30 days** without requiring a credit card number.

ProductPlan: Also a popular software providing tons of popular roadmap templates. You are given a possibility to try it for free during a **30-day trial period**.

OpenProject: Open source software for Agile/Scrum teams. Their leading open source project management software is free (as they say "*forever free*"), and you can check their other pricing plans to see what works for you the best. They give a 14-day **free trial**.

Roadmap Planner: Open source tool for Linux. They give different package plans for individuals, businesses, and custom for your specific needs. Roadmap Planner provides **14 days of free trial**, so you can try it out and see how it fits your needs.

Venngage: **Easy-to-use** website for making stylish content for websites, presentations, ads, and more. There are templates for a wide range of projects (*infographics, posters, social media images*, etc.); however, they also provide some templates for product roadmaps along with tips on how to create them more easily. Although it's not as detailed as the preceding software, it may be a nice change for participants.

Since the product roadmap should provide only key points, avoid adding too much detail to the roadmap, yet better use supporting documentation along with the roadmap:

Release plan: Sets out strict and precise dates for a certain feature to be released.

Product backlog: Used in Scrum and provides a list of high-level requirements and features—they consist of user stories and represent a to-do list defining the development process.

Technology roadmap: Often used as a separate document when developing a digital product—displays technologies as well as technical aids to use in order to achieve business objectives.

Each product is important for your business and ROI—if you don't carefully plan the development and maintenance process, it will surely turn out badly at some point.

That's where a roadmap comes into place—an essential document for any product development team.

A good idea is to look at the examples of different roadmap types and see which one would be the best fit for your needs.

Your needs are the ones that will provide you with an answer on which roadmap you should use.

3.3. Usability Issues to Avoid When Developing a Mobile App

Even though the user interface (UI) is a crucial part of user experience, it is the *usability* that should always be a priority.

If your mobile app is difficult to use, no matter its appealing design, the overall feeling will be negative. And let's get real—a mobile app's success depends only on one thing: **how the users perceive it**.

Firstly, don't confuse UX with usability.

Usability is an element of user experience (UX) that covers an overall relationship between the user and the product. Mobile app usability relates to efficiency and simplicity of achieving the goals within the app. The shorter the time a user needs to get to know the interface, the more usable it is.

You should implement an onboarding process to guide the users through your app as it improves usability.

What are the usability issues that you should pay attention to?

Different Platforms and OSs

Android and iOS are two different platforms, and each sticks to different development.

Hence, you cannot copy an iOS app to the Android platform and vice versa. For example, the Android **"back"** button differs completely from the iOS one, so you should create an app that follows a natural flow of the platform that the users can interact with intuitively.

The same goes for each operating system (OS). An app that simulates the look and the feel of the OS is essential—it helps the users adapt to an app faster and prevents any discrepancies within the UX.

Another thing you must include is different mobile screen resolutions—the same content may look awesome on one device and completely wrong on another just due to the resolution nevertheless that it's the same OS and the same version (Figure 3-5).

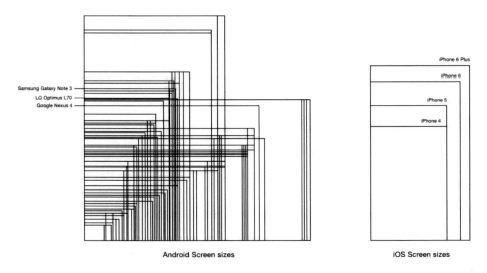

Figure 3-5. *Different mobile screen resolutions (Max Nitser)*

Landscape Mode Bypass

A phone can operate in two orientations—portrait, which is described as used by one hand and on the go, and landscape mode , described as used while stagnant and with both hands.

When developing a mobile app, people usually discard landscape mode as not being necessary.

If you want to have a good mobile app, you should take into account both portrait and landscape mode for optimal usability and UX, especially if your app contains video content.

Too Many Steps

None of us want the hassle with endless typing for a single task especially if the steps aren't as necessary as they seem.

Each action an app requires is seen as another obstacle in the way for the users, so make sure to examine the action and if there's an alternative to make it easier for them.

The simpler you make it for the users, the longer they will stay with your app.

Examples are registration with social networks like Facebook, Twitter, Google, etc. instead of making the users type in their email address, one-click payment instead of typing in the credit card number and other info, etc.

Reduce the number of steps for the users, and they will respond back with their loyalty.

Never-Ending Scrolling

Prioritizing the most important information adds to the usability effectiveness—it's inevitable to scroll down in certain cases, but most of the time you should try to reduce it as much as possible.

Users should be able to get the most of the needed information within the limits of the screen. There is also side scrolling, which is said to be avoided since it usually hides valuable content.

Poor Navigation

App developers can create great features, but sometimes the same features don't fit together in an organized way.

When users enter your app, they need to understand how to navigate and quickly do what they want: *play a game, make a purchase, check their balance*, etc.

Don't add buttons that aren't necessary as it may lead to the user being irritated trying to memorize how to reach a certain place within the app. If that happens, it is highly unlikely they'll come back to figure it out—instead, they will just leave and won't come back.

No Autofilled User Data

Auto-suggestion is a powerful way to reduce data input and help users get instant search results.

Google support indicates that auto-suggestions should consider

- User search terms

- Trending searches

- Related searches performed in the past

Apps that don't have autofilled data nowadays are regarded as poor in terms of usability.

Typically, auto-suggestions should appear after a certain number of input characters (*usually after three characters*), but the important thing is to leave the "EDIT" button visible so that users can modify the suggestion in case it appears as incorrect.

Incomplete Onboarding

It's widely known that the majority of users abandon the app after only a single use—the best way to avoid this and to instantly show users the value of your app is through onboarding.

Onboarding is a process of getting new users to understand and engage with your app enough to keep using it. It's important to design an interesting onboarding process that encourages users to return to your app again.

There are multiple app onboarding flows that you can use to engage the users. One way is sending single push notifications to new customers within their first week on the app—there are also others like benefit approach, features approach, interactive or combination approach, etc.

Check onboarding examples of similar apps to get more ideas on how to create your own.

Unclear Content

When making the content for mobile, don't copy-paste from the Web directly as it won't be the same. You should adjust the mobile content so not to include too much information displayed on the mobile screen.

Pop-up content can do wonders for a mobile app—it can provide additional info and help users get instant feedback. If you want to do it properly, choose the right content for your pop-ups and choose the right timing—only when relevant to the user (Figure 3-6). Adding too much information will result in poor UX and may frustrate the users digging to find specific content.

The best approach is to make it as easy as possible for the users to handle the content, which must be shown in a clear and concise way.

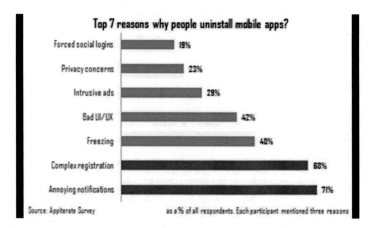

Figure 3-6. *Seven reasons people uninstall mobile apps (Appiterate)*

Unresponsive Gesturization

Nothing annoys people more than when you tap a button within an app and nothing happens.

It may happen that an app is really "broken" or just unresponsive at that time, or maybe a user navigates an app in their own way that is logical to them, but the result remains the same— frustration.

Sometimes the app has no navigation as the user feel it should, so the best practice is to include "touch heatmaps"—a qualitative analytics tool that can show where your users interact on a certain screen, where most users tap on each screen, and what is being ignored as well as spotting the unresponsive gestures with ease.

Once you pinpoint the weak spots, you can improve the usability.

Lack of User Feedback

If you want to test your usability, start with A/B testing.

Such testing allows you to assess two different layouts or designs, for example, *you can test the effectiveness of the buttons or how they differ in driving conversions or retention.* There are many tools for A/B testing (*StoreMaven, SplitMetrics, Optimizely, LeanPlum*), and it's always better to test rather than assume what the users prefer in an app.

You need to get the feedback outside your company testers and determine the needs and usability obstacles through measures such as surveys.

Additionally, you should check eye tracking and click tracking studies that can provide insights into how the users browse and click within the app to pinpoint the areas of confusion.

As per international standard ISO 9241-11, usability is the capability of the product to be understood, learned, and operated.

The usability of the product must consider the three aspects: **efficiency, easiness to learn, and user satisfaction**.

Usability means paying attention to little things that can make or break the success of your mobile app.

3.4. BONUS: Beware of These App Development Mistakes

Great mobile apps aren't cheap—imagine you invested to build an app for both platforms and then you discovered that very few people downloaded the app and even fewer could be counted as retained users.

So basically, your app lived only for a single day.

To prevent the headache, let's list a few simple mistakes that you should avoid at any cost.

No Plan or Target Audience

Before you decide to start building an app, you need to set up a plan.

As this is an important decision, take some time and think about some details like why you are developing an app, what do you want to achieve, who is your target audience, and what are their current habits.

Always bear in mind your target audience and the problem your app will resolve for its users.

No Defined Platform

Building an app for both platforms at once can cost you an arm and leg.

Almost every mobile app gets modified along the way—there is a long way from the MVP to the final product, especially as each app needs user feedback to implement updates and adjust it to serve the users better.

Although Android and iOS apps rule the existing app market, you should always think about the market you're targeting and what works the best for your users.

Last-Minute Marketing

A marketing plan should start way before the launch of your app—more precisely, in a pre-launch phase.

It's always a good idea to start a buzz around your app (*or just an app idea*) to test it and let the people become your fans and wait for the launch eagerly.

Some of the things you can do are to create a landing page, increase your web presence through social media, create a promo video catching the core of your app, and embed it into your social posts.

So mingle a bit and share your ideas on social media as it can help you boost your conversion.

Feature Creep

Many businesses strive to include as many features as possible in their app, but that is a cardinal mistake. Mobile apps are meant to allow users to quickly accomplish the task that would otherwise take longer.

Think about the core features necessary for your app to streamline the user experience and perform the very same features quickly and without delays.

As you move on with your MVP app, you can add more features along the way relying on the user feedback and behavior.

Troubling UI and Performance

If you choose a pretty layout but complex for your users to grasp, it will probably be uninstalled and deleted.

Always strive for a unique experience by choosing a simple and clear layout with functionalities easy to understand to ensure maximum user engagement.

If your mobile app takes ages to load, uses too much device memory, or drains the battery, it will deliver an unsatisfactory user experience, leading to poor app reputation. Users will leave negative reviews, and other users will decide to download some other app rather than yours.

In case your app shows signs of poor performance, you must sort these problems out as soon as possible to be able to stay in the game.

Insufficient Testing

Prior to releasing your app, you **MUST** test it for possible crashes and bugs.

Making sure that your app is not failing and has been beta tested extensively will surely provide a positive brand growth for your business.

Ignoring Negative Feedback

Don't ignore negative feedback from your users—those are the reviews you want to be able to resolve the issues.

You cannot please everyone, but those reviews contain valuable insight on possible problems and which is more important—they reflect the opinion of your users, and thus you can learn a bit more about their behavior as well as their preference with the app working process.

Annoying Ads

Try to avoid in-app ads although they are working wonders for app monetization. Those ads are loaded with graphics and can impact app usability.

If you still need to use such ads, then testing is mandatory to ensure the ads are customized as per layout design and don't compromise on user experience (UX).

What's more, pop-up notifications can be really annoying if used excessively. These can be a powerful medium to help your retention rates, but be careful—only send these notifications to the right user and at the right time.

Instant Rating

If you continually ask your users to rate your app, you will definitely end up getting on their nerves.

Those requests should be relevant and should come at the right time, for example, if the users want to uninstall your app or if any major update is available.

If you wish positive ratings, you need to keep those requests at a slower pace to give users a chance to onboard your app without nuisance messages.

The same goes for updates—if you introduce new updates every other week, it will be inconvenient for the users, and you may risk losing them. Always check if the update is really necessary, and if it is, then let the users know why it is important to get the update.

Don't impose the need for rates or updates—let it come spontaneously from users.

Copycat

You cannot simply copy and paste other application elements into yours and hope for success over the competition.

You'll know that you've done a great job if your app is unique—offering a range of functionalities like no other apps. If users figure out that your app is just a copy of other apps, your app will not survive in the crowded digital market.

So take your time when planning and try to offer your users an exclusive opportunity to benefit from downloading and using your app.

The key is to walk *a bit in the users' shoes* and create an app that adds value to your customers' lives.

Key Takeaways

- There are many ways to write a mobile app specification, and **ALL** of them are correct. It all depends on your business needs, but following some simple principles will make it easier for you: always include basic details like description of your company, mobile app, and target audience as well as a contact person, followed with a list of features, admin features, and more. Then you can move to wireframing if necessary and defining your budget, timeframe, and acceptance criteria.

- The product roadmapping can be time-consuming, but it is highly important for your product to be developed successfully. Since product roadmaps should provide only key points, try to avoid adding too much detailed information, yet better use supporting documentation along with the roadmap. Remember to check the available templates online as well as cloud-based applications as it can make it a lot easier for you. A good idea also can be to check different roadmap types to see which one would be the best fit for your needs. You can find examples of such tools in Section "Roadmap Template Tools".

- Although you do not need to be a tech expert to develop your own mobile app, there are some basic mistakes to be aware of: poor navigation, too many steps, long scrolling, incomplete onboarding, or unresponsive gesturization. All these can annoy the app user triggering them to abandon your app. Some additional DO-NOT elements include annoying ads, instant asking for rating/review, slow performance, or too many features that do not work. Keep it simple and keep it successful!

CHAPTER 4

Balance of Features in Mobile Development

In Chapter 3, we reviewed how to plan out and prevent mistakes in your mobile app development. Now, we will go into more details and explain further how to select and prioritize desired features and how to start with an MVP for your mobile app.

I will list the most important design features and trends, as well as a complete guide through mobile app development stages to better understand the app monetization process and increase chances for your app success on the future market.

4.1. Learn to Outline MVP Must-Haves

Success is not delivering a feature; success is learning how to solve the customer's problem.

—Eric Ries, *The Lean Startup*

© Maja Dakić 2023
M. Dakić, *Mobile App Development for Businesses*,
https://doi.org/10.1007/978-1-4842-9476-5_4

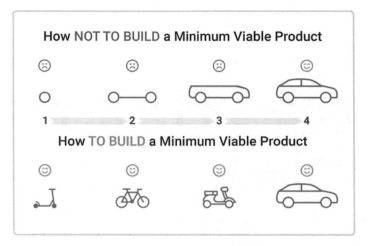

Figure 4-1. *How to build a Minimum Viable Product (Pinterest)*

Check Figure 4-1 below which shows a simple step-by-step guide to ensure successful development of your Minimum Viable Product (MVP).

Do Your Research

The first step is to **gain understanding of the problem you focus on** and solutions you can offer.

Address crucial points like *"What is the market like?"*, *"Who are the people that have this problem?"*, *"Is there a market need that my product is addressing?"*, etc.

These questions will help you in the planning stage and market research of your MVP.

Apart from these, the three most important questions that you need to ask yourself are

- **What is the exact problem your MVP will solve?**

- **Who are users interested in your product?**

- **What are the available options for the same problem on the market?**

Prioritize Features

The next step is **identifying key features for your product.**

Think about and write down different features that could be useful for your users. Once you do that, you should timebox them for further development. If they do not meet your planned launch date, reduce them to the essential ones only.

The features you intend to include should be prioritized by their importance. The specifications and features should be divided into *must-haves* and *could-haves.*

It is vital to have **one top-priority feature** that reflects the product's primary value during this MVP stage.

The MVP concept isn't about perfection, but rather a blueprint for a successful tech product.

Choose an MVP Approach

As already mentioned in Section 2.4, an MVP is the simplest product edition released to the market to collect feedback and reactions of customers for further improvements.

There is a variety of approaches available when creating an MVP—choose the one according to your needs and resources.

Your **MVP development procedure** should follow some of the following MVP methods.

No-Product

In the "*no-product MVP*" strategy, you validate your product idea and receive feedback without programming. An example is an idea visualization where you test an idea potential with marketing campaigns. It is just a way to explain how the product will look and what it will do. This method can be utilized through surveys, landing page advertisements, videos, blogs, etc.

The biggest benefit of this approach is cost and time efficiency.

There are also crowdfunding campaigns using relevant platforms, like Kickstarter. Your idea must be liked by people to raise money from contributors. Simply put, you create an ad to market a product that is yet to be developed.

A good example is the MVP of Dropbox—it began with a basic demo video and brought thousands of users to their website. The company further developed their product based on user feedback.

Product Mockup

A product mockup lets you design a portion of your new product's features. Utilizing the method of mockups for product development, you can select a range of alternatives to pick from when you are creating your MVP.

Multi-featured MVP

As the name suggests, this method focuses on core functions to ensure your customers understand what the product is intended for. This is why it is essential to design the MVP to meet the users' core requirements at least 80%.

MLP

The *Minimum Lovable Product* or MLP focuses on user satisfaction using the least viable product. The idea of the MLP is to boost a product's basic set of features. It is designed to enhance user experience through attractive design, illustrations, and micro-interactions. It uses intuitive information architecture to simplify the flow and more.

Identify Success Criteria

How will you know whether your MVP is a success or not?

To identify success criteria, you must define the **most important metrics** that include

- Activations

- Active users

- Customer feedback

- NPS (Net Promoter Score)

- MRR (Monthly Recurring Revenue)

- CAC (Customer Acquisition Cost)

- ARPU (Average Revenue per User)

Make a Story Map

Story mapping consists of four parts that are

Goals ➤ Activities ➤ User stories ➤ Tasks

This is essential for prioritizing features and creating a breakdown of your product's backlog. Goals are the primary focus of any product and require taking certain actions and features. You can turn goals into user or job stories, which will further break into tasks.

A story map enables you to comprehend your product's benefits and weaknesses.

B-M-L-I (Build-Measure-Learn-Iterate)

Finally, when your app is launched, exercise the BMLI (*build-measure-learn-iterate*) method.

When you have your MVP, try to see it as an ongoing process of learning. Do not forget for users to try out your product and to collect useful feedback from them. Quality Assurance (QA) engineers will conduct the initial testing phase and improve the overall quality of your product.

You must review every aspect of your MVP. From your customers' reactions up to their feedback, anything can help you estimate the value of your product on the marketplace.

Personally, I would define an MVP as the **initial adaptation of an original product concept** enabling you to collect validated knowledge about consumers of your product.

During the process, you may come up with a lengthy wish list of attractive features that you may not actually need at the start. Creating an MVP will help you understand how your target users respond to the purpose of your app and show if the goal is achieved.

Having understood the importance of an MVP, we are going to consider how to create a priority list of features for a mobile app MVP in accordance with your objectives and goals.

How to Prioritize Features for Your MVP

Whether you are a founder, product manager, CEO, or CTO, your aim should be to see how you can put together efforts to achieve your strategic goals. This entails identifying your target user and the market value of your mobile application.

Focus on making a minimal version of the product (MVP) that validates the concept of your mobile app with the lowest form of risk. Separate features that should be in the initial product launch from features that will be added later.

At times, during a project, more features appear as necessary. If you don't assess properly between the "*must be, should be, could be, and won't be*" (**MoSCoW**; see Figure 4-2) features for the MVP, it can affect the product negatively.

Initial prioritized app features should cover only those that will help your app attain market value through user demand.

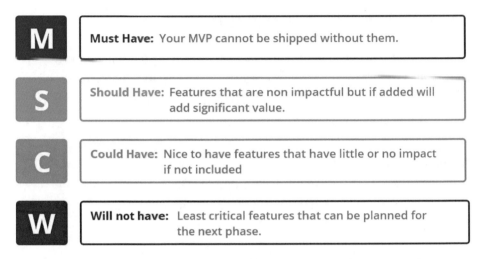

Figure 4-2. MoSCoW prioritization (www.linkedin.com/pulse/ mvp-moscow-prioritization-its-advantages/)

Distinguish User Wishes and Needs

Draw a clear line of understanding between what your users want and what they need. Consult your team about the importance of every feature listed and how to strike a balance between the must-haves and nice-to-haves.

The adaptation of numerous customer-requested features in the early stages can bring confusing user experience, beating the true purpose of the mobile app product.

Consider the Ratio of Feature Value to the Number of Users

The value of some features can only be appreciated with a large and substantial product user base.

Such features don't have to be implemented from the word go. Instead, such features can be restored from your product roadmap for future app iterations.

Research Third-Party Services

When making your choice of features, you have to consider how much time it takes to implement them. For instance, you want your users to be able to message each other. You don't have to make a chatting service from scratch as it will waste your time and resources.

There are many third-party chat services for iOS and Android (*WhatsApp, Facebook Messenger, Line, Skype, WeChat,* etc.) that will take a very short interval of time to implement. Dedicate time to do some research to find the third-party services that will be necessary for your app and consult your development partner about it.

Use Metrics to Drive Your Roadmap

Define the primary key performance indicators (KPIs) at the earliest. It will help you determine which areas to focus upon to improve future versions of the app.

The nature of your app is the dependent factor—your production stage, business type, and product type will determine your choice of key primary indicators.

An MVP will be a pointer to what KPIs are important to you.

Take a business approach in deciding your choices of customer success metrics. Some of them are

- **Customer satisfaction** (*how content users are with your product*)

- **Increase in lifetime value** (*total worth to a business of a customer over the entire period of their relationship*)

- **Adoption rates** (*number of people that adopt your app and become users*)

- **Retention rates** (*the percentage of users that remain active with your app after a certain period of time*)

- **Churn rate** (*the percentage of users who uninstall your app within a certain period*)

- **Daily/monthly active user (MAU)** (*your total number of active users in a day/month*)

- **User growth** (*speed at which you get new users over a certain period of time, usually monthly*)

- **Acquisition costs** (*how much you spend to attain new users*)

- **Average Revenue per User** (*how much revenue you generate for each active user*)

- **Return on Investment** (**ROI**; *efficiency or profitability of an investment*)

Monitoring these metrics will help you understand how users interact with your MVP.

Monitor Functional Customer Feedback Channels

Make provisions for receiving your user feedback.

This is technically mandatory for a mobile app MVP. The feedback will help your product development team make data-driven decisions concerning every stage of the development.

It will also help decide what features to prioritize in future upgrades of the app.

Do Competition Analysis

Comments on similar products from blogs, support pages, product reviews, and social networks can be your chance to find out what is fascinating for your users and what is not.

You will also get insights into what your users expect from an app and how you can stand out from your competitors.

Restructure Your Roadmap

Mobile app development roadmaps are open to change—consider such changes after you launch your MVP.

To make a winning mobile app, you need to focus on success metrics and gear upon them. With the details from your users, you can track user behavior and observe what is done well and what needs to be improved.

Your development team can then make improvements on lacking issues and decide what should be predominant changes in the main product. After this, you can proceed to apply strategic changes.

The changes you implement should align with key performance indicators for the product and with the new roadmap.

Top Techniques to Prioritize Features

We mentioned previously some tips on how to prioritize the features for an MVP.

There are several proven methods that can help you efficiently define the key features of your mobile app and organize the entire process.

Before using any prioritization method, review them all to understand which one would suit your business and could bring maximum value.

The most common approaches for your mobile product feature prioritization will allow you to compare features, highlight the most critical ones, and take into consideration the users' preferences.

These common methods include the following:

- **MoSCoW matrix**

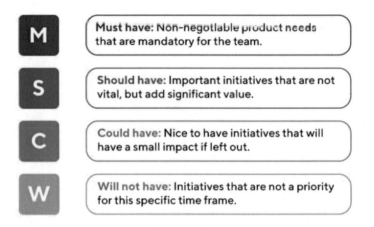

Figure 4-3. *MoSCoW prioritization (pinterest.com)*

- **RICE scoring**

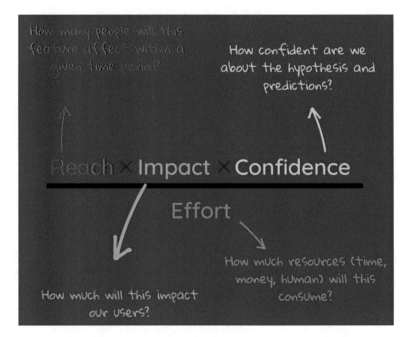

Figure 4-4. *RICE scoring (medium.com)*

- **Kano model**

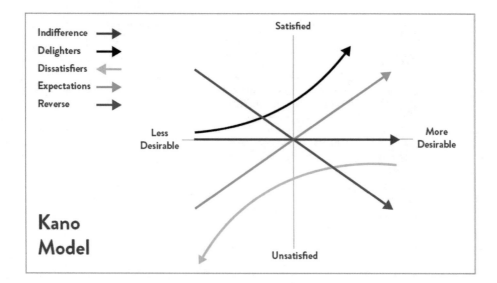

Figure 4-5. *Kano model (mightybytes.com)*

- **Bubble sort technique**

Bubble sort prioritization

Taxi app features	Comparisson	Decision
Rating system	Having a geopositioning feature in taxi app is more critical, so we need to swap theese two items	1. Geopositioning
Geopositioning		2. Rating system

Taxi app features	Comparisson	Decision
Rating system	Having a feature to call a taxi is more critical, so we swap theese two items	1. Call a taxi
Call a taxi		2. Rating system

Priotirized features for a taxi app MVP
1. Geopositioning
2. Call a taxi
3. Rating system

Figure 4-6. *Bubble sort method (easternpeak.com)*

- **Effort and impact**

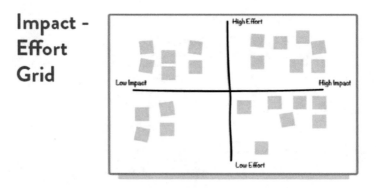

Figure 4-7. *Effort and impact grid (mightybytes.com)*

- **User story mapping**

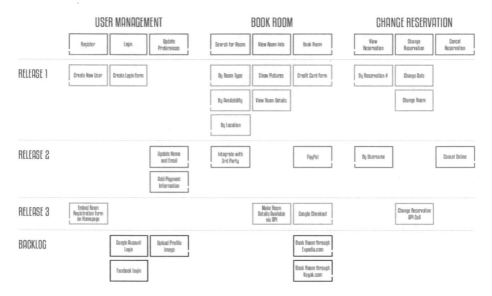

Figure 4-8. *User story map (productplan.com)*

Sorting the subsequent set of deliverables into themes is the next step after fully defining your product path. These themes can be groups of related features and initiatives that help the user accomplish a specific task.

Your theme for a shopping app can be "*shop in 5 taps*," and it will encompass all the support features, enhancements, design, or even bug fixing.

Themes help you maintain a qualitative roadmap where you can switch the lane of features while keeping to the work plan.

4.2. The Most Important Design Features

An awesome UX design leaves a long-lasting impression, and that's what makes a difference between popular apps and the ones that are not.

UX design is a dynamic process. To offer your users the best experience possible, listen to their feedback on what they like or dislike about your product—it will help you improve with each released version of your app.

You should always follow a user-centric design so that your app grows to fit the needs of the user as ***everything revolves around the END USER***.

How to start?

Start with exploring similar mobile apps and their features, but don't be a copycat as what works for one mobile app might not work for the other.

Learn from your competition and analyze why certain design trends work and why others don't. Combine your research with your own brand— repeat, customize, and learn from it as it will make your UX stronger in the long run.

If you're a designer or a developer, you should check the online documentation created by Apple and Google created specifically for developers and designers:

- *For iOS apps*: Human Interface Guidelines

- *For Android apps*: Design for Android/Material Design

The most common way of validating your product is testing it with your target audience. Develop an MVP (check Section 4.1) to figure out if your idea's well-accepted by its core users.

Here are some rules to follow when thinking about UX design for your mobile app.

Quick-Loading Elements

Google/SOASTA Research states that if a page takes more than 5 seconds to load, the probability of bounce increases by staggering 90%!

There are many ways to **speed up your mobile page** such as optimizing images, reducing plugins, etc., so check these and make your pages load as quickly as possible.

The functionality of the app must help users to complete designated tasks, and it's the first motivation for downloading your app. Prioritize core features crucial for completing the tasks and offer only relevant features encouraging more users to "*taste*" your mobile app.

Include Onboarding

When users try your mobile app and encounter issues within the first few screens, onboarding will retain them by showing how to do what they want.

Delivering a good onboarding experience is the cornerstone for attracting and retaining the users. If you **include efficient onboarding**, not only will it lower abandonment rates but it will also help boost long-term success metrics like user retention and user lifetime value.

You can show which icons can be tapped or swiped; then, considering the size of buttons and links, make it easy for users to tap them. Remain consistent with gestures within your app to optimize usability and prevent any selection errors.

Ensure Minimal User Input

Reduce search effort for your users with some search solutions like *barcode scan* or *keyword search*. It guides the users directly to what they're looking for, and simplicity of the process can significantly increase conversion rates.

User input (*entering a credit card number, registration data, checkout information*, etc.) should be minimal as users can get frustrated with the smaller screens.

To avoid high abandon rates, limit the number of fields required and include only the necessary information. You may also add autocomplete, shortcuts, spell-check, and prediction text assistance to build better user experience.

Intuitive Gesturization

Gesturization involves actions that users make while interacting with your app like *swiping, tapping, scrolling,* or *pinching.* **Knowing your users' behavior is crucial** for gesturization as it helps understand the actions they're familiar with.

Gestures enable users to engage with the technology through the sense of touch, and some popular gestures are *tap, double-tap, swipe, drag, pinch,* and *press.*

A good strategy is to keep swipe gestures out of hard-to-reach areas, provide enough tapping space, etc., as these gestures are just a cherry on the top of UX cake for smartphone users.

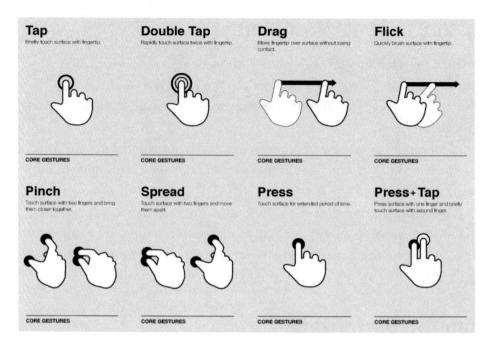

Figure 4-9. *Core gestures (Smashing Magazine)*

Make Clean UI

Your design should be *glanceable*—meaning your visual design should convey the message easily and quickly, at a glance.

Maintain visual consistency with the color palette, typography, and other elements; create a seamless visual flow from first toward other elements and facilitate for the users to complete their goals with ease.

Be consistent with UI design and keep it simple—less actions, darker/brighter colors, shorter navigation, and limited background services.

Keep the unwanted features away from users as it can slow them down from achieving the goal, thus leading them to abandoning the app.

A minimalistic approach to your mobile app design is always the best choice.

"THE MORE MINIMAL, THE BETTER."

Transparent Permission Policy

When a user downloads the app and instantly gets overrun with permissions to accept, even before actually using the app, it can be frustrating.

Make sure to **provide transparent permission policies** and allow your users to control how their personal information is shared within a mobile app.

If you clearly outline your business policies and practices, your users will be more secure when accepting permissions. You can include links to your privacy regulations or display trusted badges of security, especially if your users use your app for their personal and financial information.

Clear CTA (Call-to-Action) Button

When defining action buttons for your mobile app, you must define your action clearly.

An action button should be **easily visible and approachable**, so create bigger buttons and place them at a fair distance to allow easier app navigation.

Sometimes, a plain wording does a trick, for example, to put the "*Request a cab*" button instead of "*Submit an order*" as it will explain the purpose better.

Personalized User Experience (UX)

Personalization provides a unique UX.

Personalize whenever possible because if you **align user experience with users' preferences**, they're more likely to continue using your mobile app.

Make sure to display only relevant content—trivial content or too many push notifications will create a counter-effect.

You can use location data to suggest specific retail or ecommerce deals to certain users, or you can include the user's name in messaging—all these are effective ways to personalize.

Offer a Support Option

Users usually need assistance, so **provide them with multiple ways for customer support** like *self-serve FAQs, live support, click to call buttons,* or *live chats.* As per a survey, customers today prefer a self-service rather than contacting a support agent, so it is a wise move to offer them such a feature.

It will help users reach their goal quickly, and in return, you will get a happy customer and increase your user retention.

The preceding tips show that your app must be intuitive for users along with visually pleasing design and reliable without draining the battery. UX design itself should be natural and decluttered—the users must feel the obvious navigation flow.

Remember: Your app **MUST** fulfil the users' needs and **MUST NOT** be faulty.

Effective UX is a foundation of a mobile app—every brand needs to provide a positive experience with their digital content to their customers, users, and clients.

In the next section, let's explore how to create good-quality mobile interaction design as it is different from general design features.

Tips on Successful Mobile Interaction Design

How can you know great-quality mobile interaction design when you see it?

The thing is you cannot.

However, ***bad*** design is much more noticeable.

Despite the relatively short experience with smartphones, most users quickly get tired of the burdensome content like buttons in the wrong spot or too much text that kills attention span

A great interaction design is welcoming and instructive, helping users figure out how to operate a mobile app instinctively. These qualities don't come easy—it takes hard work, lots of practice, and plenty of patience during the design development.

Let's check some useful tips based on our experience at Zesium, which can help you.

Keep a Simple and Plain Flow

One of the biggest mistakes for any app is to be complex, failing to take the user smoothly from one screen to another.

Your application must be **intuitive**, meaning it must intuitively indicate to users each phase of the app experience. You can use contrasting colors to indicate important buttons, bold typography to emphasize things when necessary, and visual cues to point users to the desired direction (e.g., *thumbs-up for LIKE or + for ADD and similar*).

Also, the **system should be logical** so that users could recognize the iterative patterns and use mobile apps intuitively.

Match Interactions to the Platform

Sometimes app designers create an interface on one platform and try to imitate the exact interaction design on another platform.

Now, if you plan to take your app across multiple platforms—Android, Apple, Windows, or any other mobile operating system (OS)—bear in mind that users select their operating system for a reason.

Each operating system (OS) has a specific set of human interface and interaction design guidelines, which are strictly followed by their designers when developing apps for the specific platform.

Apply Familiar Patterns

A designer can say they did a good job when an app can be used intuitively, meaning UI design has to **contain recognition patterns**.

Those are the elements that users are already familiar with and that give slight hints on how the app works (*like CTA buttons such as "Add to cart" and others*). Users adapt to things quickly, and in the absence of the same, they feel uncomfortable.

If you plan to use custom interactive elements, don't forget to add some standard components so that your new app doesn't overwhelm users with a completely unfamiliar environment.

Declutter and Declutter

Mobile small screens cannot display much info at a time, and your design team should keep this in mind during your work. The best approach to mitigate such pitfalls is a method of elimination.

Try to **apply only core functional elements** that will get users right to the point they need. If a function is not essential, remove it. The simplicity will help users to concentrate on the purpose of your app, making it functional for users of all skill levels.

Don't be afraid that a minimal number of actions will make your app look primitive—it will just help your app be more effective and easy to use.

Bear in mind that people mostly rate the quality of an app based on how helpful it is.

Add Gamelike Elements

Standard apps have fewer chances to get users' attention. That is the reason you should bring some emotional aspects to the app if it seems ordinary at first glance.

To make the whole process more captivating, it can be a good idea to **use gamification**—*various challenges, boards, and stickers* will motivate users to interact with a product more and return to it regularly.

This is an effective way to create a clear layout, plus it adds the element of fun. Users enjoy entertainment, challenges, and competitions as those encourage them to come back. By adding the fun element into a casual application, you help users reduce stress and relax while using your app.

Keep It Short

Mobile phones' advantage over the Web is that they have a lot of great hardware like *accelerometer, GPS, Bluetooth, gesture recognition*, etc., so designers can effectively utilize those features to match your needs.

The primary activities on the mobile are **swipe**, **tap**, and **long press**, so options like sliding, swiping, tapping, or using fingerprint should be used instead of typing. You can reduce many form fields by utilizing all these hardware, so try different interactions to make it short and plain.

Make a perfect search work—users usually like the traditional model of swiping down for searching. Also, show the options for a **recent search** and a favorite search time.

What's more, always include **filter and sort options**—you should afford effective filter and sort options, which will give a key choice based on the context.

Check Orientation

If the users use your app 30% of the time in the landscape mode, you must design it for the landscape mode. But a majority of designers test their app in the portrait mode alone.

You should test your app both in landscape and portrait modes.

Landscape mode is usually the primary mode for apps related to driving, finance, books, and games.

Ask for In-Context Permission

The first interaction with the app plays a key role in creating an overall impression about it (*good or bad*).

When users open the new app, the last thing they want to see are multiple popups asking for permissions (*the app would like to access your camera/contacts/location and so on*). This action has a negative impact on user experience (UX) and usually leads to the app being uninstalled.

The strategy of permission consent should rely upon the clarity and importance of the permission type you are requesting. You should make a distinction between

- Critical (up-front) permissions

- Secondary (in-context) permissions

Users are very serious about their data and don't have a tendency just to tap and give all the authority to the app. Asking for the right permission at the right time will make users trust your app.

Popular Design Trends

The design trends usually follow the advancements in technology each year, and you should check for such designers who continuously update their choice of UI tools per the latest trends.

First impressions greatly matter to users, especially when 94% are design-related as per some research.

Developing good design can be done firstly by gathering relevant information as much as possible.

In order to stay on top and make your design alluring for users along with a great user experience (UX), here is the list of some latest UI design trends.

Doodles and Sketches

Doodles and sketches were popular a few years ago, but they made a comeback in 2022—welcome, creative doodles and freeform sketches.

Doodles and drawings are easy to work with and animate, and they bring personalized experience and human touch to such designs.

That is the reason doodles and sketches are a great choice for companies that wish to humanize their brand and transform it to being more relatable to customers.

Figure 4-10. *404 page example (Pinterest)*

Metaverse

From the moment Facebook rebranded as Meta, there were a lot of speculations on what would the future hold related to the way we communicate and live our lives in Metaverse.

Metaverse is a digital universe—it is a combination of technologies, including Virtual Reality (VR), Augmented Reality (AR), and video, where users can "live" within that digital universe. It is said that Metaverse is the "*next Internet*," and if it becomes common, the use of VR and AR will skyrocket.

The UI trends in Metaverse involve thinking outside of the box. In the Augmented Reality segment, Google and Apple have already introduced their AR development platforms: ARCore and ARKit, combining physical and digital worlds.

There are several ways to approach the AI (Artificial Intelligence) user interface:

- *Object-related*: Real-world objects that have tethered interaction.

- *Fixed to screen*: The user has to position the camera in a specific way.

- *Real world–related*: Using the surrounding physical world.

Figure 4-11. *Metaverse marketplace (dribbble.com)*

Design for Foldable

Foldable phones are already a hype—as this technology becomes better and more affordable, we will see other manufacturers delivering such products in this market. Samsung had a great year—they've "unfolded" the Z Fold and Z Flip 3, which sold much better than their predecessors.

Google released Android 12 and included all the conditions and limitations to consider when adapting mobile apps for foldable screens. That is the first step in involving foldable screens into a product design workflow. Another aspect is for designers to get used to creating more adaptable screen design for foldable devices as these might be a new frontier for innovation.

Figure 4-12. *Foldable devices (letsgodigital.org)*

Dark Mode

The option of "**dark mode**" is already gaining popularity among the latest UI/UX design trends. A dark theme is a low light that displays a dark surface. Users prefer such dark themes mostly because it saves battery life and reduces eye strain (it has been proven that exposure to bright light can affect your eyesight).

Dark mode has been in use in the new Android 10 and iOS 13, and with the new operating systems, users can toggle between dark and light themes at their own choice and will. If you wish to follow the trends and retain your users, this feature is a must for a future-ready UI design.

Here are the benefits of dark mode within your app:

- Highlights the design elements

- Saves battery usage to a greater extent

- Looks attractive and more appealing to most of the users

Figure 4-13. *Car assist app in dark mode (https://dribbble.com/ shots/15987513-Car-Control-App)*

Minimalism

Minimalism is already a known trend in UI—the term *minimal* refers to anything that is stripped to its essentials.

Uncluttered design makes the entire interface easy to use, plus it brings aesthetic satisfaction to the user. Additionally, minimal design is connected with a buttonless tendency, which is the base for simplified design.

Minimalism includes some of the following features:

- Simplicity and clarity

- Attention to proportions and composition

115

- Enhanced attention ratio to core details

- Elimination of nonfunctional elements

- Large volume of spare space

Figure 4-14. *Cuddly Vitamins app (`https://igorivankovic.com/ project/cuddly-vitamins`)*

Illustrations

Illustrations in UI design enable users to interact in an easier and clearer way.

Custom illustrations establish artistic harmony, add creativity to the user interface (UI), and make your design stand out among the competitors.

Hand-drawn illustrations are usually used to leave an organic impression on users connecting them to their usage.

Some illustration methods for UI images are as follows:

- Ignite emotions with illustrations like facial expressions, shapes, colors, and curves.

- Design visual stimuli to send the right message.

- Use as main images for landing pages, reviews, etc. while they must be balanced well with the business goals.

- Build brand recognizability with informative illustrations created as per your target audience.

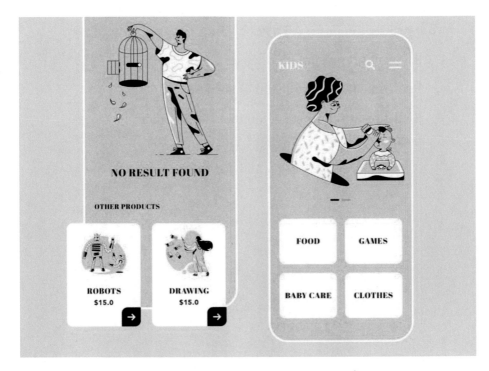

Figure 4-15. *Examples of illustrations in a mobile app (mindinventory.com)*

Augmented and Virtual Reality (AR and VR)

Augmented (AR) and Virtual Reality (VR) will definitely be a long-lasting trend for the future.

The AR-driven features make the understanding of the features easier, more accurate, and better. Augmented Reality (AR) allows users to get real-time feedback about the app, and for the design purposes, the best is to study users' habits like time spent on the app or possible expectations. A great example is within the medical sector—AR can be integrated into telemedicine or online medical consultation purposes.

Virtual Reality (VR) is considered by designers for more than just basic aspects (*photography*, *motion design*, etc.) but for other elements like interactions, sound design, curved design, and surroundings/environment.

Here are some trends for AR used in UI:

- AR avatar representing the user

- Real-time face filters (Snapchat-like)

- Real-time animations when the user interacts with the app

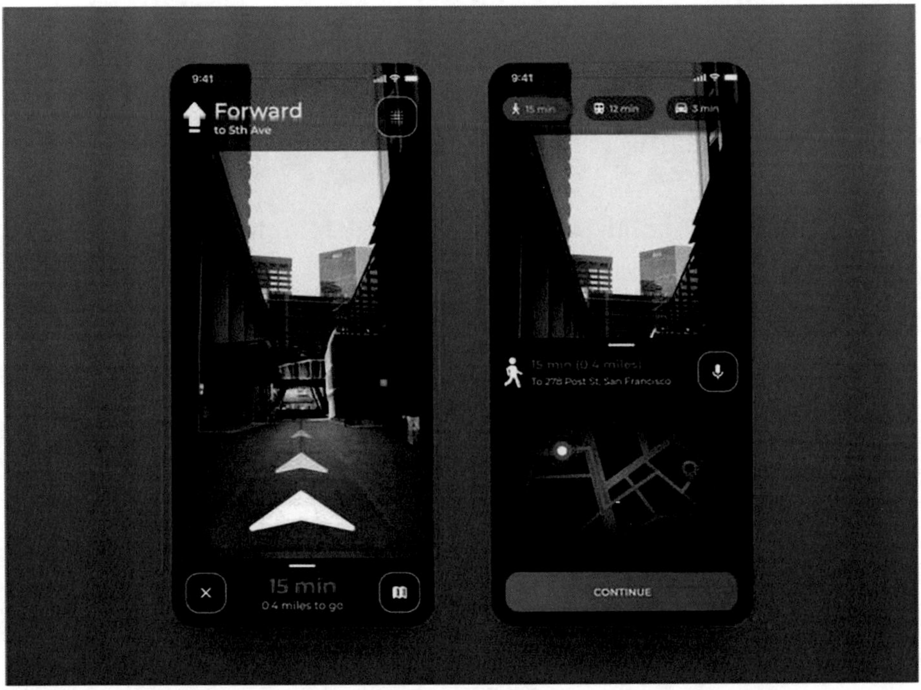

Figure 4-16. *AR Navigation App by Bohdan Kozachok (www. pinterest.com/pin/778489485608367212/)*

Some recommended trends for usage of VR in design are

- 360 degrees of vision

- Curved design to make it easier for the users to read the text or images

- Display the same depth of all UI elements, menu, text, etc.

Voice UI and Artificial Intelligence (AI)

We live in the age of Alexa, Siri, etc., and per Edison research, at least 35% of Americans own a smart speaker in 2023.

If you want some innovation in your application, check with the app developers about a voice user interface (VUI). The voice-based UI can be implemented into your UI/UX design process—it provides missing information, allowing users to interact with a system through speech commands.

The visitors of your business website search for information or services with the help of the voice assistant. As people have gotten accustomed to voice chatbots and virtual assistants (VAs), it can be a good move for designers to incorporate VUI within the app and make it more interesting for users.

Here are tips on creating UX with voice interaction:

- Lead the users through the used functionalities.

- Implement different design guidelines for the voice interface.

- Understand the natural communication of people with their voice.

- Provide users with options as opposed to graphical UI.

Figure 4-17. *AI Coffee Ordering App by Vlad Tyzun (https://dribbble.com/shots/4450154-AI-Coffee-Ordering-App)*

Dynamic Color Palette and Bolder Typography

Colors are one of the must-have aspects for UI designers to consider.

Designers should be familiar with color theory to apply them effectively to your product. The trends may vary, but using vibrant colors and gradients for websites and apps is somewhat an unwritten rule.

The latest of some UI trends is a simple monochrome choice when it comes to colors—as simplicity is the key, such choice makes the apps more meaningful. Thus, usage of bold colors has increased recently, and designers should make the color gradients and contrasts more enticing for the users. Within 2022, brands have started to accept the effect of much bolder or oversized fonts in their UI. Chunky fonts and bolder contrast greatly bounce off the space, inciting a stronger emphasis on the written content.

Based on your theme colors, you can check a palette that can match it in color, hue, tone, and more for harmonious results.

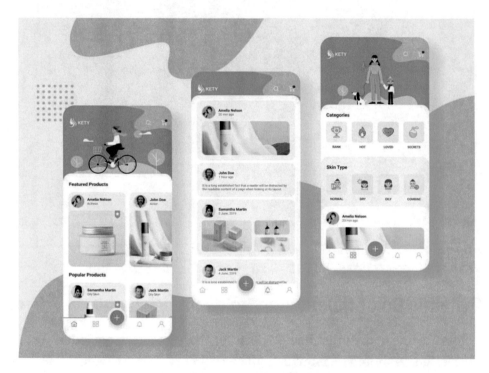

Figure 4-18. *Beauty App (https://dribbble.com/shots/9173004-Beauty-app)*

Some benefits of dynamic UI and gradients are as follows:

- Clear navigation and an intuitive interactive system— highlighting and contrasting of important elements.

- Increased readability—usage of high-contrast colors should be applied only for highlighting elements.

- One color applied to several elements to show the connection between them.

- Applying the same of similar colors within logos, websites, and mobile apps to increase brand awareness.

- Trendy colors catch users' attention even within high competition.

Figure 4-19. *Smart Home App (https://dribbble.com/ shots/6706511-Smart-Home-App)*

Animations

Animation is enticing to people of all ages; thus, there has been an increase in usage of animated illustrations to attract masses.

Using animations in illustrations within web or mobile apps and others brings a natural feel to the entire UX design—it can perfectly narrate a story that would otherwise be tedious to read if in text.

Using animated illustrations is a wise approach to convey messages to the users in a more effective way.

Benefits of animated illustrations are

- Effective way to narrate a story on the product, service, or brand

- Increased user engagement with your product or a service

- Increasingly grabs user attention

Neomorphism

Neomorphism has become one of the biggest design trends as of 2020.

Its name is coined from NEO + skeuomorphism = neomorphism. Neomorphism is a method of creating an image of extruded shapes by combining shadows to match the real-life objects.

Both lower and raised shapes are made of exactly the same material as the background, which is easily created by playing with two shadows (at positive and negative values). However, if you want it to work out, the background cannot be completely black or completely white. It requires a bit of hue so both dark and light shadows are visible.

Benefits of neomorphism are as follows:

- Lifeless representations are moved into reality offering a new feel.

- Represents a detailed design with highlights and shadows.

- Using neomorphic cards as a raised shape provides the depth within design.

Figure 4-20. *Neomorphism examples by Sulagaev Agency (Dribbble,* `https://dribbble.com/Sulagaev-Agency)`

Asymmetry

There's nothing wrong with working under the umbrella of traditional UI principles, but making your design stand out means that you must break the rules sometimes.

Instead of complying to the traditional grid system , you should challenge the basic principles and push the boundaries with asymmetrical grids and layouts.

Try to experiment with more dynamic compositions to provide character and personality to your design.

Consider the following for the asymmetrical design:

- Experiment with more dynamic compositions.

- Design per users' needs.

- Use typography and imagery for creative design.

- Collapse gutters and overlay multiple elements for more effective design.

- Use white space of the surface area.

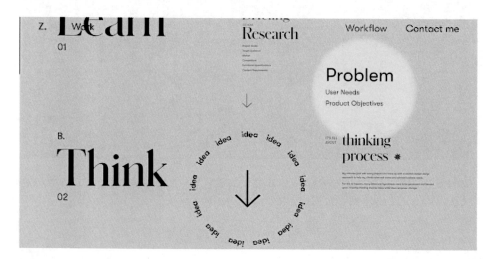

Figure 4-21. *About page example (https://zhenyary.com/about/)*

Storytelling

The capacity to tell captivating stories through digital experience will continue to be one of the main trends.

Storytelling is a visual way of telling the user what they need to know based on user testing and research.

It creates positive emotions between the brand and the user as you can convey your message within one (or more) image or in a 20-second video. The storytelling conveys the story to the users in a more creative and digestible way.

Educate your users through your product or a service with storytelling consisting of images and short text—it will help users quickly understand your message much easier than reading a list of tedious tech specs. Another plus is that storytelling can solidify your brand's first impression with the users.

Modifying information to a catchy story will help users remember your brand in the future. Copywriting has become one of the most important elements for a great user experience—while the style captures users' attention, the story itself engages them with your brand. This approach ensures that users can feel like a part of your story, thus preventing them from simply scanning your content.

Benefits of storytelling in UI design are as follows:

- Enables an easier user journey

- Creates effective design for customer touchpoints allowing them to get back again

- Makes use of a plot and a conflict for more captivating story of your brand

3D Graphics

3D design elements are still on the top of the list of UI design trends—they gained popularity by using the underlying principles of photorealism, which increases user engagement.

They are being integrated with the latest technologies like Augmented Reality (AR) and Virtual Reality (VR), allowing UX designers to create hyper-realistic 3D visuals. This way, you can keep the users engaged, but be careful as these elements may reduce the speed of your website and always make sure they're properly optimized. Animated elements will thrive on screens helping users distinguish the interactive parts.

3D visuals look more appealing to users, which trigger their long-time engagement.

3D graphics include the following:

- 360-degree presentation for improved UX design

- 3D graphics for mobile and user interfaces

- Use of background elements in order to balance readability and effective user navigation

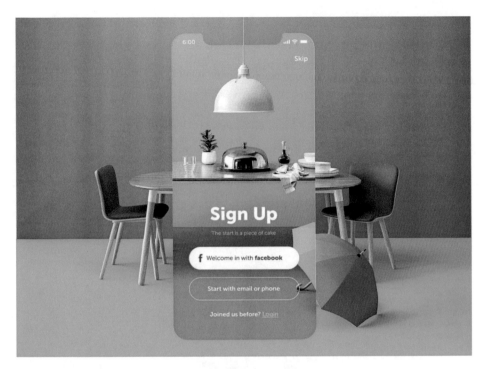

Figure 4-22. *UX Planet, 3D Graphics in UI Design Concepts*
(`https://uxplanet.org/ui-inspiration-in-volume-3d-`
`graphics-in-creative-ui-design-concepts`)

Passwordless Login

With technology, people always seek ways to save time. The importance of
skipping the typing of passwords leads us to another important element for
users—login without passwords.

A majority of users usually tend to forget the passwords when dealing
with online web platforms, and as passwords usually contain letters,
numbers, and special characters, it is hard for users to remember or
recollect.

With **biometrics** (fingerprints or facial recognition), **one-time
passwords** (OTPs), or a **PIN code**, users no longer have to worry about
remembering all their 50 passwords.

Mobile app designers can keep this UI/UX design trend in mind when they are designing the login page of the web or mobile apps.

Benefits of such passwordless login are as follows:

- Enables easier and long-term user engagement

- Creates easy accessibility to your website or app providing a user-friendly service

- Effective passwordless method with protected user data

- Keep this method in mind when designing your login page on your app.

Figure 4-23. *Face verification feature for an ewallet (Dribbble,*
`https://dribbble.com/shots/15901276-Face-Verification-`
`Interaction-for-E-Wallet)`

The trends listed are only some of the most popular that have a tendency to stay for the coming decade as they satisfy the aesthetics of user requirements.

Primary benefits provided by these trends relate to accessibility and usability of the UI design, providing higher user engagement along with the enriched user experience.

The important thing to remember is that UI/UX design trends do not focus only on visual aesthetics, but they tend to significantly improve usability for the end user.

If you apply those trends wisely, it can bring lots of benefits to your product.

4.3. What Functionalities to Include to Your Mobile App

The best apps have a few things in common: they all have a simple user interface, an easy way to navigate through, and absolutely no showstopper bugs. A skilled app development agency can help you get the most out of each of these important attributes.

Before you contact an app development agency or a freelance developer, try to understand the mobile app development process so you're not jumping in blindfolded.

Take a look at the guide that will walk you through the process so you know exactly what it takes.

Phase 1: Plan

Brainstorm App Features

Having a carefully considered plan is going to build the foundation for everything that comes later—do your homework before calling the developers.

When thinking about the features for your mobile app, the best strategy is to put yourself in "*users' shoes*." Think about the reasons people would install your app and how they would interact with it.

Download similar apps, and as you explore them, make notes, for example:

- Is registration required?

- Can users access all or only particular features?

- What steps are required to perform a certain task (e.g., *creating a profile, navigating to payment options*, etc.)?

- What hardware components may be necessary to perform a certain action (i.e., *the camera, GPS, speakers*, etc.)?

- What did you dislike about this similar app (*buttons, illogical gestures*, etc.)? How would you improve it?

- What is good within the similar app?

Finding a similar app (or a similar feature) can provide you and your development partner with a benchmark when building your application.

Let's go over a list of some common features you can include into your mobile app, no matter the industry you operate in.

Log In/Register

This is a common feature where users can sign in or register for an account if the nature of your app requires it (*shopping/delivery/car sharing apps*). Consider that you can also include social login (via *Instagram*, *Twitter*, *LinkedIn*, etc.) to facilitate for your users.

Profile

Registration is a type of page where users can enter their details and create their profile, update their account details, and configure profile settings.

Allowing your users to personalize their account will ensure better user satisfaction.

Onboarding Process

This is one of the essential features to include in your mobile app—it is an effective way to ensure your users understand all features and value of your app.

No matter how intuitive it is to navigate your app, it will still be beneficial to remind users on certain steps.

Effective onboarding can help users get the best from your app, increasing satisfaction and frequency in interaction.

Search Filter/Categories

Mobile users want results quickly, and they would appreciate help when searching for information or trying to perform a task.

Build your app with fast loading times and incorporate filtering options to make the browsing process as seamless as possible.

For apps with rich content, the search button must be prominent and visible on the home screen for users who want to do their own search quickly.

Home Screen

A home screen is one of the main elements of a mobile application, presenting its menu and features. Keep your home screen menu accessible and functional—this screen can vary a lot due to the app's purpose, but you should keep your common features at hand for users.

For example, it is great if the home screen displays your business colors, containing search fields with visible and meaningful icons.

Share and Comment Options

Messaging apps or any other apps that wish to enable communication among users should offer users the option to share and comment or chat options.

This is an opportunity for users to share the content or comment on the posted content and make your app content more visible to a wider audience.

Feedback Option

No matter how great your app is, there will always be areas you can improve—pay attention to user feedback as the best people to provide insightful inputs are your actual customers.

Make it easy for users to provide the feedback as it will show them you value their opinion. Mobile app development requires you to focus on features most important to your users, but resist the urge to add too many—users appreciate speed and simplicity, so focus on these qualities in your development strategy.

Catalogue or Product Page

This particular feature fits ecommerce businesses the most—visual presentation plays an important role in ecommerce apps. Catalogue or product screens act as shop windows, and the better the product list is displayed, the more users would be willing to purchase your products.

Make your catalogue screen fit any screen size, and you can organize products in columns for users to scroll through.

Once you obtain and retain users, a good move is to present your products in a specific order depending on users' preferences and past activities.

Newsfeed

If your app's nature requires, you can have a newsfeed page where users can follow the latest updates from their app connections or updates from your company.

It allows them to engage with the content most relevant to them and also share the same, contributing to your app's visibility and popularity.

Since people often scroll feeds during breaks, the best option would be to create a design without overloading visual details. Remove any redundant details, improve feed typography, and do not clog entries with too many UI controls such as like, save, follow, etc.

Posting Interface

The posting interface is needed if you plan to offer your users to post text, images, videos, links, and more.

For example, in social apps, the newsfeed is constantly updated with activities by users so other app users can follow.

Private Messaging Interface

If your mobile app needs for chat services to be implemented, you should offer your users an option to post private messages to specific users they want to contact. It can be organized as live chat or comment-based chat depending on the needs and preferences. You should consult your development partner related to many types of chat features and which one would match your business needs and your mobile app.

Offline Capabilities

Users can get annoyed when an app is entirely useless just because they have a weak or no Internet signal.

Consider how to build in content or interactivity that can work offline, and it will positively impact user experience while they are on the go, online or not.

Checkout

Checkout screens must be well designed for users to feel comfortable while performing this last task in their shopping experience. Checkout screens contain a form where users fill in all the necessary data like name, address, and credit card number.

As per Baymard Institute, the average cart abandonment rate is 70%—users have left the order in the middle due to its long or confusing process.

Some good practices for checkout screens would be the following:

- The checkout button must be clearly visible and accessible.

- All methods of payment should be clearly presented with the help of visual elements.

- Ensure users that the personal data they provide is secure with you.

Analytics

One key component to incorporate into your mobile app is analytics—a business must be able to track and identify their user experience and actions. Such an insight will enable you to overview users' preferences and habits, helping you improve or tweak your app for better.

If users provide their consent, the data gathered will only help you encourage better updates.

Battery Preservation

No matter how beautiful or popular the features your mobile app has, if the battery drain is significant causing end users to not sustain the life of their device, then those features go to the wayside.

Solutions must account for battery preservation methods that ensure a prolonged experience and sustained battery life for the users.

Push Notifications

If you wish to make your mobile app interactive, push notifications are the best solution.

The push notifications feature is integrated into the mobile app and serves for consistent communication between the users and the app, even if the app is not used.

Push notifications can be text, graphic, or mix of the two sending your users to the content they may be interested in. Personalized messages are much better than unsolicited ones since they are usually targeting a particular user and are likely to be of interest to them.

Send relevant and timely notification messages to users and do not overrun them with countless messages.

If done properly, push notifications bring many benefits like the following:

- *Minimal cost*: It doesn't require a separate medium for sending; thus, the investment is minimal.

- *User control*: Users can set their preferences through your mobile app settings, reducing the risk of users getting annoyed by too many notifications.

- *Brand consistency*: Last-minute deals, discounts, coupons, and special offers sent to users tend to enhance the brand consistency as users will appreciate information that adds value.

- *Engagement*: Excellent to increase app engagement and improve retention rates.

- *Tracking analytics*: Analyzing complex analytics within open rates, delivery receipts, engagement, interaction time, and click-through rates as well as other types of analytics.

- Push notifications **provide more interaction with users** by conveying the latest updates and news. Make your notifications short containing appropriate keywords.

- Push notifications can **boost your engagement** with every alert on the latest news or events—even if users don't have time for it, it may bring escalation in involvement with your mobile app.

- The instant ping sound of a notification will drive users to open it up, ultimately **driving the app's traffic**. Pay attention to send relevant content as too frequent or rare alerts can result in loss of interest.

- Push notifications **provide insights into user behavior** like tracking interaction time and duration, devices, platforms, etc. Having these insights enables you to serve users the best way possible.

Once you have your list of features for your mobile app, you will need to prioritize them and determine how they will fit into your development plan.

Mobile development in stages is the most common practice, as it allows you to steadily grow your application while implementing user feedback along the process.

Consider key questions like

- What features are essential for users to perform the core action in the initial release?

- Will users still find the app useful if I remove a particular feature at launch?

- Which additional features could benefit from user feedback?

- And so on.

Don't be surprised if your target audience triggers the modifications following the initial release.

The best approach would be to note down the steps users would usually take when using your app.

With most mobile apps, no one reinvented the wheel—remember, even the most popular or ingenious applications have similarities to the existing ones.

Form a Strategy

After thinking about the questions and features mentioned previously, consider how your app is going to make you money as there are pros and cons to each payment structure. For more details on app monetization methods, see Section "The Best Mobile App Monetization Methods".

Completely Free

One approach is for your app to be free for users and paid for by in-app advertising banners. There are several mobile advertising platforms, and they each offer their own monetization structure. Check Google AdMob, AdColony, Unity Ads, and Epom to see which one works for you the best.

You should also consider the type of in-app ad style you want to include, for example:

- Banners (*small rectangular ads embedded on the app screens*)

- Interstitial ads (*appear when switching between screens*)

- Native ads (*designed to look like part of the app and less intrusive*)

- Video ads (*can offer rewards for clicking*)

One-Time Payment

Require a one-time payment for unlimited use of your app.

This used to be the only alternative to free apps, but its popularity has dwindled with the introduction of subscription and micro-transaction payments.

Ongoing Subscription

This is the most popular revenue-generating model for apps, especially on the Apple store. In 2020 annual spending on the top 100 subscription apps in the United States was led by Apple's App Store at 4.5 billion US dollars followed by Google's Play Store at 1.4 billion US dollars.

Micro-transactional Payments

Another very popular payment method and only surpassed by subscription-based payments.

Micro-transactions are small payments within the app that expand the features of the app, either for lifetime or for a limited time. This is an especially popular method used by gaming publishers.

Analyze Your Competition

It's important to understand the market niche of your app and determine the competition. Since the mobile app market is saturated with various apps, make sure your idea is truly unique.

It doesn't matter if there are many similar apps already available and similar to your app idea, because yours could be the one to beat them all.

Analyze your competition as it will indicate their pain points, and if you read the reviews, you'll also find out what people would like to include in the app.

Based on your findings, add favored features and highlight these when you promote your app.

If you offer useful extras, people will be more prone to onboard and switch to your app.

Phase 2: Design and Develop

Visualize Your App

Wireframes are simple drafts created to outline the look and feel of your app. They are similar to blueprint drawings for a building, except that they outline every screen, interactive object, and interaction between them.

You can put down the sketches on paper initially, but it's recommended to use one of the online tools. Digital wireframes will make it easier to make changes, especially as your wireframes become more detailed and complex in structure.

Figure 4-24. *Wireframe process (wildnettechnologies.com)*

Once your wireframes are completed, you can share them with your colleagues for feedback on navigation and app structure. If there are any glitches or bugs, this is the best time to find out—before you move onto the design and development of the actual product. Modifying wireframes at this stage is much more cost-effective than having to do it later.

If you have no idea what tools are available, don't fret. Your development team will help you at this stage, and the list of three best tools for you is coming up.

The listed wireframe tools in the following are perfect for beginners with tutorials available for any additional guidance needed:

- **Axure**

  Axure is widely popular allowing designers to create flowcharts, wireframes, and mockups. It provides an option to build app prototypes, meaning functional wireframes that can be navigated by clicking around.

  Another great feature for teams is the option to collaborate with team members and add comments throughout for feedback.

- **Moqups**

  With Moqups it's possible to wireframe any app you can think of. It also supports mockups, mind maps, diagrams, and prototypes in a small efficient package.

  The tool is entirely web based, so you will need an Internet connection to build your app project.

  Like other wireframe tools, it also supports team collaboration. Since it's all done online, there's no issue working with a remote team placed in different locations in the world.

- **Mockplus**

  In Mockplus, there are plenty of drag-and-drop elements available to build the interface you are envisioning.

By scanning a QR code, it's possible to preview wireframes on a real device in real time. Since it's all built in HTML, the compatibility is pretty much universal, and if you are somewhere without an Internet connection, wireframes can be downloaded for offline use.

It supports app team collaboration, so multiple people can work on it simultaneously.

Design Screens

Once you have a sign-off on the wireframes, the fun part starts: ***making your app pretty***.

Here's where you decide what color palette you want to be applied to your app and what fonts and icons to use.

If you are a designer yourself, you can try sketching up some designs yourself, but you have to know all the limitations of designing for the device(s) you are targeting. You also have to know what the current trends and visual styles are or, even better, what's soon to come.

A probably better option would be to hire an app development company and work with their designer. The advantage of hiring the entire team is that they'll be on the same page throughout the project.

Hiring people individually can be a recipe for disaster unless you are a pro project manager.

Put the Pieces Together

You're now at the phase where the design is ready to be handed over to the development team. They will review the technical requirements and choose the best technology stack for the app.

A common procedure is to design the development in sprints. Sprints are usually done in 2-week phases, and at the end of each phase, the app should be tested by the QA team to be sure no bugs are present for the final release.

During this phase your app is programmed natively for either Android or iOS or as a cross-platform solution for both devices in one source code. Any back-end integration with servers and APIs is also performed in this step.

In addition to the developers, another team is also brought in through this phase. They are the Quality Assurance team. More about QA in the next phase.

Test It (Early)

The Quality Assurance (QA) team tests the app throughout development for any bugs, inconsistencies, or anything not looking according to the requirements. All issues are logged in a bug tracking tool and sent back to the developer until the issues are resolved.

Usually app development includes an alpha and a beta test phase. The alpha test phase is the test phase described previously and is all happening internally.

The beta phase is when your app is almost ready to be launched in the app store. At this point you do a soft launch in a live environment similar to the final environment. The app is hosted on the publisher's app repository, but in an invite-only status.

A selected group of people are then asked to download the app and give feedback and report any bugs or issues they experience during use.

Generally speaking, a QA team can be included in the early stages of the development (*planning, defining requirements*, etc.) since that is the time when you define acceptance criteria by which the QA team will test the application later. Since not all development companies include QA at the beginning, the best is to check about this with your development partner.

Once you have gotten feedback from everyone and adjusted the app accordingly, your app is ready for the official launch in the app stores.

Phase 3: Launch

All there is left now is getting your app ready for **the launch**!

You have to write descriptions, compile enticing screenshots and videos, and figure out what geographic locations your app should be available in and of course the price of your app or payment model. For more details on your mobile app launch, check Section 6.1.

If you are launching on Google Play Store (for Android devices), always check their document that describes what conditions must be met in order for your application to be published. Apple's App Store has stricter rules; thus, always consult their detailed guidelines in order not to get rejected. However, your development team should be familiar with these policies—they will help your app to complete the required conditions to reduce the delay in releasing your application.

Once your app is live, don't rest on your laurels.

An app has to be maintained regularly to stay up to date and bug-free. Sometimes new programming functions are introduced by Apple or Google, and others are removed, so it's necessary to keep an eye on crash reports coming in and fix any issues immediately.

Developing your mobile app is an exciting venture—enjoy your app ride and make it a long-lasting one.

The Best Mobile App Monetization Methods

When you're developing your mobile app, do not forget to include planning on how you will make money out of your app.

There are many ways you can generate money, and you need to figure out the best method that matches your app idea.

Check the following mobile app monetization models that will help you benefit on each penny you have invested in your own mobile app.

How to do it?

- Prior to deciding on any monetization method, you should get to **know your target audience** to understand their behavior and the way they may use the app. If you understand your users and the way they use your mobile app, you will learn quickly what can be the best way to monetize it.

- Another important factor is **whether your mobile app is free or paid**, meaning that a free app can be downloaded and installed without any charges, while a paid app requires payment for downloading.

Always remember that each mobile app is different, so make sure to choose the best strategy that can monetize your app in the best way possible.

App Monetization Models

The most common types of app monetization models you need to understand prior to implementing any method are as follows.

Cost per Mile (eCPM) Model

Cost per mile is the preferred model for the publisher due to the fact that no matter the action taken by the user, it still brings some reward.

The common formula to use for calculation is shown in Figure 4-25.

Figure 4-25. *Cost per mile model (Zesium)*

Total earnings represent the revenue generated by the app publisher with a specific ad.

Total impressions stand for the number of clicks registered with an ad throughout the ad campaign duration.

Cost per Click (CPC) Model

As opposed to eCPM, this monetization model is regulated by a mobile user taking an action on an ad. The good thing about this model is that it attracts diverse types of advertisers aiming to deliver better ROI.

The CPC model brings risks as it will not be successful unless it generates a high click-through ratio, plus it is really difficult to predict the revenue up front.

CPC can be calculated using the formula shown in Figure 4-26.

Figure 4-26. *Cost per click model (Zesium)*

Total ad spent stands for the amount spent on the ad campaign, while total measured clicks is the number of clicks registered over a specific period of time.

Cost per Action (CPA) Model

The app revenue in the CPA model is generated only if a user takes a specific action like downloading the app or using it, clicking the ad, making in-app purchases, and so on.

It can bring a fruitful return on such ads, but it is also prone to a variety of fraud hard to detect by the publisher. Check how to calculate cost per action in Figure 4-27.

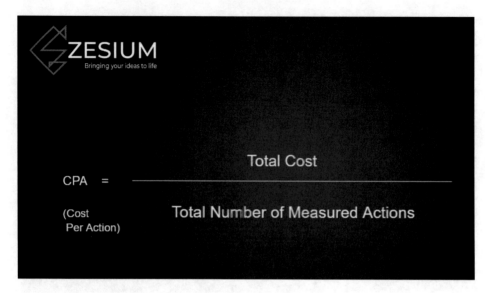

Figure 4-27. *Cost per action (Zesium)*

Some examples of monetization strategies are as follows.

In-App Advertising

In-app advertising is one of the most popular ways to monetize your mobile app. As per statistics, the potential of advertising brings the core value to your revenue model.

The important thing at the beginning is to plan how you will display the ads.

Be careful as no one wants to be bothered by a series of ads popping up when browsing through your mobile app. Figure out a way to educate your users without affecting the user experience.

Some ways to include online advertising can be

- Displaying ads on the mobile or company website

- More specific ad networks like Facebook, Google, LinkedIn, or Twitter

- Marketing strategies similar to marketplaces like eBay or Amazon

There are many types of in-app advertising within this model, and the following can be considered as the best:

- *Video ads*: The publisher gets paid if the user watches the in-app ad video.

- *Offer walls*: The user is rewarded with virtual content or additional in-game features for completing an action, and it is preferred with a cost per mile model.

- *Banners*: Banners are constantly displayed when the app is used; however, it does not generate much traffic.

- *Notification ads*: Notifications pop up within the notification bar to make the user aware of the ad.

- *Playable ads*: A new type of in-app advertising allowing users to experience the app prior to downloading it, decreasing nonessential downloads.

In-App Purchasing

In-app purchasing (IAP) is an excellent way to monetize your mobile app including a simple strategy with the apps that come for *"free to play"* but with a "pay to win" model.

Although in-app purchases aren't a much guaranteed revenue generator, they can be applied to both free or paid apps to increase the revenue.

If not done properly, it can lead to bad reviews and frustrated users, so consider these potential drawbacks prior to choosing this method. The process itself must be smooth and convenient to drive sales.

The best advice is to place your mobile app for free, add more or additional features and functionalities, and only then ask your users to pay for them.

Subscription

If your mobile app is used on a regular basis, you have a chance to monetize your mobile app by offering a subscription as it works the best for apps that deliver content.

You can create a strategy on providing content to your users for a subscription fee. However, you must take care that your content is relevant and original as users won't see the purpose of subscription unless the content is updated regularly.

This way you will attract users to visit your app more frequently and encourage them to spend more time with your app.

Subscriptions can be a steady revenue generator but only if your content follows the rule of being brand-new and relevant.

The Freemium Model

The freemium or free to play model is usually followed by web-based services.

It firstly offers the app for free for users to be able to "*experience*" the value—users can download the app but cannot access the FULL sets of features without upgrading.

Only when the users try out your app you can ask the users to pay for unlocking the additional features or an upgraded version.

The users who are satisfied or impressed by the app's features will surely pay a little more for it.

The downside is that it takes more time to generate revenue, although freemium apps usually generate more money than the paid apps. The common situation is that users decide to keep only the free app version, but don't worry—you can still earn some profit by offering upgrades or premium content.

If you implement the freemium model properly, you can easily make money through your mobile app.

Affiliate Marketing

Affiliate marketing involves earning a commission when users buy a product or service by following the link on your website or within your mobile application.

Affiliate marketing can bring you some advantages like referrals for praising others' services/products or a new sales medium for your company.

There are many affiliate programs that you can try out—check the commission rates and decide which one can be the best for you.

Another benefit affiliate marketing can bring is additional traffic for your app through hosting ads on the website as this can help you generate leads for your app.

Sponsorship

If you have no success with the ads, you can try getting sponsors for your app—it can be done in partnership with advertisers as well.

This model offers relevant rewards to customers when they complete any designated action within your app where revenue is shared among marketers and advertisers.

Sponsorship can offer personalization for users and can enrich user engagement as well as monetize the mobile app.

Some examples of the sponsorship model are

- *Sponsor banner*: Highly visible, bringing to the app visibility.

- *Sponsor tweets*: Tweets are a great medium for advertisers.

- *Sponsor pools*: Brings traffic directly to the website.

Crowdfunding

Although referred to as the LAST resort, the crowdfunding market is expected to witness a growth at a CAGR of over 16% during the period from 2021 to 2026, as per Mordor Intelligence study.

Crowdfunding is a process where a project is funded publicly over the Internet. This method can be a bit tricky because you can never be sure of the amount the public will fund for your project.

Some of the best-known crowdfunding platforms that can generate funds for your app are

- Kickstarter

- Indiegogo

- GoFundMe

- Patreon

- RocketHub

Considering that the crowdfunding method is unpredictable, it is better to use it as an additional channel to bring extra income rather than the main channel for your mobile app monetization.

Paid Download

This method is a way to generate revenue by selling your mobile app in the app store and involves users to pay once for downloading the mobile app.

If you wish to generate revenue this way, it is crucial to show your mobile app as exceptional with brand-new functionalities. If you provide value to your users that other apps fail to provide, only then you will get high visibility.

This method can be challenging as it can be rather difficult to convince users to pay for your mobile app they haven't used yet when there are a plethora of other available apps free of charge.

When trying with paid downloads, think about some downfalls—a price on the app creates a barrier for the people to download, it is not suitable for every app, the app may fail to meet users' expectation resulting in reduced download number, plus app stores take 30% of the price from the app publisher. This percentage applies to paid download mobile apps or if a user needs to pay for an upgrade package and/or addition of certain features—this does not apply on transactions related to third-party payment systems since the transactions do not go through the app stores' purchase system.

Those can be the reasons not to choose this method, but if your app offers value over other apps or if you want to tie your revenue directly to the downloads, then this might be your perfect match.

Email Listing

Email is still a very popular marketing channel, and it can help you generate revenue through your mobile app as people don't change their email addresses frequently—it gives you a chance to run some targeted campaigns.

Promotional emails are an excellent way to make people aware of your app as everyone communicates through email nowadays. Chances will eventually be on your side as it is highly likely that the email will be read at some time.

In marketing, there is a lifespan of posts on various mediums, and email is definitely on the top with a lifespan of 12 days as opposed to Facebook posts, which "*live*" only for a few hours.

You can also try to gather email addresses by enclosing your app subscription form within the email.

The email strategy can turn out to be an exceptional method as you can send your users some promotions or enable them to get some benefits if they download your app, thus increasing the chances of success.

SMS Marketing

An old-school method being SMS marketing cannot be overlooked when you want to monetize your mobile app.

SMS marketing does not require any special arrangements to function, and as almost everyone has smartphones, SMSs can be sent to users easily. The only thing you need to do, as an app publisher, is to obtain the database of smartphone users' contacts available for such purposes.

Once you have your user database, create an SMS that will be compelling for users to open—text should be simple and polite with an attractive offer and a bit of humor to trigger people's emotions and make them open the message and read the text.

White Labeling

White labeling is another way to monetize your mobile app—it involves selling a product/service under the brand name of another company. A company produces a product and then sells it to another one for further marketing, and for users, the product appears under the brand name it is advertised by.

For example, if a mobile app is developed for providing a highly positive user experience, it can be sold to other companies with an excellent marketing model for final delivery to the users.

White labeling can save a lot of money as some companies prefer to get ready-to-use applications to advertise them under their own brand name.

This model has proven practical as both sides work on the areas they are experts in—the development company can focus on the product developments, while another company will focus on promotion, distribution, and marketing.

Every mobile app requires a specific strategy.

I've listed several monetization methods, but this is just the tip of an iceberg—each method has its own pros and cons, and the trick is to choose the best one depending on the type of your mobile app and the business you're running.

The most important thing is to figure out the benefits of each method to make the best revenue out of these monetization methods.

4.4. Why Is Early Testing the Best for Your Product Success

Application maintenance is necessary for every product—it includes different processes from updating to stabilizing and securing the product's application.

If the secured application maintenance process is not initiated seriously, clients and companies could face a huge level of financial penalty while also suffering consequences of different maintenance problems.

That is the reason proper application maintenance is extremely important to rectify any issues that may be arising during the course of product functioning.

Bug Fixes

Both the application maintenance and development process encounter bugs in many ways, and these bugs can occur due to several reasons, making the application maintenance process a difficult one.

The bugs enter code during the application maintenance for the product—these specifically include last-minute changes, buggy third-party tools, and lack of version controls. Other areas of bug coding are unrealistic release schedules, miscommunications, and human mistakes.

The bugs usually occur in different varieties—some of them are seriously causing interruption in application functionality, while others frequently cause improper operation. Any kind of bugs can cause a huge problem for the entire product, so their elimination is necessary before raising a critical issue.

App bugs can cause great disappointment and annoyance with users. The users' inconvenience can be better avoided by eliminating different types of bugs on time, considering that most projects face bug elimination issues around 5–10%.

Security Patches/Updates

The application maintenance process involves an automatic update of the product system; however, both apps and software are required to support updates through the manual process as well.

The process of updating the product enables acquiring more users while gaining "*out-of-the-box*" features and an impressive brand at the same time.

The important changes come during the course of the update although it mostly consists of security stability and web application performance. The systemic functioning of updates' installation necessitates an effective working on the web application maintenance and its product review. It is good to know that the process of patching and updating software and apps is automatically resolved with the latest security problems.

Third-Party API Updates

The application maintenance process involves a direct link with the third-party service, and it mostly comprises Twitter, Facebook, and other social media sites.

The API continues to change from the third-party service, meaning that it requires a timely update of the application maintenance. The newly developed service-based APIs should be used to update the entire product.

A slow working of the product occurs if the application maintenance is not carefully and timely updated with the right API system. This kind of maintenance is not regularly overseen where both old and newly developed APIs are continuously supported with the latest web application services.

Most commonly, programmers initiate 8–16 hours to update the product with the application maintenance process, and it is usually done to support a new development of third-party API, making the overall product functions and systems functional, quicker, and more accurate.

Application Maintenance Scaling

A leading factor for the product's application maintenance is its top-most scaling. It is similar to developing an MVP of the product where the app becomes highly popular with great expectations.

The user base of the product expands regularly, increasing the challenges for maintenance and support. However, there are many actions to introduce in order to resolve such maintenance issues.

Facilitating New Functionality

Another aspect of application maintenance is facilitating a new functionality of the product, and it is quite common, involving various features. It includes value-added work while facing tough rivals in terms of applications and products. It provides better product functioning due to the addition of new features during the application maintenance process.

Amid the course of application maintenance, development of new features comes as a leading factor. The clients and businesses are required to focus on the specific problems encountered during the product development process. The users' feedback should be used for improving the overall functionality of the software or application.

Monitoring

The final step of the application maintenance of the product is its overall monitoring. Bugs cause a great issue for the product, making its functionality a serious issue. Bugs can crash apps and alter the API, forcing developers to focus attention on the application maintenance daily.

A wise strategy to ensure robust monitoring of the product and its application maintenance is to hire an IT company that has experience in monitoring the product's app. It can help developers save time from everyday app maintenance issues while receiving direct alerts regarding the product's development. Moreover, IT companies can develop the products in terms of updates, constant changes, web app development, and timely resolution of the app issues.

The timely updates enable the users to enjoy stable functioning with the latest app or software versions. It finally saves companies from a financial penalty caused by poor application maintenance, thereby improving your brand with the latest app development trends.

Maintaining the application requires the same amount of time as developing one—once you implement measures to maintain your product, you will be able to grow your application and acquire more users.

Further and regular monitoring will enable you to upgrade your application easily and efficiently.

Developing new software applications is a challenging process riddled with difficulties, especially without proper bug tracking.

As projects get more complex and ambitious in scale, software developers have a hard time tracking software defects properly. This is exactly why effective reports on found bugs are essential to successful software development.

Why Are Software Defect Reports Important

Every software development project involves certain resources and deliverables, and software companies need to deliver top-quality products.

The best recipe is to handle the defect report writing process correctly—if you fail to address critical software errors prior to launch, it may backfire on your company reputation.

Writing such software defect reports throughout your software development can bring significant benefits such as

- *Streamlined development*

- *Reduced number of defects in the launched product*

- *Higher user satisfaction with the product*

- *Easier tracking of bugs for later patching*

- *Improved reputation and reliability of your business/brand*

- *Attracting more lucrative future software projects*

Mobile App Security

Mobile app security is a critical consideration for any company today no matter the industry. If you're collecting and storing personal data, financial information, or any other sensitive info, then you will need to implement security measures to protect such data.

Mobile apps without security protocols put extreme risks to both users and developers as unprotected vulnerabilities may become targets to hackers for malware attacks or data breach.

Mobile app security must be the top concern as any unsecured mobile app is at a high-risk level.

Mobile app security is the process of defending a mobile app from fraudulent attacks like malware, hacking, or other criminal manipulations. It represents the amount of protection an app has from malware, phishing, and other harmful hacker crimes.

Android is a good example—being an open framework, it is more vulnerable to MITM (*man-in-the-middle*) attacks, data breaches, or malware assaults as opposed to the iOS platform, which is exclusive to Apple users.

Reasons to Secure Your Mobile App

More and more of the world's workforce is working remotely— freelance workers use their own laptop or computer to do the company's work, and such an approach carries risks of attacks.

A single breach is enough to invade the privacy of your company's system and customers. Hackers' usual targets are high-ranked officers in the company as they hold more valuable data; thus, it is crucial for developers to inspect the app security—developers have to provide the latest security features to protect user privacy and data.

Mobile app security, if done properly, enables users to protect confidential data and protect themselves from data loss, malware, and virus attacks as well as from lawsuits of unprotected systems.

Important mobile app features for security are

- Secure login

- Re-authentication for important actions

- Encrypting all data (*your developers can use additional layers of encryption*)

- Using secure coding techniques

- Using SSL

- Limiting login capability to online-only mode

Here are important steps in mobile app security.

Secure Database

In order to secure a database, you must fully encrypt and backup storage with well-defined data access to prevent any data breach.

Developers have to store all critical data in a secured place, no matter if it is a device or a cloud-based server.

Secure Source Code

If your developers provide a high level of security, hackers will not be able to access your app's code or decode it with diverse methods like obfuscation or conceal code.

For example, Android has ProGuard, a built-in feature making codes into confusing characters. Since being an open source platform, it is more prone to cyber attacks; thus, developers must ensure safe source code to prevent any possibility of alterations by cyber threats.

Secure Data Transmission

This is especially critical for businesses dealing with sensitive data like private users' information or banking details. Your developers must encrypt data to secure data transmission—you should use secure channels via VPN tunnels, SSL, TLS, or HTTPS communication.

If encryption-decryption algorithms are weak, they can be easily decoded by hackers, leaving the app data in the open.

You should use strong cryptography to prevent snoopers, packet sniffers, and MITM attacks:

- *Input validation tests*: These prevent malformed data from entering the app database. Such validations are already available in most mobile frameworks.

- *Data portability*: Data that can be accessed across different platforms or services like "social login" being a process of login to apps or sites with your Google, Facebook, Instagram, or other login info.

These actions help developers complete a thorough data protection and add user privacy and authentication from square one.

Perform Penetration Testing

Penetration testing is a process where malware is reproduced on your device to search for any defects that can be exploited. Such testing is commonly used to improve web application firewalls (WAFs).

Adapt your WAF security policies and patch the bugs before launching your mobile app. Both pen testing and standard software testing are crucial to boost your app's security.

Make it a regular practice to test previously written code lines to test defects and implement improvements.

Use Tokens for High-Level Authentication

A token is a unit that securely transmits information about user identities between the applications and websites. A security token authenticates a person's identity electronically by storing some sort of personal information.

Usage of complex passwords should be applied—if your mobile app requires it, design your app to accept only medium to strong passwords with alphanumeric characters. Keep in mind that it must be renewed regularly, for example, every 6 months or so.

OTP (one-time PIN/password) is valid only for one login session on a computer or any other device. You should add two-factor verifications and also additional encryption to make your app even more secure.

Other authentication methods can include fingerprint or retina scan—biometric access systems have already been introduced to level up the security measures and will be even more in the future.

An experienced development partner can offer a security recommendation, helping you choose the most appropriate features for your mobile app. If you operate in specific industries (*finances, healthcare,* etc.), make sure to be compliant with the prescribed regulations (GDPR or other relevant regulations).

Having a mobile phone is a large part of our everyday lives, and many underestimate the value a phone holds when it comes to the information it stores. Your phone contains much data from social media data to banking information.

As a business owner, always prioritize a robust level of protection and data privacy in the app for your users.

Key Takeaways

- First, **start with an MVP**—do market research, prioritize the most relevant features, choose an MVP approach, identify success criteria, and make a story map. Always keep in mind BMLI (*build-measure-learn-iterate*) as the mobile app development process includes many tweaks and repeated updates. When prioritizing features, firstly distinguish user needs and how they match your business goals and consider the ratio of feature value to the number of users. Always check on third-party services and use metrics to guide your roadmap. Pay attention to your users and monitor functional customer feedback channels while keeping an eye on competition for analysis. In case of any alteration necessary, restructure your roadmap.

Some methods you can use to prioritize your mobile app features can be the *MoSCoW matrix, RICE scoring, Kano model, bubble sort, effort and impact,* or *user story mapping.*

- When talking about design features, consider quick-loading elements, along with onboarding and minimal user input. Ensure intuitive gesturization and clean UI and always pay attention to transparent permission policies. Clear and visible CTA buttons will help your users navigate through an app, but nonetheless, include a support option. Try to provide personalized user experience as much as you can. Successful mobile interaction design for your mobile app should follow and match interactions to the platform (iOS, Android, etc.) and apply familiar patterns. Declutter and keep it short and simple—add gamelike elements to engage your users and ask for in-context permissions prior to any action from your side. Some recent popular UX design trends include doodles, illustrations, animations, asymmetry, 3D graphics, storytelling through design, and more. More tech design trends also involve Metaverse as well as design for foldable, AR and VR technologies, and Artificial Intelligence, and voice UI.

- Your development process should contain a few phases:

  - *Planning and brainstorming*: Add functionalities that are relevant to your mobile app and industry you operate in. Some common functionalities include log in/register, profile, onboarding, home screen, search bar, feedback, newsfeed, posting, share and comment sections, analytics, and more.

- *Design and development*: Visualize your app via help of your development company, or you can try some tools to help you display your idea. Design screens, put the pieces together, and test it for eventual bugs or glitches.

- *Launch*: The last phase followed by an extensive feedback and support process.

- There are many app monetization models, and you should pick the one matching your app's nature: cost per mile, cost per click (CPC), cost per action (CPA), in-app advertising or purchasing, subscription, freemium model, affiliate marketing, sponsorships, crowdfunding, email listing, or SMS marketing. ALWAYS keep your mobile app security the highest priority—secure database, source code, and data transmission. Perform penetration testing and use tokens for high-level authentication.

- If you test your mobile app early and perform actions like bug fixes, security patches or updates, and third-party updates and maintain the over application functionality, users will be more comfortable with your mobile app. Thus, you will increase retention and regular usage.

CHAPTER 5

Why Are Users Essential for Your App's Life?

In the previous chapter, we covered most of the important elements necessary for your mobile app development, but there is the most essential ingredient—YOUR USERS.

In this chapter, we will analyze how to provide great user experience through best onboarding practices and relevant user feedback. I will bring you a step-by-step guide for the user feedback process from collecting data to validating the results, as well as benefits that are essential for your product development.

5.1. How to Onboard Users to Your Mobile App

"The first impression is everything!"

This is the motto to live by when thinking about your mobile app.

Sometimes, the initial interaction with an app can be confusing instead of an intuitive flow you wished for.

© Maja Dakić 2023
M. Dakić, *Mobile App Development for Businesses*,
https://doi.org/10.1007/978-1-4842-9476-5_5

That's where app onboarding comes handy—it's one of the most crucial phases of a user's journey ensuring a great first impression.

What Is App Onboarding?

Mobile app onboarding is a set of screens leading users through your app's benefits and features.

The onboarding process is important as it educates users about the app functions and gathers profile information to deliver personalized content.

The entire process facilitates a positive user experience, leading toward a higher user acquisition and retention.

Why Do You Need Onboarding?

It can be complicated for new users to know how to navigate your app, especially if your interface is different from what they're used to.

Statistics outline that average users lose interest quickly if the onboarding is too long (*over 1 minute*) or if it takes too long to figure out how the app works.

Check Figure 5-1.

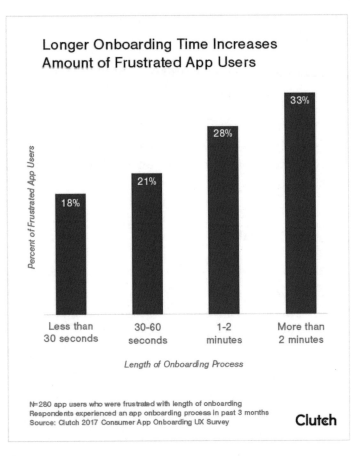

Figure 5-1. *Mobile app onboarding survey (clutch.co)*

Including an app onboarding can help the first-time usage be as seamless as possible, reducing the percentage of users abandoning the app.

User retention can be divided into three phases:

- *Short-term retention*: The most important phase—
  the initial interaction with a user can either make a
  positive or a negative effect. This phase also affects the
  following two phases.

- *Midterm retention*: The goal is to form new habits and create repetition in the routine.

- *Long-term retention*: It focuses on improving the existing product.

Following these categories, your goal should be ensuring your app is used more than once during the first week of the phase.

If you provide solid onboarding, you can activate the app's early usage and gradually increase retention.

Types of Onboarding

As there are many different types of apps and businesses today, there are also different methods of onboarding users.

All onboarding methods have one thing in common: **encourage and educate users to navigate your app**.

The most common types of onboarding are the following.

Benefits-Oriented Onboarding

This method displays the benefits and what your app does for your users rather than how to use the app.

Benefits-oriented onboarding screens, as shown in Figure 5-2 below, can also include permission requests that the users can opt in for like accessing the location and sending push notifications.

Some guidelines for a successful benefits-oriented onboarding are as follows:

- *Set a limit to display three key benefits max.*

- *Each slide must contain only one benefit.*

- *Prioritize the main benefits only for display.*

- *Consistent vocabulary.*

- *Onboarding prior to any registration process.*

- *As brief as possible.*

Figure 5-2. *Benefits-oriented onboarding example (WowMakers Blog)*

Function-Oriented Onboarding

The common example is a short tour through the app with instructions on how to get started and/or how to perform specific actions. The example of function-oriented onboarding is shown below in Figure 5-3.

Here are guidelines that can help if you want to use this method:

- *No need to explain obvious functionality.*

- *Set a limit to three slides with one function per slide.*

- *Set a clear focus, for example, helping a user get started, process a payment, etc.*

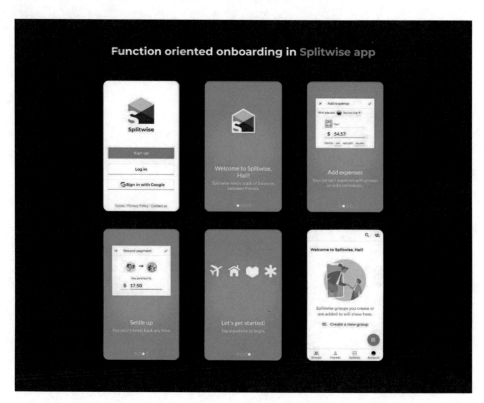

Figure 5-3. *Function-oriented onboarding example (WowMakers Blog)*

Progressive Onboarding

The method shows users new information as they progress through the app, as displayed in Figure 5-4 below.

The instructions displayed on the screen relate to the page the user is at—it resembles a live tour. For example, if users are on the registration screen, they will see only registration-related information.

It's a bit more practical as users learn as they navigate through the app instead of getting instructions up front.

Guidelines that can help if you decide for this method are as follows:

- *Use it to show complex workflow.*

- *Use it for hidden functionalities.*

- *Ideal method for gesture-driven interactions.*

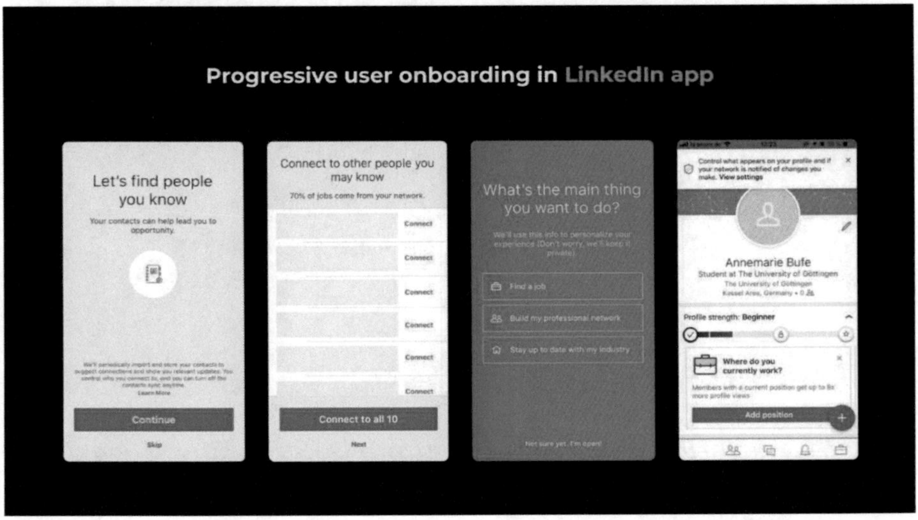

Figure 5-4. *Progressive app onboarding example (WowMakers Blog)*

Alternatives

The above-described methods are the most common ones, but you can always combine and modify them to your advantage.

Check the following examples.

Alternative 1: Hybrid

A hybrid method is nothing more than blending one, two, or all three methods together for the best service. Although it is not always possible, it can be proven useful sometimes as in the following example from the past by Flink. Check out the example of hybrid onboarding method in Figure 5-5 below.

Figure 5-5. *Hybrid app orientation example (Smashing Magazine)*

Alternative 2: Video

Some apps use videos to onboard their users, and it has proven worthy of the risk.

There are different types of videos for you to choose—some can be more practical in the form of tutorials, while others can be advertisements in nature.

Videos can be a great means of onboarding, as shown in Figure 5-6 below, but you should be careful with videos on websites—no matter the quality, avoid playing them automatically as users can find it inappropriate, thus causing a counter-effect.

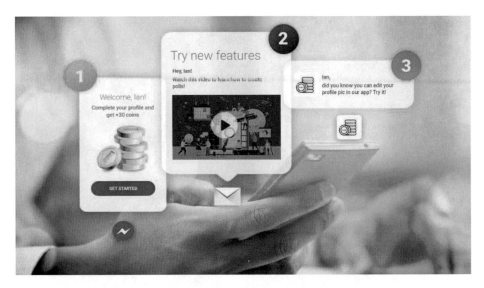

Figure 5-6. *Video onboarding example (pushwoosh.com)*

Alternative 3: Sample Data

Another onboarding method can be providing sample data for your users to experience, as in Figure 5-7. This is helpful with apps that handle delicate data like HR or finances.

Sample data allows users to feel comfortable by trying out and making mistakes while learning how your app works. If you provide such an option, users will feel more ready for a real data input.

These are some of the most common techniques for user onboarding, yet if you're still unsure which one to use, test one or two methods and check what works and what doesn't.

Figure 5-7. Data sample onboarding example (Smashing Magazine)

There is no unisize solution that fits all, so use the data to make the most of your onboarding flow.

There are many websites that provide a variety of onboarding patterns to get inspiration from such as Pttrns, Mobile Patterns, UXArchive, and Pinterest, so try to check them out if you need some fresh ideas.

The Best Practices for Onboarding Users to Your Mobile App

The initial interaction with your app should help users decide that your app is worth using regularly.

Implementing some of the following best onboarding practices can help successfully engage and retain users.

Offer Value First

People who download your app do it for a reason, and onboarding needs to show that you will meet their expectations.

Don't show off with your best features or with how your app works— it's more important to explain **what users will get from your app** and **what's in it for them** and to promote its value. Users are driven by their needs, and your app should be the tool helping them achieve their goals.

For example, mobile payment Venmo immediately shows their core value through a live feed of their transactions, showcasing diverse uses of the app as well as the popularity as in Figure 5-8.

Stick to the key features that are necessary to help users experience the app's value.

Figure 5-8. *Value promotion by the Venmo app (justinmind.com)*

Ask for Essentials Only

When creating any action (*signup/registration/payment/onboarding*), make it as easy as possible for users and ask only for essential details and permissions.

For example, if you have an event app, you can request a location access (*with explanation that it's needed to find nearby events*), but don't ask for access to their camera or contacts as it can cause counter-effects, eventually leading to users abandoning the app.

Once the users complete brief onboarding, you can later display additional options like signing up for a reward process, promo coupons, or other incentives.

Don't ask for more than you need and give your users an idea of exactly what they're signing up for.

Make It Simple and Brief

People quickly get tired of pages of instructions, and it's important not to overrun them with too many input fields at once.

A good choice can be illustrations and app screenshots to convey important messages, as shown in Figure 5-9, as it will avoid heavy text explanations that can discourage new users.

Some complex apps requiring detailed instructions may use the progressive onboarding method as it will break the process into a step-by-step guide making it less tedious.

Make sure the content is short and just tell users what they need to know in as few words as possible.

Figure 5-9. *Compact onboarding screen examples (orangemantra.com)*

Ensure Concise Signup

A complicated signup process can be a main cause of churn.

Remember, people use your app *on the go*, and no one wants to spend a long time completing input fields.

You can provide social signup options via Facebook, LinkedIn, Gmail, etc. as it will save them time and energy and remove a great deal of friction points from the process.

For example, WhatsApp or Viber automatically detects SMS to simplify phone verification so that users don't have to leave the app for a code to enter. This makes the process super-fast along with a great user experience.

Ensure that the registration process is as easy as possible.

Promote Your App's Content

Sometimes, the signup process itself can represent a barrier between the user and your app.

You should let users jump into your app and experience it before asking them to sign up—it's a good way to speed up the process of new users recognizing your app's value.

For instance, if you have an ecommerce app, you should allow users to browse your products prior to creating an account. If a user tries to purchase a product, then you can ask them to make a new account.

A good example is Airbnb, as in Figure 5-10—their users can browse available accommodations and dates, but they are only asked to sign up once they're ready to book a trip.

If you let users see what your app offers beforehand, they will know how worthy your app is to them.

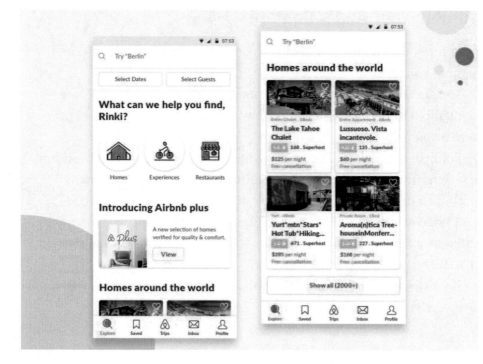

Figure 5-10. *Content promotion by the Airbnb app (Airbnb)*

Provide a "SKIP" Option

Keep in mind that some people may want to jump right into the app and explore it on their own.

A good idea is to provide your users with an option to skip the process while you can monitor to see what performs better with your users.

Today, many apps offer the **"SKIP"** option, which has been proven worthy—one example is a video streaming app Vevo that added the **"SKIP"** option and reported increased logins by almost 10%.

Another example is Slack, Figure 5-11 below—as opposed to other apps that offer a **"SKIP"** button at the beginning of the onboarding flow, Slack provides the option on each onboarding screen.

This way, users can leave the process as soon as they feel ready to use the app, and it gives them a choice in case they get bored or frustrated—instead of leaving the app, they just exit the onboarding flow.

Providing users with a choice to SKIP onboarding will fit their needs and make them stick around.

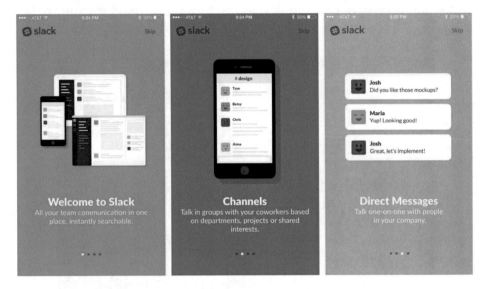

Figure 5-11. *Example of an onboarding feature (Slack)*

Motivate First Conversions

If you wish for people who download your app to keep using it, you may offer them certain incentives for completing onboarding tasks.

The ways you can motivate your users will depend on the nature of your app—apps using in-app purchasing as monetization will benefit from *time-limited discounts*, while freemium apps can motivate users by *usage-based rewards*.

Reward points, coupons, specialized content access, promo codes, free shipping, and other offers will help you activate new users and encourage user engagement as well as help drive conversions.

A great example is Starbucks—their app prompts users to create an account where rewards play a major role in the app's value proposition.

On the following screen, Starbucks even says *"Join Rewards"* instead of *"Sign Up,"* making it clear to users that they can save money by joining their app - check it out in Figure 5-12.

A small incentive from your side can be a great deal for your app's success.

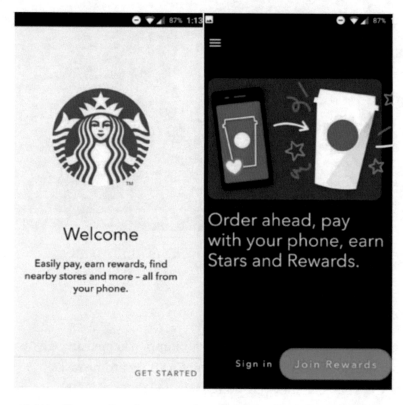

Figure 5-12. Example of an app loyalty program (Starbucks)

Use Cross-Channel Messaging

Your app should communicate with your users via short tips and notifications to guide them through the process.

Don't display unexpected pop-ups, but rather communicate how much is left in the process and make users feel welcome and thank them for their time.

Welcome emails, push notifications, and in-app messages can work together to help users experience your app's value and drive them to complete the onboarding process.

You can combine text (e.g., *to check out a new feature*), emails, and push notifications (e.g., *to complete a registration process*) to engage users and encourage them to open the app again and do specific tasks.

All your onboarding messages should be simple and direct with a visible CTA (call to action).

Don't spam users with numerous messages and don't try to cover all features or benefits in a single email.

Measure Results

In order to achieve effective onboarding, you'll have to monitor your results.

Analytics is a powerful insight tool to understand users' behavior—there are various tools for user segmentation, which can help you group users by specific actions and create custom messages for each group.

Monitoring usage and app analytics provide insights into which users experience problems and where. Tracking the pain spot for users can help you mitigate any potential friction points.

There are various platforms to help you monitor app use and track its success.

Finally, do not forget to test the entire process before offering—make sure that you offer your users a process that is short and easy.

Good onboarding displays a proper mix of educating users on how to use your app and showcasing the value you offer.

The result is a worthwhile user engagement that can increase your app's success.

5.2. Methods to Collect User Feedback

Before Collecting the Feedback

Before you start collecting user feedback, it would be wise to **prepare the ground**.

#1. Specify the Objectives

Don't make a mistake and jump into collecting feedback with no clear goal—**define the objectives first** as it will help you choose the right method and the right tool.

You should understand clearly which category your app belongs to and **what kind of feedback** you need to collect from users.

#2. Select the Right Method

When you define your feedback goal and resources, review and **choose the proper method**.

Review the automation user feedback tools that require little effort to set up and manage so to help your team.

#3. Experiment

Be open to experiment!

Example: If your feedback results are low, **try changing the feedback approach** or use different methods.

Such experiments will help you gain more valuable feedback, thus improving your app and overall user experience.

#4. Consider the Cost

You should figure out which different feedback system to implement to **determine the cost** and organize your team and the delivery plan.

Adding a feedback to an app mainly involves three tasks:

- Design and develop the app UI for the implementation of the user feedback.

- Design and develop the back-end system to manage feedback data.

- Process and analyze the amount of collected data and interact with users.

User Feedback Methods

There are various methods to collect user feedback, so make sure to review them and choose the most appropriate as per your defined app goals.

The common forms of feedback in mobile applications include the following.

Ask for a Like

Users pick one option, YES or NO, from a simple question: "*Do you like the app?*"

If the choice is YES, the user can be guided to rate your app and write comments at the store. If the answer is NO, you should display a simple feedback form in the app, allowing users to send additional information.

The technique can greatly increase the positive evaluation rate of an app and reduce the influence of negative comments. It enables for all feedback to be managed the same way in the back end, which is more convenient for reviewing and tracking of feedback state and others.

This can also bring extra cost within the development of a back-end management platform except when using third-party services.

Ask for Rates and Reviews

Another way to collect the feedback is to simply ask users to rate or review your app—both platforms (*Android and iOS*) support such requests. Mobile app ratings directly affect how easily your app can be found at the stores.

The important thing is to find the perfect timing—many apps ask for reviews instantly, but this usually annoys users as they did not have enough time to get familiar with your app to give a score.

For example, if your app has a low star rating, it may indicate that there's an issue within the app or other parts.

Selecting the appropriate people to prompt ensures getting valuable feedback from your satisfied users but also triggering unhappy or inactive users to provide direct feedback.

In-App Net Promoter Score

Net Promoter Score (NPS) is another method to measure general sentiment but also allows users to send personalized feedback. An example is given in Figure 5-13 below.

Such a process divides users into three groups: ***promoters***, ***passives***, and ***detractors*** based on their answers.

How likely are you to recommend this product to a friend or colleague?

Not at all likely 0 1 2 3 4 5 6 7 8 9 10 Extremely likely

Figure 5-13. *Net Promoter Score method (Pinterest)*

Measuring how many people would recommend your product will help you learn more about general sentiment among your users. You can also add follow-up questions asking to explain their score and get more personalized feedback you can act upon.

NPS is easily added to your mobile app—the process is smooth for users, and they don't have to leave your app to give feedback.

Support Communities

You shouldn't do everything "*INSIDE*" your app—you can create communities outside of your app where users can express their opinions and concerns, ask for support, or just engage with your team.

Here are few ways app companies can create communities:

- Support through social media and email

- Web forum on your site to help users connect and share their experiences

- Multiple ways for customers to get in touch directly with your team

Beta Tests

Developers frequently use beta tests to get insight into user experience, especially before the official release.

You can gather potential beta testers through your website via a simple web form asking for their email addresses.

Beta testing ensures that any bugs that designers, developers, and alpha testers failed to see are discovered and eliminated. Beta testing will enable you to understand how users will perceive your product in the future, which is very important as it can improve the QA of the final product.

Beta testing can save you from a lot of potential PR issues if you launch a poorly made product; thus, a proper beta launch can cut your costs significantly.

Feedback Surveys

Creating useful surveys takes more challenges than you can expect, considering there are plenty of questions you can ask and you need to select only a few to collect valuable feedback.

Try to follow some simple practices:

- Ask only relevant questions.

- Create friendly open-ended questions.

- Create consistent rating scales.

- Avoid leading questions.

A good tool to understand your users' sentiment is a mobile survey—short mobile surveys with specific questions (e.g., *feedback on a new feature*) are the most efficient ones.

Always remember that the timing of surveys is critical—if your survey interrupts customer in-app experience, it may result in more harm.

Companies can collect and analyze both quantitative and qualitative feedback from users with the help of such surveys.

Email and User Contact Forms

Email is the easiest way to gather user feedback as you can use each interaction to gather feedback. Try to follow some steps to maximize chances of reply.

Set Clear Expectations

Users usually don't leave feedback as they believe they will never hear back from you.

If you add a short sentence to your communication messages advising users you will soon reply to them, for example, *"We'll get back to you within 24 hours,"* you will build trust with your community.

Organize Email Feedback

Use some tools (e.g., *Trello*) to assign tasks for the whole team to access so that no insight is left overseen.

Automation tools will facilitate the process and keep tabs on requests while also giving the employee a clear roadmap for the future user interactions.

Send Personalized Responses

Emails enable you to request more personalized feedback than in a survey.

Ask your users about the issues they struggle with or what features they would like to see or just ask why they chose your app! You can see the example of a simple Contact us form in Figure 5-14.

Set a defined process of replying to these emails, or the entire process will be futile.

The greatest benefit of email is low cost—considering that most of the time users willing to send an email with feedback tend to be more loyal, it is more likely they will provide valuable data or interesting ideas.

On the other hand, the collected feedback would be scattered over the email messages, making it more difficult for a review and data analysis.

This approach is suitable for limited budget cases, short development time, and/or a development team not skilled enough for back-end development.

Figure 5-14. *Contact Us form (*ventureharbour.com*)*

Usability Tests

Usability tests for mobile apps are created to observe test users while they use your app—the goal is to measure the user friendliness of the app and support your brand better.

Such testing helps you add value to your business and meet the requirements of your end users.

Ensuring to have good usability for your mobile app will help you improve user satisfaction and increase revenue.

From understanding your product better, detecting loopholes, and more, here are some benefits of mobile usability testing:

- Understanding the user's in-app behavior

- Identifying bugs

- Saving on development costs

- Getting repeat customers

- Creating outstanding UX

Social Listening

Social listening is another great strategy for user feedback—comments or direct mentions on social networks and also built-in polling tools.

Social media is invaluable when it comes to client feedback—there are different social listening tools available to collect what people say about your product or brand.

Keeping track of such mentions serves to improve your user experience and respond quickly to any reports.

You can set up alerts for your brand mentions via Google Alerts, Mention, or other tools and always keep in mind that **TIME** plays a significant role! You should quickly address any negative comments as it can have a huge impact on your brand's reputation.

Many brands now combine in-house employees and third-party tools to monitor all their social channels.

Message Center

A good way to provide a good user experience is to have a channel where users can turn to easily in case they need a quick response or have feedback—a message center, as in Figure 5-15, can be an excellent conversation channel for that.

Another good point is that your feedback system directs the messages to your center rather than to the app store, thus eliminating friction for the user and reducing your bad reviews on the store.

Gathering the right people and guiding them to your most efficient communication channel is the right recipe for improved user experience.

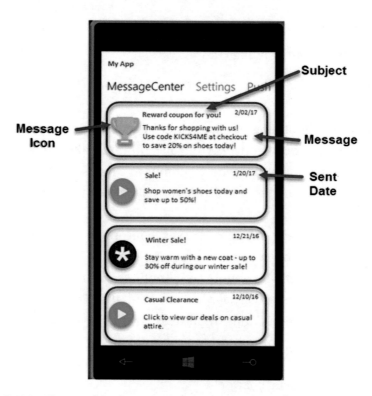

Figure 5-15. *Example of an app message center (oracle.com)*

Questionnaire

Another effective way for feedback is a questionnaire, which lists targeted questions and multiple-choice answers for users. If you keep it simple, users will happily answer questionnaires, but if questions are too long, it can trigger users' resistance.

This approach requires determining the feedback goals in advance, defining what is more urgent at the current stage, and then creating questions and forms. Designing questionnaires requires drawing as many details as possible out of the least amount of questions.

In terms of development, web page–like forms can provide a powerful back-end data analysis function.

Content-Rich Feedback

Since textual feedback can be inconvenient for users when describing some complex scenarios, more and more apps allow feedback combining text and voice for users to express their thoughts more easily. This greatly increases the probability of users taking the initiative to provide feedback.

If you want to take screenshots faster, in addition to the default screenshot feature of the system, there are also apps supporting the "*shake*" gesture to trigger the screenshot. One of the biggest advantages of screenshot feedback is that there is no need to take up any screen space with dedicated controls.

The downside of voice feedback is the operation cost as it uses analysis and classification of a great number of collected recordings.

Other Tools

Some other tools you can use to review for collecting user feedback are mParticle, Apptimize and more.

Incorporating such automation tools will help you drive more engagement, collect valuable user feedback, and adjust your product roadmap.

Review all of the tools and choose the best tool that corresponds to your mobile app, your strategy, and your targeted users.

While Collecting the Feedback, Respond to User Feedback in Time!

Once you have successfully integrated the module into your app, you should retrieve first-hand user feedback.

Whether feedback is positive or not, users will want to know whether it's received—replying to user feedback in due time is a giant leap toward improving customer satisfaction:

- *Contact users advising their feedback was received and will be processed in a timely manner and express sincere appreciation.*

- *Contact users based on their feedback content— answer their questions or clarify the future product improvement plan and so on.*

- *Notify users when their suggestions have been accepted. This will allow them to better use the app, but also let them take some pride in improving your app.*

Email is one of the means that is most unlikely to disturb the user; thus, it is important here that the design of any form of feedback takes into account the provisioning of users' email addresses for later tracking.

Sticking with these principles will help you find the balance between not bothering users and compiling the necessary data to determine which elements of your app need improvement.

Upon Collected User Feedback

Once you've got feedback from your mobile users, you need to act upon it.

Otherwise, your users will feel like their opinions don't matter and that you're not interested in creating a better experience for them.

That is why you should do the following.

Track the Right Metrics

Focus on things that are easily measurable and track the right metrics:

- The percentage of purchases made through mobile devices

- The number of visits from mobile

- Time on site on mobile vs. your website

- Number of daily installs and their sources

- Measuring the effectiveness of marketing initiatives

For example, if you're using NPS (Net Promoter Score), you'll be able to determine how many users like your app or a feature and so on, while if you do not use it, you must search the feedback for the common strains like how many people are complaining about bugs or unhappy with how slow the app is and similar.

Encourage Users for Continuous Feedback

In order to encourage customers to give continuous feedback, build feedback channels into the app experience. Come up with a schedule that's triggered by a user's actions.

For example, when they've been using the app for 10 days, ask for a review. After 3 months of active use, ask them to update their review.

Analyze Feedback Data and Adjust the Roadmap

Ultimately, you should summarize, classify, and analyze the feedback data to identify the issues within your product as well as to prioritize them. That way, you can adjust your product roadmap accordingly.

If necessary, you can perform further user surveys and interviews with the aim to plan the next development and release.

Identify Sources

Once you've gathered the input, identify sources and categorize the feedback. Where does it come from? Surveys, support emails, tweets?

Make sure to document inventory or try to visualize the streams of feedback.

Organize and Categorize

Read through the data that comes in—note down the things you observe as sidenotes and try not to jump to conclusions. Dig in and understand what your users are saying, but remember, proposals are not to be taken literally.

Structure your data and categorize it—was it a complaint, a compliment, an idea, or a feature request? Make a clear structure and find an easy way to tag your content.

Sort the Input

With sorting, you will be able to clearly identify patterns and make those actionable. You will be able to distinguish the large from the small stacks and clear from the ambiguous ones.

See threads, patterns, and things that belong together or recur throughout the data. Label each stack with a category name and a short description. You can also add quotes or audio/video if you think it will represent the underlying data better.

This will usually serve as input for design helping reach informed decisions with specific design challenges.

Unify Data

The next step is understanding—some things can be obvious like "*a button that does not work*," but some other things can be tricky to fully grasp, for example, if the app appears to be sluggish or causes confusion related to the pricing models.

Write a Story

Start to formulate your specific insights from these.

- What is new about the feedback and why is it important?

- What have you learned that you didn't know before you started?

Instead of jumping to solutions, formulate "*how might we*" statements. As an example, "*How might we provide clarity in our subscription pricing?*"

Each insight might lead to one or several ideas. Some might be as clear as "*fix xyz*" and others more ambiguous such as "*people feel uncomfortable about their own behavior in relation to this technology.*" Write a to-do, a user story, or an epic that can be used for the next build cycle.

Validate and Share

Not all insights are created equal; therefore, carefully weigh the importance of each insight.

A great way to order your insights by importance is how closely the insight connects to your mission. What are you trying to achieve, and what stands in the way of that success? If you feel your team is still unclear about where you are headed, spend more time there.

Share your most important insights and what you have learned with your users or customers and with your team. This is the fastest way to see if what you have done actually makes sense. If not, ask yourself if it is because of the content or the presentation of the content.

Here are a few ideas on how to do this:

- The all-hands meetings for sharing and having your findings challenged. Keep the number of insights low and back them up with video/audio/snippets.

- Keep an internal blog and share the stories there.

- Put them in a Slack (or similar) channel. This way your team can consume them in *"by the way"* mode.

Rinse and Repeat

Now that you have set up a structured approach to user insights, repeat the process and make it a part of each iteration.

You'll become more aligned with your users' needs over time.

Make sure to conduct wide data analysis on your results and adequately adjust your mobile app roadmap. Also important: Don't forget to thank your users for their feedback and inform them on recent improvements.

If you try to follow these steps, the feedback automation will perform its magic and let users help in improving your mobile application.

User feedback will help you get an overview of your product from a fresh perspective, allowing you to adjust your product roadmap and improve your app for the better. No matter if you follow Agile development or not, quick and frequent feedback is one of the important factors that can make your app more successful.

Implementing the right feedback system and defining a user journey map will help you motivate your mobile app users at the right time.

In the following sections, we will review some of the best practices for you to maximize your app value and functionality.

5.3. How to Prioritize Feedback and Put It in Action

Before analyzing, make sure you have gathered all the feedback in one place.

There are some common ways on how to prioritize user feedback and turn it into your biggest strength.

Here's how you can turn user feedback into an advantage for your business.

Collect and Consolidate Your Data

Firstly, sort all user feedback that you want to analyze into a spreadsheet and add key metadata about each user (*you can include how long a person has been a user, how much they spent, the date and source of the feedback, etc.*).

Your table could look similar to Table 5-1.

Table 5-1. Example of the Feedback Sort Method (Intercom.com)

Product area	Customer feedback	Feedback type	Feedback theme	Feedback code	Customer since	Customer type	Monthly spend	Feedback submitted	Source	Customer ID
Rewards team	"I love your product! I really wish I could send stickers to my teammates to say thank you"	Feature request	Stickers	Ability to send stickers to teammates	6/7/2014	5 DAU	$150	1/11/2016	Website feedback form	NC295473

After you collect the feedback, such systematization will consolidate incomplete or inconsistent data. There are many different segments of users, and grouping them per different aspects (*frequency* and others) will be helpful as each user has their own expectations from your company.

Upon carefully examining the data, discover common themes as well as repetition of the feedback. For example, if many users from different segments complain about the same thing (e.g., *onboarding process* and others), then you should act on it.

Categorize Feedback

If you take your time to review the comments and try to uncover patterns within responses by categorizing them, you will get even more valuable insights.

Once you start reviewing the comments, you will notice categories that can contain elements like speed, availability, registration, price, and so on.

Create categories and review the comments again to mark them with an appropriate category, the example of categorization is given in Figure 5-16. If a single comment refers to more than one category, you can divide it into parts and mark each part of the comment.

Expect that comments will be both positive and negative, and you can start dividing them into matching columns in your table (e.g., *Excel*) with proper sections.

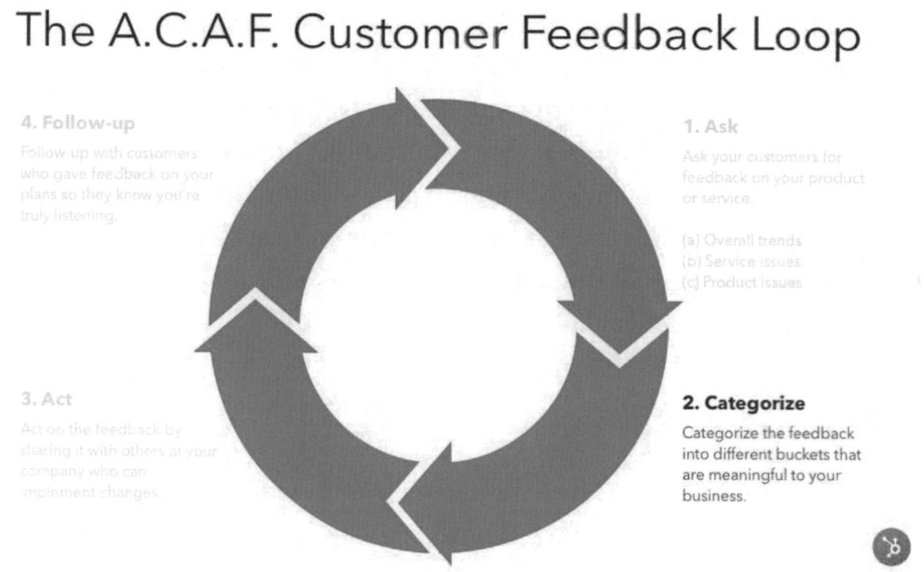

The A.C.A.F. Customer Feedback Loop

4. Follow-up

Follow-up with customers who gave feedback on your plans so they know you're truly listening.

1. Ask

Ask your customers for feedback on your product or service.

(a) Overall trends
(b) Service issues
(c) Product issues

3. Act

Act on the feedback by sharing it with others at your company who can implement changes.

2. Categorize

Categorize the feedback into different buckets that are meaningful to your business.

Figure 5-16. *The A.C.A.F. customer loop (hubspot.com)*

Some common rule to help you to understand the feedback is to group it by

Feedback Type

Categorizing feedback into different types is helpful if dealing with inconsistent feedback from your customer support or customers who wrote anything they wanted in your survey field.

Some common categories that can be useful are

- Usability issues

- New feature requests

- Bugs

- Pricing

- Generic positive comments

- Generic negative comments

- Junk (*nonsense feedback*)

- Other (*for feedback hard to categorize where you can later come back and re-categorize if any patterns appear within the rest of the data*)

Feedback Theme

Sorting out feedback per theme is useful if you're trying to make sense of the high volume of different feedback. If you have a small data set (*around 50 pieces of feedback*), you may not need it.

The themes you create will be unique to the feedback you get and will relate to the aspects of your product.

For example, if you received a lot of user feedback, your themes can look like a list of product features such as

- Profile

- Mentions

- Newsfeed

- Onboarding

- Etc.

Such categorization can help you even more when you have to provide your insights to more than one team (*if one team works on mentions and another on your profile and so on*).

You can also create team-related themes (*marketing, sales, customer support*, etc.) for better efficiency—try to create some themes and see if such category types can be useful to your teams.

Feedback Code

Feedback code is necessary to clarify unsorted feedback from users and to rephrase it in a more actionable way.

Create the feedback code detailed enough so that even an inexperienced person can understand the subject of the feedback.

The feedback code should be concise and matching user feedback as possible—you must refine the feedback whether you like it or not.

An example can be like that in Table 5-2.

Table 5-2. Example of Feedback Code (producthabits.com)

Customer feedback	Feedback type	Feedback theme	Feedback code
"I love your product! I really wish I could send stickers to my teammates though; it would be really nice to use them to say thank you"	Feature request	Stickers	Ability to send stickers to teammates

In order to uncover such details, you should segregate your feedback data. A common practice is to create a table with Excel or Google Sheets or any other tool you find suitable and import all your feedback data.

Your feedback will come in both structured (*ratings or ranking indicators*) and unstructured forms (*comments, complaints*, etc.), so you can also add a category to help you consolidate your data more efficiently.

You can make a list of all complaints or praises in one place. After you fix and test it, update the app and request more feedback again.

When new feedback arrives, assess the situation again for better insights—if there's no improvement, then the issue might be elsewhere, and if the problem is resolved, it's a win for you.

This process is repetitive—analyze the data, fix specific issues, and repeat the feedback loop until everything is working properly.

Get a Quick Overview

Before you start coding your feedback data, you should review the feedback to understand the variety in responses.

If you review feedback and end up with almost each customer giving different feedback, you will most likely have to analyze a higher volume of data to discover the patterns.

However, if you scan through the first batch of feedback and the majority relate to a particular issue within your app, you will have to review less.

Code the Feedback

There are different ways to code your feedback, but the usual manual procedure is to create two spreadsheets, as shown in Figure 5-17—one to keep your code frame and the other for coding each piece of feedback per specific code frame.

You can structure your feedback by code frame to separate positive from negative comments, or you can code each piece of feedback per several codes from the code frame.

Another method of manual coding is to use feedback types as one of hierarchy levels such as usability issues, bugs, new feature requests, etc.

	A	B	C	D	E	F	G	H	I	J	K
	ID	NPS	Type	NPS catego	Why	Code1	Code2	Code3	Code4	Code5	Code6
M1		5	NPS	Detractor	Nice campu	10	36				
M2		8	NPS	Passive	I love it ove	23					
M3		7	NPS	Passive	Paper recoֲ	16	7				
M4		8	NPS	Passive	Possibility	7					
M5		1	NPS	Detractor	I do not likֳ	45					
M6		4	NPS	Detractor	The lecture	40	32				
M7		3	NPS	Detractor	Very poor r	31					
M8		8	NPS	Passive	One focuseֳ	37					
M9		6	NPS	Detractor	Because we	23					
M10		6	NPS	Detractor	I will recom	1	13	10	20	39	
M11		7	NPS	Passive	Many choiֳ	7					
M12		6	NPS	Detractor	For the priֳ	17	1	42			
M13		8	NPS	Passive	It gets a ver	1	11				
M14		4	NPS	Detractor	Yes for the ֳ	3	42	31			
M15		9	NPS	Promoter	We are tauֳ	24					
M16		10	NPS	Promoter	Because it i	18					
M17		6	NPS	Detractor	Because the	6	33				

Figure 5-17. *Example of a coding feedback sheet* (`reviewmonitoring.com`)

When you go through the entire feedback and carefully code each row, your exact feedback codes will be specific to the product/service that the feedback relates to.

For example, a few analysis codes you can use to a new feature request can be

- The ability to send emojis

- Assigning tasks to multiple clients

- Onboarding process

If any piece of feedback talks about multiple points (*two different feature requests and so on*), it is useful to capture these two separate points in separate columns.

Whether positive or negative feedback, if you spot certain words that appear frequently (e.g., *negative, bad experience; positive: easy to use and so on*), it will instantly indicate widespread use.

It can also help color your spreadsheet to easily see the emerging patterns or to run a sentiment analysis and get an overview whether customers are mainly satisfied, neutral, or dissatisfied.

Refine Your Coding

You can start with higher-level codes and break them down later.

Focus on the exact language people use as sometimes, similar issues can turn out to be quite different issues after all. As you go through more feedback, you can realize that you have to break a single popular code into several pieces of more specific code.

For example, you realize you have a lot of user feedback related to *email issues*, but as you read more, you realize that these can be divided into separate issues like *"email delivery bug"* or similar, which are quite different.

Always remember to go back and recode the earlier codes if necessary.

Analyze the Popularity of Each Code

Once you've finished coding your feedback, the next step can be to determine the total amount of feedback per a single code—it will help you see what kind of feedback is the most common and which patterns exist in your user feedback.

A great way to do this is to sort the data into *"feedback type," "feedback topic,"* and *"feedback code"* columns and group similar items together. After that, you can highlight all items with the same feedback code, and a total count will appear—create a summary table to record all total counts for each feedback code.

If you have a large data set (*more than 500 pieces of feedback*), you can create a pivot table for these calculations—it is valuable to analyze the other user attributes that you collected. For example, put your user attributes (*user type and so on*) into a spreadsheet and look for other correlations you received, for example, what is the monthly spend of users demanding a new feature and similar.

Summarize and Share

You've coded your data, and now you can create a summary of user feedback data based on the popularity and discuss it with your team.

If you have little feedback (*less than 50 pieces*), you can summarize actionable feedback in a simple table or a document.

A large set of feedback can be broken down by other variables like "*feedback type*," "*feedback topic*," etc.

Such practice will make it much easier for you to identify different groups of feedback and channel them to different people in your team who should act on them.

Keep in mind that the most powerful thing you can do with feedback is to prioritize.

You can create top ten user issues that you can then use to adjust your product roadmap.

Take Action

Implementing feedback successfully is a significant part of product development.

If poorly managed, user feedback can divert you from the real problems, and you can end up wasting time and resources.

However, if you manage your feedback properly, you can come up with new ideas and plan your improvements more effectively.

Summarize previously reviewed feedback into a short document and share it with your team for further planning.

An effective method is to try to incorporate user feedback at each stage of the development process leading to the final "***thank you***" email. Never forget to thank your users no matter if the feedback is positive or negative. The example of a 'Thank you' email is shown in Figure 5-18.

Figure 5-18. *Example of a "Thank you for your feedback" email (Pinterest)*

Unstructured insight is the one that will help you build a better product, but other data can help as well, like product purchase history, lifetime value, and more.

Automate User Feedback Analysis with Third-Party Software

There are many specialized solutions for automating user feedback analysis where some are more DIY than others.

Some of these solutions are

- Text analytics solutions like Lexalytics, RapidMiner, Thematic, and similar

- Qualitative data analysis solutions like NVivo, Dovetail, ATLAS.ti, Quirkos, etc.

- Voice of the customer (VoC) platforms like Medallia, Qualtrics, Clarabridge, Confirmit, and more

You should check each solution and confirm its features and if they correspond to your needs for analyzing the feedback. For example, some tools have both manual and automatic methods for coding feedback, while others can unify user data no matter the feedback channel and so on.

Check each of the solutions and decide which one suits your needs best.

Without a feedback process in place, your company might overlook some apparent mistakes, which can prevent you from achieving the revenue you want. When it comes to feedback, the more details you have, the better.

Start with consolidating the data for a preliminary analysis, look for patterns and correlations, and then tackle the issues—afterward, test until you notice the improvement in feedback.

In case you get stuck, you can always use some tools that can give you further insight.

Keep in mind that the feedback process is a never-ending process. You should ensure that your feedback process is a loop—listen to your users, make improvements, and continue to collect feedback.

Benefits of User Feedback for Your Mobile App

Your most unhappy customers are your greatest source of learning.

—Bill Gates

The best way for your mobile app to thrive is through user feedback as it is one of the main elements in improving user satisfaction and growing your business.

Although a high average rating can be really great, it can also shift your focus from quality customer feedback behind each star. Ratings don't provide valuable information but only show whether your users like your app or not—in other words, you cannot identify the features for improvement or modify your product roadmap to make the changes quickly.

You will also need qualitative data to provide context and insight—ratings are important, but reviews are even more so as they help maintain the health of your app.

When used together, brands can really understand their customers' needs and pain points.

As competition is tough, it is vital for you to develop an app that provides value to its users and that is functional and engaging.

Let's list some reasons it is essential to regularly receive feedback from your users.

Locates Improvement Areas

You know your product inside out, yet sometimes you cannot see all the imperfections.

It is extremely important to get insight into what your users like, but make sure to listen only to the most relevant feedback.

Create a feedback system where users can express their opinions so you can decide which features to keep, which ones aren't so relevant, and which new features should be created.

Once you receive the feedback, don't put everything into a feature backlog but rather in a *"feedback bank"*—no matter how much you love users for sharing their concerns, you must be careful about applying them to product management. Each feature has a lifetime cost that includes maintenance, debugging, additional server load, etc.

For example, a bug could sometimes take days to fix, or adding a new feature could take a month to implement—investing your resources into something that is not relevant for your app could turn out to be a waste of time.

That's why it is essential to filter the feedback and sort your priorities— only then you implement a new feature and stay assured that your company will produce the app that meets user expectations.

Makes Users Feel Involved

By asking your users to provide feedback, you show them they are an active participant in making the app better for them. When users feel appreciated, they start having positive connotations of your brand, which they display by sharing their good user experience to other potential users—the result could be more *"sales"* in the future.

Make sure you use collected opinions to reach decisions about your app and communicate it to your users to keep them engaged. By not doing so, you risk your users feeling neglected or ignored.

A good try is to implement a customer feedback loop that is a strategy for constant product improvement based on users' feedback.

Remember, communication should always be a two-way street—try to create in-app surveys and specifically ask about their pain points within an app—this way, users can state the issues they face in the app or rate certain services, thus giving further understanding to developers what is needed in the app.

Such a method provides a feeling of direct involvement of users within upgrading your app.

Produces Personal Recommendation

Personal recommendations are the top reason for purchase decisions within users. Referrals are the most effective yet free way of advertising, and it resembles word-of-mouth type of advertising.

Some other factors like advertising or price comparison influence users' decision at some point, but referrals remain important during each stage of the purchase process.

It is said that 71% of consumers are more likely to make a purchase following a recommendation or word of mouth.

Such referrals usually come from trusted people like friends or family, and it can be the most convincing tool.

If you wish to get users through referrals, first make sure that users' feedback is positive. Do not forget to thank your users for making a referral—a good idea is to consider some appropriate way to reward them, through a discount, unlocking certain premium features, etc.

Bad Feedback for the Better

Do not worry if you receive some bad feedback—bad ones should be valued even more than the good ones (*as my colleague Vladimir Nikić from Zesium would say, "I don't want to hear good stuff. Tell me what's bugging you"*) as those users stepped out to share their bad experience expecting from you to act on it.

Firstly, it is highly important to create an action plan to deal with the bad feedback. Contact the users, address the issue, and advise them on the exact date when you will follow them up. If the problem is more complex to resolve, make sure to compensate the user for the unhappy experience.

You do not have to give your app for free, but certain incentives can trigger much more positive response. In such cases, the user will give you another chance and treat your oversight as a minor mistake.

In case you don't have such a plan, things can go sideways and turn out badly for you.

Helps with New and Existing Users

Whenever someone wants to download your app, the first thing they do is reading reviews and checking ratings. Although personal recommendations are more powerful, reviews and ratings should not be underestimated.

You would be surprised that 93% of users read online reviews before deciding whether to purchase according to Qualtrics.

You should care about your online reviews—track the situation, ask your users for their opinions, and react appropriately. This way, you can even prevent any surprises before appearing on the Internet.

Even if you don't get only positive reviews, such unique insight will help you understand the concept of the users' desired approach and result in regular users.

Builds Loyalty for Your Brand

Feedback communication creates a relationship that will make the whole experience more personal for users. Users will start to personalize your business and see it as a *"person"* (*group of people*) who cares about their experience.

User-generated content (UGC) can be in the form of user reviews, testimonials, or other visual content crucial to building your brand loyalty, making you more visible to the rest of the audience.

User reviews can be a potential goldmine of ideas on how you can separate yourself from competitors. For example, maybe your app is *"faster when loading"* or *"more reliable"*—the sooner you find your angle, the better.

One of the key things of building brand loyalty is being **"real"** to your users—not only having a distinct tone but also trying to respond to callouts because you **WANT TO**.

Creating and maintaining such relationships will pay off—instead of being just a company (or an app), you create a connection between your users and your brand.

Combines Data for Better Results

You should combine data analytics and user feedback for developers to have a clearer picture on what caused the issues.

Analytics can locate some issues like short sessions, but you cannot know why users are logging out unless we have users' feedback.

When you combine feedback with analytic data, you can gain deeper insight into a user's app experience. It can help you answer some complex questions like *Why are users abandoning my app after only one usage or why do users leave from a specific app screen*?

When talking about metrics, you should always track the right metrics:

- *Growth*: The number of downloads

- *Retention*: Monthly actives out of the total number of downloads

- *Engagement* (or stickiness): How frequently users use your app

Key Takeaways

- Include onboarding to your app as it can only bring positive user experience—check which onboarding suits your audience the most: benefits- or function-oriented or possibly progressive onboarding. The onboarding process should follow some steps— first, offer value and ask for essentials only. Ensure concise signup and promote your app's content while motivating first conversions. Provide a SKIP option for users that don't like being bored with such a process but use a cross-channel messaging system to stay updated with your users and measure results.

- Remember that user feedback is a goldmine for your app.

  - Prior to collecting feedback, specify the objective, select the right method, and consider the cost. You can start with simple methods like asking for likes, rates, or reviews and in-app net score promotions, but you can also try out support communities, beta testing, and feedback surveys. Do not underestimate the power of email—reach out to your users via email or through user contact forms to ask for their opinion. Usability tests can help pinpoint weak aspects, while social listening can empower you to gain more insight into what users like or dislike with your app.

  - While collecting the feedback, always respond to user feedback in a timely manner.

- Upon collected feedback, track the right metrics, analyze feedback data, and identify its source. Organize and categorize feedback, sort the input, and unify data for easier management. Once alterations are validated and shared, encourage users for continuous feedback, repeat the process, and make it a part of each iteration. Some tools that can help you pinpoint weak spots can be session recordings, touch heatmaps, navigation paths, conversion tunnels, and action cohorts.

- Prioritizing feedback is essential—once feedback is collected and consolidated, categorize it as per your specific parameters (type, theme, etc.). Code the feedback and analyze the popularity of each code to get more insights. After you've summarized and shared the findings, take action! A good idea would be to automate user feedback analysis with third-party tools (text analytics, qualitative data analysis, voice of the customer, etc.).

- User feedback can help you locate improvement areas and combine data for better results. It helps produce personal recommendations, helping new and existing users. Taking feedback into consideration makes users feel involved—even bad feedback is for the better of your app! Such a relationship builds loyalty for your brand.

CHAPTER 6

How to Promote Your Mobile App in the Market

Chapter 5 was all about your users and how to listen to their needs and show them that your mobile app offers great value for them.

In this chapter, we will focus on the business side—I will list the best practices for your brand and mobile application promotion in the market, including precisely described steps before, during, and upon the launch of your product. Additionally, a list of online tools will help you monitor your app's success and increase your mobile downloads after the launch.

6.1. The Most Important Steps for Mobile App Launch

According to the InMobi survey from 2016 as in Figure 6-1, **the biggest challenge** for app developers was not design or development but **marketing**.

The funny thing is that the **same challenge has remained** to date as number one.

© Maja Dakić 2023
M. Dakić, *Mobile App Development for Businesses*,
https://doi.org/10.1007/978-1-4842-9476-5_6

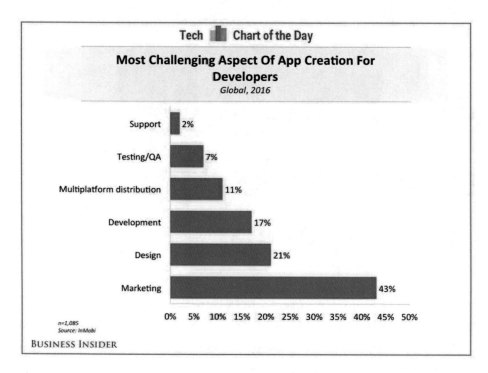

Figure 6-1. *Most Challenging Aspect of App Creation for Developers survey (businessinsider.com)*

Most app owners and developers still state that they have trouble raising awareness for their app—it's not surprising, given that millions of app launches happen every year, and only 1% will skyrocket.

How can you ensure your app launch goes smoothly?

There are a few stages you should follow, but bear in mind that you should be flexible with the deadlines.

Pre-launch Stage

1. Identify the Target Audience and Unique Value Proposition (UVP)

The first step is a **MARKET RESEARCH**—getting to know users before the launch will save you time and money. It will help better understand users' pain points and what they dislike about the apps that are already on the market. It's highly important to discover reasons for the users' pain points by analyzing their behavior.

If you prepare your app with all the collected info, you will have a steady process and will be able to anticipate any possible pitfalls.

Think about a few questions to get the clearer picture of your next step:

- *Whom is your app built for?*

- *What is the problem your app will resolve for the users?*

- *How is your app delivering **value** to the users?*

- *Why is your app better than the competitor's in delivering that value?*

Once you compile the details, you can focus on your marketing plan—don't forget that for a consistent brand image, all your marketing activities should communicate and reinforce this message.

2. Create a Landing Page and Promo Material and Engage on Social Media Popular with Your Target Audience

After the market research, it's time for your app to be tested. It's always a good idea to **create a buzz around your app** and let people become fans and wait for its launch.

You should set up a landing page with the basic info like the app's name, a short description, and a signup form for the visitors. After, start with collecting leads, offering a preview of your app to the press and early adopters. Don't forget about integrating with analytics or A/B testing tools to check insights on your messaging strategy (Google Analytics, Optimizely, Instapage, etc.).

Next, the best is to **increase your web presence**—you should identify social networks popular with your target audience and start posting content related to the upcoming launch of your app. Share your ideas on social media and ask for likes, tweets, and signups. Mingle a bit!

Try to create a promo video that catches the core of your app in a 1-minute pitch—a promo video can be embedded to your social posts and landing pages, and it can boost conversion by up to 80%.

3. Identify Influencers/Communities Popular to Your Target Audience

Mingle through message boards and blogs to find an appropriate existing online community in your line of work—invest some time online and **join their conversations** since participating in these groups may be a great benefit as a direct feedback tool.

You should also track top influencers whose content is being shared in those groups—create a list of all influencers in your work niche who might be interested in writing about your app.

4. Prepare Launch Activities

After you've done all your market research, focus on the realization of the launch.

Here are a few tips for that:

- *Content marketing*: **Great content can help** you succeed in the launch since it shows your potential users how useful your app is, allowing them to understand better how to use it. You can embody your content with blog posts, infographics, videos, and press releases to boost your brand image.

- *Creating a press kit*: Make sure that **users can access information about your app easily** and do not go back and forth through the Web. Compile all your assets into one online press kit that should contain, for example, *your app's logo, icon, screenshots, promo video, links to social media accounts, recent press releases*, and other relevant info. Once you do that, your influencers can quickly go through your press kit and find the details they need in one place if they will write about it.

- *Product curation sites*: You should check some **websites that curate new products** since they can help you create some hype about your app. Make sure that you are ready with your Minimum Viable Product since the ratings on these websites have an upvote/downvote or review section. Some of these websites are Product Hunt (best to launch around 7 AM PST), BetaList, Hacker News, Crunchbase, etc., so choose the appropriate product curation site for your mobile app.

- *Creating your product page*: The **users can see only the first few lines of your app description** in the app store, so you need to ignite their interest in those five lines— your app store description should be like advertising copy. Keep in mind that every successful app solves the problem for users, so ensure this is clearly described. Additionally, it's great to try to follow ASO best practices to help your app rank higher in the app store by including keyword(s) in the title and description of your app.

5. Beta Launch

There are many websites for the newest apps that are coming soon, and some of those are BetaList, ErliBird, IdeaSquares, etc.

Once you've created a list of beta testers, remember, **feedback is the key**!

You can use UserVoice where testers can send feedback directly to you or Crashlytics to help you identify where exactly your app breaks and eliminate those bugs.

Analytics are extremely useful to determine who comes back and uses your app and to proactively reach out to those that don't and find out why.

The app stores always show the highly rated apps first, so make sure to **ask your users to review your app**. Instead of intrusive pop-up messages, ask them after they perform the core action in your app—do not bother them in a screen that flows directly with your app's UI/UX. For example, if they're not enjoying it, ask for feedback via UserVoice, or if they are, just ask them to rate it.

Make this process as smooth as possible to get the best user feedback and ratings.

Launch Stage

The BIG day is finally here!

Now it's time to submit your app to the app store(s). At this step, you should be aware of the submission guidelines to get your app approved. For Android mobile apps, check Google Play Policies, and for iOS devices, check the App Store Review Guidelines. (For more on app positioning in the app stores, see Section "Brand Positioning Strategies for the App Stores".)

If you want higher download and user retention rates, your app needs to leave a good first impression within the first few days prior to launch. If you fail to do this, you'll likely lose users' interest soon.

Once you've submitted your app, spread the word loud and proud to a press list, influencers, and communities to inform them about your app's release.

Send an email to everyone on your list encouraging them to test the app and thank them for their loyalty. You should also promote your app on social platforms such as Facebook, Twitter, Instagram, etc.

Create a system for regularly recording your previously identified KPIs. This dashboard will present all your metrics in one place and help you stay goal-oriented. You can also make your own mobile app KPI calculator, which can be adapted to include the most important metrics for your app's success.

Additionally, if you have some good contacts at TechCrunch/Verge/VentureBeat, you should check with them about getting an article.

See Section 6.2 for more on best mobile app promotion practices for you.

Post-launch Stage

When you launch your app, your work isn't done—you should continue doing a couple more things in order to secure your app's success.

- *Measure*: After the launch, your assessment should include customer satisfaction, engagement and retention rates. Reasons like *why users abandon the app* can help you adapt to the shifts in user expectations.

- *Listen*: Make sure that you improve the app experience and add new features and personalized content regularly as this will keep your users engaged.

Use analytics, track user behavior, and listen to user feedback to determine what your users want to ensure compelling updates. Always make sure when updating your app that the features meet your business goals as you cannot meet everyone's needs.

- *Stimulate regular usage*: If you want to drive engagement and retention, you should stimulate users to use your app to ensure the long run. It can be through mobile-specific rewards, promotions, coupons, or specific content access. How you stimulate your users will depend on the nature of your app.

- *Re-engage users with marketing communication*: Be careful when communicating with your users—people don't like to get "*over-spammed*," so choose wisely. Push notifications can engage, encourage activity, and re-engage inactive users when done appropriately.

- *Keep ratings high*: Ratings are a reflection of user experience, so it would be good to keep those numbers at 4.5 or higher. Positive user experience and a useful app will often end up with high ratings and positive reviews. Always be careful in managing and resolving negative reviews and keep communication channels open to user feedback.

You can always use various tools to help you monitor your *app's health*, and you can check on these tools on Section 6.3.

Remember, a mobile app launch isn't a one-time event.

It's a cyclic process requiring re-assessment since the market needs change.

Since there's always room for improvement, make sure to do it on a regular basis to keep users engaged through new updates and functionalities.

6.2. The Best Practices on How to Promote Your Mobile App and Brand Strategy Examples

Promotion of your mobile app and brand strategies go hand in hand. While promoting your mobile application, you can also apply brand positioning methods along the way, strengthening your reputation and increasing visibility.

The Best Practices to Promote Your Mobile App Successfully

A good starting point can be to promote your app before the launch and create a community around it, giving them a chance to subscribe to your mobile app and wait for the official release.

Mobile app recognition brings many challenges—usually, the challenges are not about the apps themselves, yet about a lack of promotion. If you do not promote your app effectively, all your hard work may end up "*unpaid.*"

Remember, the more you promote your mobile app, the easier and faster the entire process becomes.

Let's check some ideas on mobile app promotion, depending on the nature of your app.

Get in Touch

Every mobile app owner needs to understand their users' expectations—reach out, and your audience will help you discover gaps you may have missed. In addition, you will connect even more with them.

Keep your users engaged during your app's development as they are the foundation of your business—it can increase your app downloads within your target audience.

Get in touch with your users and **ask about their opinions or suggestions** for your app to make it more beneficial for them.

No matter how you reach out to your users, your new app needs to be imprinted into every aspect of your marketing—**add it to your email footer** with a one-line ad and a link directing toward your app download page. **Include the links to your website**, **blog**, **and social media** profiles in your email signature to get the most of your reach.

Reach Out to Relevant People

Sponsorships can help your brand to build a substantial community—developing **beneficial relationships with influences** can help you promote your app. A website like BuzzSumo is a great place to find a list of relevant influencers within your mobile app niche.

Working with influencers can be arranged in different ways:

- Joint venture (*promoting your app for a price or an exchange*)

- Share option (*if your app is relevant to them*)

Reach out and ask if you can get some of their time to discuss the idea and gather some feedback.

Not only influencers but **other people can help you as well**—if you find people who would care to write about your industry or niche, they might be interested to write about your awesome solution as well.

Just make sure not to be pushy as it can turn people away.

Build Your Landing Page

Create a great landing page and make a simple and clear introduction with one or two sentences.

A landing page has all the elements necessary to inform users and engage and help them share info about your app easily.

Make **download buttons larger** and **more noticeable** for visitors to try it out. As you scroll down, each action should have a **single call to action (CTA)** leading directly to download your app.

Make an **eye-catching app icon** as it will attract people to check out your app. Some tips would be to have a unique shape that stands out, choose a limited palette of colors, avoid using photos or a lot of text as it can turn out to be ineffective (*text in icons can be barely readable*), etc.

You can try and create **a separate section on your website** reserved exclusively for your app or try alternatives and create a pop-up page display whenever someone visits your site.

Do not forget **social media**, so make use of that space to promote your app—a simple banner with the name of your app and a logo along with the link will do the work.

Create Teasers

Create a teaser **promo video** prior to app launch and collect beta subscribers via an email submission form.

Videos are an easy way to showcase your mobile app's value—create a simple 30-second commercial video and make sure to leverage your social media to promote your app. Include your video to your blog post, Instagram, YouTube channel, and more.

The additional benefit is that you can also take advantage of video SEO, plus always **add your main hashtag** and/or descriptive hashtags to maximize exposure on social media.

However, be careful with videos—don't spend too much money to produce a video for an app that has changed multiple times since its launch.

Use Different Methods

You should maintain consistency with **regular updates** on topics relevant to your mobile app as it will separate you as a niche expert (*possibly increasing your downloads*).

Another way to get your users updated on major changes is to write **a blog** post announcing your mobile app launch as a **company update**. Including your app into your regular blog is another promotion—you can dedicate the entire blog post solely to your app or include a **call-to-action (CTA) button** at the end of each blog post inviting your audience to download your mobile app. **Include app links, screenshots, and videos** to help them understand the value of your app better.

You can also start a **podcast** and talk about the problem your app resolves in your talk show. A good idea is to create your own logo stamp and customize it to resemble your style, which you can later distribute around your preferred locations.

Another option is to create a **SlideShare presentation**—it can help someone else in the development of their project, plus it can bring a few more downloads along the way.

Use Social Media

When you launch a mobile app, it represents a big achievement for your business.

Make sure to share it with the world and use social media in different ways—do it wisely as many people think that copy-and-paste of the link is enough. Be creative with **your intro text**, engage your audience, **post interesting content**, and make your app click-worthy. You can repost the same content with a different message post to make sure your audience actually receives your message.

Other ways are to run a **Facebook ad campaign** to get more installs or to try AdWords but only if you have defined keywords and enough time to adjust your campaigns.

Pinterest can be a good choice—**share interesting content** here, but just make sure to watermark all your images with your app logo. Users who like your app will flow directly from Pinterest to your website.

An effective way to reach your audience is sharing **interesting infographics**—you can use tools to create infographics and share them with your audience via social media profiles.

You can make things more fun—**throw a launch party online** and host a live broadcast, which will be available on various social media networks. That way, you give people a chance to participate and join the party!

You can take your promotion a step further enabling your **users to share their screens** or in-app content. It will increase your app's visibility and create a place where your users can express themselves.

Start a Community

You can find several good places to **start your community** like Reddit, Facebook (*online groups*), Meetup (*for local groups*), Slack, LinkedIn (*for professional groups*), and more. Make sure you choose the one that matches your target audience. Surround yourself with people who follow the same things as you do, engage in discussions, and share your own relevant content.

You can increase your app's visibility through communities also, to become better known among your audience.

A community is a great place **to ask for the feedback** and hand out **promo codes** for them to try your app—you can discuss the current features, bug fixes or future updates, etc. as it will show them you value their opinion.

Build strong relationships with your community as it will present the opportunity to grow not only your app's community but mobile app install rate as well.

Apply for App Awards

Many organizations award prizes to innovative applications within various categories like functionality, design, and more.

Taking part in such app awards is one of the best ways—it can reveal your app to new audiences and increase your reviews and downloads. Explore such contests online and apply for the ones you think match your app the most.

Some of the most popular app award sites are

- Appy Awards

- Appcircus Competition

- Apple Design Awards

- The Webby Awards

- Best Mobile App Awards

Get Featured on Mobile App Review Sites

If you want to get featured on any app review site, you must send them **a pitch for your mobile app**—basically, your pitch should explain in a few words why your mobile app is good enough to be reviewed and featured at their site.

Many of such sites look for, for example

- Pretty graphical design in high quality

- Original content, themes, etc.

- Stable app without glitches, bugs, long loading times, or other crashes

You will have to provide material to support your app, and you can do it via document form listing the following items:

- A link to your app within in the app store

- A summary describing your app and why it is unique

- Screenshots of your app logo, home screen, and in-app content

- Videos of your app (*YouTube, Vimeo*, etc.)

- A promo code for a free app download (*if it's paid*)

Receiving reviews about your app is an easy way to take advantage of another's site traffic as well—check some lists of the best places to submit your app and go for it!

App Store Optimization (ASO)

App Store Optimization (ASO) is Search Engine Optimization (SEO) for the app stores (both Google Play and App Store). Check the comparison in Figure 6-2 below.

ASO pays attention to **relevance of the keywords** and search as well as to the keyword frequency in your description.

Optimize your icon, title, description, and screenshots so that your app can be found quicker in the official app stores. Choose your keywords and categories carefully as it will determine your ranking.

Google Play and App Store are the most famous but not the only app stores on the market. There are alternative app stores on the online market where you can place your app:

- GetJar

- SlideME

- AppsLib

- Amazon Appstore

- AppBrain

Figure 6-2. *Difference between ASO and SEO (appradar.com)*

Engage in Online Communication

Always **contribute to online conversations**—if your users take the time to write feedback for your mobile app, you should take time to respond to them.

Don't leave automated messages for your users as it may result in users leaving feeling you don't take care of their concerns. No matter whether the review is positive or negative, **reach out to them** and let them know you're trying to resolve the issue or have your thank-you note but keep it real.

Focus on nurturing **your existing users**—if you accomplish to build a community that can provide you with valuable feedback and help your app become better, you will manage to create a more successful campaign for new user acquisition.

Always **go for a direct conversation** with your users, ask them questions, encourage suggestions, and more—remember, not all communication has to drive downloads. Keep your communication worthy—**offer advice or help** users who have a problem, and app downloads will start increasing. Always keep in mind that **word of mouth is "*the best medium of all.*"**

You can create **an invite system if your app is paid**—offer users to choose if they will pay for the app or invite their friends. You can also re-engage with your current users since Google and Facebook have an initiative where you can run ads to drive users to try your mobile app.

Another great way is to actually help your users promote your app. Create a recommendation system and **add a button "*Tell a friend*"** that your users can use to share your app with friends—for better success, incentivize it with discounts for each new subscriber, like in the Duolingo app.

Offers and Support

Make the process of promoting your app a fun one. ☺

Set an amusing task for your audience to complete and tag themselves with your specific hashtag on social media to follow the development of your app and reward the winners publicly.

You can set up **various categories for users to climb up the ranks**: by sharing the app, engaging with your brand, or having their friends sign up as it will encourage your users to try out your mobile app.

Discount is always a good way to approach your users if you are working with in-app purchases—you can offer cheaper prices on certain days, occasions, etc. and let the users know via push notifications or a newsletter.

Similar to discounts are coupons—find a **coupon service** relevant to your market and try a campaign.

Offer your users a **free trial** if your app is paid, and you can collect potential user details. You can later reach out to them and explore if they don't sign up—ask about their needs and build a relationship.

No matter how you create your offers (*discounts, coupons, promo codes*, etc.), remember that users will more likely get onboard if they can save some money.

Track Analytics and Performance

Always check your analytics via various tools to get insight into how your users interact with your mobile app.

Track the data, draw conclusions, prepare an action plan, and go for it!

There are various ways to analyze your users' behavior—install a touch **heatmap**; **use navigation paths**, **session recordings** (Section "Tools to Track User Behavior in a Mobile App"), or other methods; and analyze what content people like or dislike.

Keep track of **your app's performance** and the overall user satisfaction— the sooner you detect any problem, the sooner you can resolve it.

Be Your App's Ambassador

You can give your contribution and engage in public speaking or **share your expertise at conferences**, webinars, and similar events. Talk about the problem your app is solving and not just about your app.

You can extend the reach and **share your expertise** via guest blogs— you can always put a backlink to your app within the blog, and it can only help for your users' list to grow.

Offer your users **a newsletter with valuable content** and keep collecting email addresses to grow your list.

In case of negative reviews, focus on **helping users solve their problems** as such action will evoke positive reactions and possibly make more ambassadors of your app.

You should always keep your content fresh and let your users know that you're making your app better for them.

Be Prepared for Press

Prepare a press kit to ensure the best chance of getting your story published. Your PR kit should include

- Your app summary guide
- Your press release
- Screenshots (app)
- Design (icons, logos, banners, etc.)
- Videos (intro or demo video, onboarding video, etc.)
- Founder's bio and photos

Once you've prepared everything, you can move forward and check the free press release distribution sites to get started.

When talking about your mobile app, **everything counts**—from placing the widgets and beautiful layout designs up to the engaging content.

Despite countless hours and attention, many businesses still do not get the adoption they hope for—instead of thousands of people downloading your app, you get a dozen or so.

The best way is to put all your efforts into promoting your mobile app once you decide to develop it—a long-term strategy will result in harvesting more downloads, more users, and more visibility for your mobile application on the market.

Brand Positioning Strategies for the App Stores

Brand positioning is incredibly important as it can do wonders for your mobile application. Effective positioning will help your mobile app stand out and get into the minds of the users.

How can brand positioning help your mobile app in reality? There are a couple of ways:

- *Makes your brand look credible*

- *Fosters brand awareness*

- *Enhances user loyalty*

- *Enables you to take control over your brand image and reputation*

- *Helps you communicate your mobile app value*

When talking about the mobile app market, Google Play Store and Apple Store are the leading stores for mobile apps and gaming. Thus, we will review these two giants in this section.

Keep in mind that not all brand positioning strategies are the same—your strategy will depend on your industry and your own product. Pay attention to having effective messaging to separate yourself from the competitors.

Some brand strategies can be applied to both stores, but there are slight differences that can help improve your app positioning in either store or both stores.

No matter the store, you need to calibrate your perfect ASO strategy—a good way is to try A/B testing. These types of tests determine which version has a better conversion (*clicks*, *installs*, etc.). During the testing, half of traffic can be pushed to A and the other half to B. Upon the results, compare them and see which one performs better.

Both Apple and Google rely on their algorithms to crawl and index keywords from the app's metadata. Keywords play an important role in both stores, but they read differently as different stores behave as per their own algorithm for the same keywords and the same apps.

Let's check some strategies for each store for you to successfully position YOUR brand/mobile app.

Google Play Store

Google Play Store sets stricter rules for both users and developers when it comes to ASO guidelines. Some new updates include the following:

- The title length is shortened from 50 to 30 characters, like in App Store.

- Restrictions to use keywords in icons, titles, and developer names suggesting promotion.

- Removal of graphic elements from app icons (featured images, screenshots, videos, short descriptions) that may be misleading.

- Emoticons and special characters are disabled and no longer allowed.

Google Play's algorithm takes almost all text elements into account for keyword indexing. Put your relevant keywords in your app title (30) and short (80) and long descriptions (4000 characters). In order for a keyword to be indexed, it needs to be included two to five times in the long description or once in the title or short description.

Here are some quick strategies you can use to increase your ASO ranking and improve app positioning in Google Play Store:

- *Target market and keyword research*: Identify your ideal user and target market niche: you need to understand the "lingo" used by your audience.

243

If you are trying to target teens with your apps, then you need to use language more natural for them. Knowing your audience and making them convert (*or install*) is integral to developing your app to get more conversions.

- *Page optimization*: An ASO-optimized listing can increase your app ranking and installs. Google Play Store optimization also makes the app rank higher in Google search results (app packs). You can follow some Play Store factors:

  - *Developer name*: Can boost the app rank in search results, especially if it's from a trusted developer. Google prioritizes apps from trusted developers with a positive history.

  - *Title*: Your title can be up to 30 characters. Place your main keyword with your title. Try to make it as unique as possible and do not use common terms. Your title should fortify your app value, so keep it short. Google Play Store displays your app's title and icon only, so make sure each word counts.

  - *Icon*: It is the first visual contact you have with your users, so make it memorable. Your app icon needs to be unique, striking, and definitely appealing because users see it in the actual search result in Google Play Store. Make sure not to place any emoticons or misleading graphics as you will be penalized by the store.

  - *Short description*: Has a strong impact on your app's ASO ranking. Keep it within 80 characters— use a sentence or two to describe your app value.

Keywords are important for ranking; thus, consider both keywords and semantics. Medium or long-tail keywords are better for a start—these have a high conversion rate yet less competition, thus less traffic as well. Android short descriptions will be seen on the app listing first after the screenshot, and its goal is to convince potential users to download your app, so make it worth.

- *Long description*: You need to include your app keywords with a compelling CTA (*call to action*). Keep it up to 4000 characters with a clear description of your app benefits and features. Keyword density and frequency is the key to ranking. Google Play will process the keywords by crawling your description. The best is to repeat any important keyword five times, but pay attention to implement them naturally into your narrative—do not embed those mechanically.

- *Promo videos (a.k.a. app preview)*: These videos are YouTube videos that can be added to your app's listing, and they appear in your app listing before the screenshots. The video may also be displayed when Google shows your app in other parts of the store. You can add only one video, and it is recommended to use landscape mode (YouTube format). You can use this opportunity to show your in-app experience or highlight how users benefit from your app. Google Play features graphics shown before your screenshots if you have a video that significantly affects your app's conversion rate optimization (CRO).

- *Screenshots*: The Android store allows eight screenshots—screenshots demonstrate how your app (or a game) looks inside, and those should be marketable and engaging. They need to catch users' attention, so use text or graphics in screenshots to present your app to users in an interesting way. Still the screenshots shown in Google Play are somewhat smaller than those in App Store, so keep this in mind when you consider adding a copy to your screenshots. As a result, screenshots play an important role in conversion rate optimization.

- *Monitoring and tracking*: You should track your app weekly. Check the install volume, both paid and unpaid, rankings of keywords, ratings, reviews, etc. and adjust your ASO strategies, such as removing or editing keywords that do not perform. Track customer feedback to get insight into the **UX (user experience)** of your app, which is also essential in ASO ranking, just like in SEO. In Google Play, you can communicate with your users, which means you can respond to feedback quickly, whether positive or a complaint. Don't ignore complaints because they can help you improve your app and product, thus better positioning your brand to your target market. Always respond quickly and positively, so you can build trust in your app and improve your app's brand positioning.

- *Drive app engagement and reviews*: The latest changes include the impact of your app engagement—this means it is not only about installs but how often your app is used. In addition, ratings and reviews are also taken into account, so respond to any review. Your response is an excellent opportunity to start a conversation about your app. Reviews will improve engagement and reinforce your brand. Keep in mind that you represent your brand, so you should keep a positive attitude and always assure your users you want to make their experience better.

Keep in mind that Google follows their own guidelines related to technical requirements and always keep an eye on guideline updates as there can be more updates or modifications. For example, in case you develop games for Android devices, you should get familiar with the latest updates in 2022 Google Play guideline adjustment.

iOS App Store

App Store has introduced certain new features that can be used for better App Store Optimization strategies. Some of the latest changes are

- Introduction of in-app events to further boost your app visibility and discoverability.

- Screenshot of installed app features.

- Introduction of widgets.

- Custom product pages allow to create multiple versions of your app pages.

- A/B testing allows you to create different types of visual representations of your app to see which version is more appropriate for your customers (app icons/ screenshots).

App Store search results contain several details like developers, in-app purchases, categories, editorial articles, and similar. Moreover, apps are shown in the search results with the app title, icon, subtitle, and description.

Depending on the platform and image orientation, a single rating and three screenshots or app previews can be displayed.

Some ASO strategies for App Store can be as follows:

- *Accurate keywords*: Only App Store includes a specific field for keywords—you are limited to 100 characters, so be concise. You may use spaces to separate words within keywords, for instance, "*Software,Buy Online,Europe.*" Choose keywords that your users search for and give descriptions of your app's purpose to increase the search results. Compromise between less and more common words. App Store rejection may be caused by trademarks, celebrity names, or other protected terms and phrases. Usage of words not applicable to the app and use of competing app names are forbidden. Using the # character is allowed only if it is part of your brand identity.

- *Title, subtitle, and description*: You can use only up to 30 characters for the title. The process is the same: a short, easy-to-spell, and unique app name describing your app value. Use a subtitle to describe the purpose of your app—your product description should concentrate on your app's value and functionality. Include a brief statement of what the app does and add an overview of the app's key features. iOS offers 30 characters for a subtitle where keywords are important—iOS subtitles will appear below the app title in search results, so focus on explaining your app's purpose in short.

- *Screenshots*: App Store allows up to ten screenshots, and since those are shown as a part of search results in App Store, they are extremely important for this store when it comes to conversion rate. You should design screenshots that will make your app stand out and grab users' attention.

- *App preview*: App previews are shown as a part of search results in App Store. The store is very strict with its requirements as you can add up to three videos, which should be short and relevant in portrait or landscape mode. App preview videos are also important for conversion optimization in App Store. The first video you add will appear in the search results along with the first two screenshots—keep in mind that the video is automatically muted as the user scrolls down.

- *Correct app primary category*: App categories help users discover new apps to meet their needs. The category you select is particularly important for your app's discoverability in App Store. App Store features include appearing in the Apps or Games tab and being in the search results. Select the main category that is most relevant to your app. If your app is not related to your idea, it will be rejected.

- *Grow your app's positive ratings and reviews*: Ratings and feedback can affect your app ranking in search results and inspire users to engage with your app or even download immediately. Ensure your app is stable before you ask for reviews, and choose an appropriate time to ask. Keep an eye out for occasions when users are likely to feel good about using your app, like right after launching or releasing an update. To promote user reviews on Mac App Store, the SKStoreReviewController API is used. Users can issue ratings up to three times a year, in a structured prompt, and request a review without leaving the app. Ensure you have your support profile and contact info accessible on your app and app store product page as it will help minimize negative interactions and the likelihood of bad reviews.

- *Encourage in-app upgrades and purchases*: In-app purchases show up in App Store's search results. It can be viewed when users click your app, along with your app's description, screenshots, and previews. You can display a total of 20 items on your product page, where each item should have a unique display name, promotional image, and description. Use these features to boost your app's ranking and increase the number of installs, active users, and revenue.

- *Make use of additional localizations*: Provide description for app ranking that will help you promote your app to people who speak other languages in the selected countries. The App Store localization table contains all additional localizations.

- *Update your app regularly*: And more frequently as apps that are updated receive a special boost in App Store.

In addition, Apple's algorithm is believed to consider the apps that generate higher revenue.

Your strategy will depend on **your industry and your specific product**, so pay attention to creating effective messaging to separate yourself from the competitors.

6.3. The Best Tools to Help You Track User Satisfaction

If you'd like to get deeper insight on how users behave with your app or what their likes or dislikes are, there are many tools on the market that can help you with it.

These tools can help you see how users interact with your app as well as improve and optimize your app for your users.

Tools to Track User Satisfaction

Google Analytics for Mobile Apps

Google Analytics for Mobile Apps is a free tool that you can use for Android and iOS platforms. There is also a premium version intended for enterprises with more detailed information.

Google Analytics primarily measures user acquisition, activation, and revenue. You just need to sign in with your Google account and start using it.

You can set goals for your users and check if they are accomplished as well as track the goal flow.

Some of the features are

- *The number of users and sessions*

- *The money spent by users*

- *Session duration*

- *Operating systems, device models, and locations of your users*

Mixpanel

Mixpanel helps with tracking and analyzing how users engage with your mobile app to be able to re-engage them with more targeted information in the future.

You can get further insights of the users' journey not only on your mobile app but also on desktop and mobile web.

No code is required to track the app's metrics, so it is really easy to use. Features cover

- *Engagement*

- *Retention analytics*

- *Conversion funnels*

- *A/B testing*

- *Automatic insights*

Localytics

Localytics offers a variety of features—from extensive quantitative analytics to smart tagging and more.

It provides understanding on how to drive targeted engagement across the user life cycle. Localytics supports Android, iOS, Windows, Blackberry, and HTML5.

Some of the features are

- *App usage information*

- *Screen flow*

- *A/B testing*

- *Funnels and segments*

CleverTap

CleverTap offers deep insights on user behavior, thorough segmentation, and personalized messaging.

It enables you to engage your users with personalized push notifications and in-app messages to better understand users' preferences as well as to track user uninstalls to better retarget them.

Some of the features are

- *Audience analytics (funnels, cohorts, uninstalls, user journey)*
- *Automated segmentation*
- *Omnichannel marketing*
- *Campaign optimization*

Flurry

Flurry analytics is extensive where you can view data of your app usage. It can be used by businesses as it monitors user interactions across multiple mobile applications.

The dashboard covers a variety of information like app usage, audience, events, etc. It can appear somewhat confusing for the first time, yet the analytics provide extensive data to better optimize your app.

Some of the features are

- *Retention analytics*
- *User sessions*
- *Events and segmentation*
- *User paths*
- *Funnels*

Apptentive

Apptentive analytics will help you uncover strengths and weaknesses in your user experience—it helps listen to, engage with, and retain your users.

The product intelligently engages customer segments and triggers users to take action through in-app messages, surveys, etc. Apptentive helps boost your app ratings, drive downloads, and build customer loyalty.

Some features include

- *Sentiment analysis*
- *Analytics*
- *Rates and reviews*
- *Surveys*

Tools to Track Your App Uninstalls

Another important insight would be to track when users uninstall your app. It will help you pinpoint the troublesome areas within your app and improve those parts.

Spotting the phase when users uninstall your app can indicate the issue within the interaction process alerting you to pay attention instantly to any emerging problems.

Some of the tools that can help you are as follows.

Google Play Developer Console

The Google platform allows you to track the app performance—you must be registered to Google Console , and after you select All applications, click your app.

You can check the number of installs and uninstalls for the previous time (*week*, *month*, or *year*), and features available for the downloadable reports include Android version, device, country, language, app version, and more.

You can use this tool for uninstall tracking for free.

MoEngage

MoEngage is another platform that can help you with tracking of your app uninstall rate and provide solutions to win them back.

You have plenty of options to follow about the users who deleted your app like gender, age, location, number of sessions, etc., and you can set a range for the criteria you choose. If you check the uninstall statistics by a period of time, you can better understand your uninstall tracking.

After you upgrade your mobile app, there is an option for you to announce it to your users by email.

MoEngage offers their analytics for free for less than 10,000 monthly active users.

Appgain.io

The Appgain platform works on both Android and iOS and will help you to know who deleted your app, re-target your app uninstallers, and reduce churn rates as well as increase your retention rates.

In case any of the users abandon your app, you can re-target your ex users and get them back on track through social media like LinkedIn, Facebook, Instagram, etc.

The features include tracking who uninstalled your app, possibility to contact them again, and more.

You can try it for free with a 14-day trial period or the basic package or upgrade if your needs expand.

AppsFlyer

The AppsFlyer platform provides SDK for both Android and iOS to track metrics and improve performance. Since tracking for iOS and Android apps is different, there are some steps to follow.

For Android, you should first register to the console and integrate with the AppsFlyer SDK, and then you can view uninstall data within the dashboard.

There is a documentation file for iOS too if you want to measure uninstalls for your app—start with finding your app, check your certificate, export the .p12 file, integrate with the AppsFlyer SDK, and test Uninstall. Then, you will be able to track uninstall data within the dashboard.

The uninstall attribution is free if you have their SDK installed, but visit AppsFlyer pricing to see which edition would suit you the best.

CleverTap

CleverTap is a well-known platform for tracking uninstalls of both Android and iOS. CleverTap focuses on minimizing the churn where you can compare uninstalls vs. new activations to better understand the cause of users' actions.

Besides behavioral and live segmentation, you have the option to reach out to users and try to win them back, and you have 14 days of free trial, while other packages start from $311 per month per 25,000 MAU.

Countly

Countly is another choice for iOS and Android app uninstall tracking with plenty of features—the Countly SDK enables you to see the missing users who didn't have a session for more than 7, 14, 30 days, etc. and create campaigns to re-engage those users via push notifications.

They offer a community edition for free forever with basic features, or you can choose between their enterprise edition or your own customized edition package.

Once the user uninstalls your app, they are unlikely to come back— tracking uninstall metrics will effectively improve your retention strategy, and you will get a complete picture of the relevant metrics.

Keep an eye on users' actions to make sure your app satisfies the users' needs and use tools to help you track relevant data to be ready in case of any alerts.

Uninstall tools will make things easier for you—decide which one suits you better based on your app and your budget.

If you've built your mobile app, you should work on popularization of your app—engage your users by tracking their entire app behavior and consider any potential usability issues or reasons they dislike your app.

There are more tools to help you, so consider each tool's pros and cons and choose the one matching your needs for the best outcome possible.

Tools to Track User Behavior in a Mobile App

If you have developed your app, one of the crucial things you need to pay attention to is user behavior.

It is important to track KPIs like downloads and retention, but do you know how your users behave? Do you know what your users like or dislike with your app?

Such information helps you "*see*" how users interact with your mobile app and improve user experience.

Users will abandon the app for various issues (*complex registration, app crashes or speed, too many or too few push notifications*, etc.) or use gestures in a totally unexpected way. Tracking their behavior can provide you with a valuable insight on what features of your app are preferred or disliked.

If you use the right methods and tools, you can understand your users much better and improve your mobile app as well as increase conversion rates.

Session Recordings

Session recordings show you exactly how users interact with your app from the moment they launch it for the first time until they leave the app, as shown in Figure 6-3.

This way, you'll see your app through users' eyes, with every tap and gesture they make—you can track user behavior at any stage of the app's life cycle.

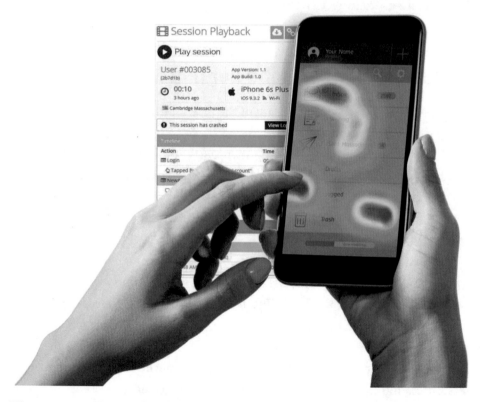

Figure 6-3. *Example of a session recording (*`medium.com/appsee`*)*

Session recordings provide a full analysis of every action taken by the user, which makes it easier to understand users' pain points better.

For example, if users quickly abandon or uninstall your app, the session recordings will alert you and pinpoint any hidden problems that may harm your conversion rates or user retention.

Pro tip:

- The first session recordings are important to understand how users navigate your onboarding process or what triggers them to abandon your app after a single use. If your sessions are under 20 seconds, you can identify the reasons for abandonment, thus increasing the retention.

- Monitor your long-term customers' sessions and learn from them what works well in your app or what can be optimized.

Touch Heatmaps

If you want to understand how users explore each menu, screen, or gesture, it would be wise to use a qualitative tool like touch heatmaps.

Touch heatmaps, as in Figure 6-4 produce a color spectrum of collected users' interactions on each app screen. These maps provide instant insight on how your users interact with each screen, enabling you to monitor user behavior and understand the issues.

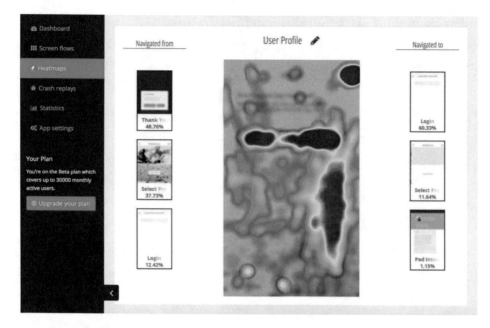

Figure 6-4. *Example of touch heatmap results (uxplanet.org)*

Touch heatmaps can be filtered by various parameters like unresponsive gestures on the screen, the first gestures users made on a screen, etc. For example, monitoring unresponsive gestures can quickly reveal any usability issue that causes the same.

Some of the reasons can be ambiguous design, error in resolution calculations, mislaid elements on the screen, etc.

Pro tip:

- Check the features that first catch users' attention on every screen and only then optimize them appropriately.

- Identify the unresponsive gestures to improve gesture UX and observe the final gestures on each screen to see if they make sense or indicate any potential problem (e.g., *if someone taps the "BACK" button instead of completing the registration process*).

Navigation Paths

Navigation paths provide a detailed map of your app's user journey—it appears as sunburst visualization where the center indicates that the user launched the app, and then the sunburst expands to show the first screen the user navigated to. It displays the screens from the first one to the second one and so on. This is especially important as it facilitates detecting interesting or problematic user journeys. Check the example of navigation path in Figure 6-5 below.

For example, if you detect users that go back and forth between the same screens, it may be a sign that they are confused about the navigation or may have encountered a usability issue.

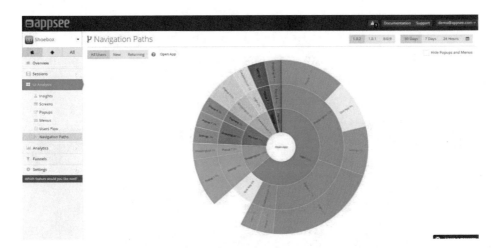

Figure 6-5. *Example of navigation path overview (*appsee.com*)*

Navigation paths can help you pin a starting point apart from the "*Open app*" to see journeys from any screen in your app, even pop-ups. These navigation paths can also guide you when choosing the most relevant session recording to review.

Pro tip:

- Improve navigation by identifying user journeys that show confusion as well as understanding why users abandoned the app by comparing new vs. returning users.

- In case you have an ecommerce mobile app, you can assess these paths from the cart screen to understand where users go if they don't complete the payment.

Conversion Funnels

Conversion funnels can show you the exact spot where the users drop out of the funnel, as shown in Figure 6-6.

Conversion funnels track user behavior in the areas of your app that are the most relevant for your company bottom line: onboarding, payment, and in-app purchases.

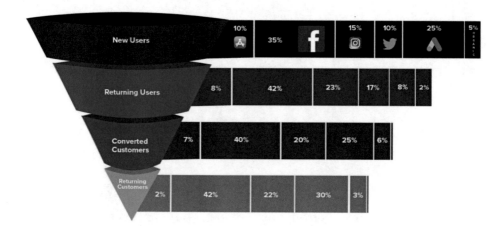

Figure 6-6. Conversion funnel (clevertap.com)

A powerful approach would be to combine the conversion funnels and session recordings—conversation funnels provide excellent data (*completion time of each step and others*), and combining it with session recordings may increase your chances to successfully improve conversion rates.

Pro tip:

- Monitor the recordings of your users as they drop out of the funnel and try to understand what made them fail if you want to increase in-app purchases.

- Another good advice is to assess the average time between each step of the funnel.

- Monitor conversion funnels and session recordings for registration, login, and onboarding to increase retention rates and improve the onboarding process.

Action Cohorts

Action cohorts enable you to analyze any user action in relation to another revealing user behavior trends and engagement over any period of time. Figure 6-7 shows an example of action cohort.

Such information can enable you to understand the relationship of your app and the users as well as what kind of behavior you'd like to see with users and how to incite it.

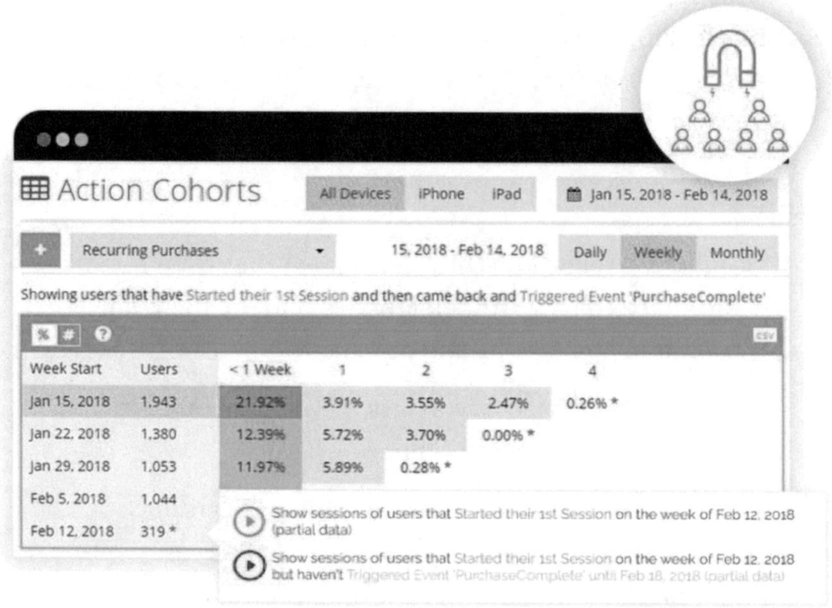

Figure 6-7. Action cohort example (business2community.com)

Action cohorts allow you to analyze the time between the initial and the following actions—it enables you to track user behavior between two specific actions over a certain period of time.

Pro tip:

- You should try to understand the entire navigation process, from the moment users completed onboarding to the moment they've created an account. You will be able to track the relationship between users' first and second in-app purchases as well as the behavior of the new users.

- Increase user retention by monitoring cohorts of users who created an account and then abandoned the app to understand the behavior better and improve any possible faults.

BONUS: Methods to Increase Your Mobile App Downloads

Another actual challenge appears when you realize that you've uploaded your mobile app and your download rate is nothing as you've hoped for.

Hold on. Not everything is lost yet!

Besides the tools I've mentioned previously for tracking user behavior and satisfaction or uninstalls, you just additionally need a few techniques to help your app become more visible.

Some of the following techniques may help you boost downloads of your app.

ASO

We've already mentioned ASO (App Store Optimization) in the previous section (see Section "Brand Positioning Strategies for the App Stores") since tweaking your ASO for the better can lead you to more downloads, increase your brand exposure, rank your app higher in the app store, and even attract more potential users to try out your app.

Let's get real—when searching for a specific app, most of us won't search more than the first page. And that's your goal—getting higher in the app store as the higher the ranking, the more people will be able to find your app.

If you succeed for the users to download your app, let's quickly repeat the factors that influence your ASO:

- *App download number*: The more downloads you have, the more downloads you'll get.

- *Positive reviews*: The more positive reviews, the higher the ranking.

- *Popular keyword relevance*: Popular keyword selection may bring more visibility and downloads.

- *Backlinks*: Include backlinks to relevant pages, and you can improve your app ranking.

- *App opening number*: This number also has significant impact on your app ranking.

- *Retention rate*: The number of people who uninstall your app vs. people who keep it within a specific amount of time (e.g., 30 days and so on).

- *Revenue records*: Apps with good revenue will get more visibility at the store.

Free App at Launch

This is an effective strategy to attract new users where your app should prove the value that you guarantee.

This strategy can drive significant growth in the number of app downloads. If your app is paid in the app store, make it free for some period of time (a week or more) as no one likes to pay for something they've never tried.

Also, if you have a free app but with paid in-app features , it would be smart to make your app "in-app feature–free" for a while until the users engage with your app and realize the potential.

Crash-Free App

If your users download your app and immediately encounter problems, they will leave bad reviews and comments, thus preventing future users from trying out your app.

In order to prevent this, you should go down the proactive path and submit your app to vigorous testing prior to making it available for the public.

No matter what happens, keep in mind that you should **ALWAYS** respond to your users' positive or negative comments.

Referrals and Reviews

Whenever we want to download a new app, we first check reviews from other users and try to get an overall picture of the app usability.

If you have a majority of bad reviews or no reviews or referrals at all, it's an instant sign that your conversion rate is extremely low.

Referrals can also demonstrate your app's quality and trust, which can help increase your downloads. Your current users can become your brand ambassadors if you offer them some kind of incentive for referring your app to their friends. Those incentives don't have to be monetary, but app related; for example, if you have a cloud storage app, you can offer free storage, or if you have an email finder tool, you can offer an additional free number of searches if your users leave a relevant review or refer it to their friends.

You can also send out requests for a review to a variety of "influencing" people or groups like relevant celebrities or critics on major tech websites with large audiences and others.

Paid Marketing

If you have allocated some budget for paid acquisition strategies, you can promote your app through the following channels:

- *Paid press releases*: There are lots of free press release services, but a paid press release offers detailed targeting.

- *Facebook-targeted ads*: Use Facebook's ad tool to target a specific audience based on their age, gender, location, and page likes.

- *Popular ad networks*: Google Ads, Unity Ads, Vungle, and Chartboost are good examples of advertising platforms you can use to promote your app.

- *App directory listings*: App directories are websites where users can search for popular apps as well as directly install and evaluate them. Rates charged by app directories are based on the number of generated installs.

Social Media and Content

Brand awareness is much more important than you think.

Creating and maintaining a strong online presence can help you reach more people and introduce your app to new customers. But be careful to place your content to the right target audience as not all social media channels are used by the same age groups. Also, find time to respond to your followers and ask them for comments as it will show them you care about their opinion.

Content may be interesting blogs, articles, sponsored content, videos, infographics, or a website or a landing page where you can place your content with the most important centerpiece—your app. Make sure that you perform SEO (Search Engine Optimization) to get the most out of your online presentations.

Present information about your app so that users can learn more about it and get more engaged. Getting more visitors, followers, and engagements on your web channels will surely improve your app downloads.

Create a buzz around your mobile app and get people to talk about your product as that will draw attention to it and hopefully will be followed by brand awareness.

Email Marketing

This less-used strategy seems to get lost among social media channels today. But it can be as powerful as any other strategy I mentioned previously. You can successfully connect to your potential users, and depending on the age of the target audience, this method proves itself as fully effective.

You can create lists through your website or other channels and win new contacts with fresh, funky, and shareable content.

As per DMA, for every $1 you spend on email marketing, you can expect $32 in return. A carefully planned email marketing strategy can make you money and keep your business steady-going.

Push Notifications or Alerts

Push notifications are also one of the biggest attention-grabbing communication channels as they provide important information like sale alerts, new feature announcements, or reminders to proceed with a task in the app.

The benefits are huge like improved user retention and valuable insights into user behavior as they represent a simple communication channel with a high response rate.

Measure, Improve, and Measure Again

In order to be able to fully grasp the effectiveness of your strategy, you will need to keep track of your metrics. These insights will help you improve your future strategies and campaigns.

Many times I read that to be a successful growth hacker, you need to work with what you have and CONSTANTLY measure your results in order to tweak your future attempts and ensure better results. You should apply the same for your mobile app.

If you've noticed that your users abandon your app, you should try to figure out the reason it happens. Once you gather the information like retention rate, uninstall rate, etc., you can redirect your strategy and focus on a more proactive approach for the best results.

Simple launch of your mobile app is not enough to ensure success on the current market—no matter if it's robust, providing unique value, or working flawlessly.

Today, you need more to get to the top—you need some of the best marketing practices in order to get your app closer to the users, and once you do that, rest assured that your mobile app will move toward a greater number of downloads and increased visibility.

Key Takeaways

- The most important stages in the mobile app launch process are

    - *Pre-launch stage*: When starting, first identify the target audience. Then create a landing page, promo video, etc. and engage on social media to your target audience. Identify influential groups and people from industry, which can help the promotion, and prepare launch activities such as a press kit, product curation sites, content marketing, and creating your product page. Once everything is in place, prepare for beta launch.

    - *Launch stage*: When all app store submission guidelines are met and you've submitted your app, spread the word out loud and inform press lists, online groups, and communities about your app's release. Send email to everyone on your list to try out your mobile app.

- *Post-launch stage*: Once launched, your work isn't done. Measure customer satisfaction, engagement, and retention. Listen to your user feedback and analyze data for more insights. Stimulate regular usage and re-engage users with marketing communication. Ask for reviews but be careful and do not spam your users.

- Promotion of your app should start prior to its official launch—you should reach out to relevant companies or communities for support. Build your landing page and create teasers, which you will distribute via different channels (*social media, podcasts, SlideShare presentations, blog, online community*, etc.). Apply for app awards and get featured on mobile app review sites—include ASO and offer support with your app for better results. Be your own app's ambassador and engage in press and speaking events to promote your idea.

- Make sure to regularly track and analyze users' satisfaction (*Google Analytics, Mixpanel, Localytics*, etc.), app uninstalls (*MoEngage, Appgain.io, AppsFlyer, CleverTap*, etc.), and user behavior (*session recordings, heatmaps, navigation paths*, etc.) for better insights. Some methods that can help you increase downloads include ASO, giving free access, and ensuring it's crash-free, with good referrals and reviews. Make use of paid and email marketing and social media. Push notifications and alerts can be a wise choice but only if managed carefully. In summary, measure, improve, and measure again.

CHAPTER 7

Outsourcing to a Technical Partner

The previous chapter guided us through launch and promotion methods for your mobile application. In this chapter, I will bring you advantages and disadvantages of outsourcing for software development as well as tips on what to pay attention to when choosing your outsourcing development partner.

7.1. Should You Outsource Your Mobile App Development

Today, remote working has become a common practice for global businesses, no matter the industry. Many companies found themselves having to alter their technical policies, but was it worth it?

As per some studies from 2023, 35% of remote employees feel more productive when working remotely. People became more prone to remote work and communication than ever before. Remote also unveiled a path toward outsourcing for more businesses, yet you should be sure that outsourcing is the right path for you.

There are many indicators showing you need to outsource your mobile app development.

Let's list some of them.

© Maja Dakić 2023
M. Dakić, *Mobile App Development for Businesses*,
https://doi.org/10.1007/978-1-4842-9476-5_7

No Required Expertise

Even if you have your own in-house development team, it can happen that they lack certain skills required for your project. Do not rely on questionable skills as some mobile applications may be more complex than they appear.

For example, if your project requires implementation of Artificial Intelligence (AI) technology and your employees lack such skills, you may end up stranded. Adopting a new team would require much resources, while training would take a lot of time affecting your product release.

In this case, outsourcing can be an excellent alternative to this. Without hiring a new team onboard or training your employees, you will significantly reduce both your time and resources with outsourcing.

No Tech Sector

Some companies do not have any kind of IT or tech department if their industry does not require it. However, it instantly means your company lacks the required knowledge for building your product.

Mobile app development calls for in-depth knowledge of certain technologies, and you will end up with high costs to build a team of mobile developers with good skills.

If this is your case, it would be better to outsource your mobile app development project. The risk will be minimal as you will hire a software vendor that has expertise in mobile app development.

No License for Development

Development of a mobile application requires certain tools and devices, meaning infrastructure. This means you will need to acquire relevant licenses and renew them regularly, especially with technology today evolving rapidly.

For example, mobile app Quality Assurance requires the volume of test cases and a variety of devices to use. Thus, you will need access to multiple devices and operating system versions as well as services—it may end up in additional cost.

Outsourcing reduces such costs because the software vendor is responsible for such tools and licenses, allowing you to focus on other business demands.

No Time

Even if you have a skilled in-house team of developers with the required expertise, it may happen that they have no time to take on this project due to other company tasks.

In case that your in-house development team cannot deliver on time, scaling up your team can be a solution. Due to time pressure, do not experiment with new hires and try to get help from an IT vendor.

For example, if you depend on the delivery time that cannot be completed, the best is to outsource your development. If you put too much pressure or workload on your employees, you will directly affect their efficiency and delivery time.

If you outsource your project, you will avoid recruiting or onboarding new members and thus will not waste your time and resources. Eventually, you can build a partnership with your software vendor for support and maintenance or in case of any future projects.

No Budget

Most of the companies do not have professionals to work on all of their business projects, and even if they do, the total amount of expenses on salaries and taxes would be quite a challenge. Finding a reliable development partner will place a project timeline and costs under your control—it would always be a wise solution to partner up with a certain software vendor in case of any future projects.

In case you have a startup business, outsourcing can act as a transition period until you build your own development team. You can enjoy the time to grow, reduce expenses, and acquire project experience.

No App Maintenance Skills

If you wish for your application to remain competitive on the market, it will have to be maintained and updated regularly.

After the successful launch, your development team can always support you in case of unexpected bugs; to include additional features, updates, or upgrades; etc.

If you do not have capacity to commit to maintenance, then outsourcing can be the right solution for you. Your outsourcing partner will be accountable for any challenges involved like updating, upgrading, or any other bugs that may appear along the way.

No Production Risk for You

Every mobile app development project carries risks.

When you outsource mobile development, all the risks involved are also shared with the company you outsource to. When contracting services of a third-party vendor, you will sign a binding contract—you may define clearly in this document the project's responsibilities and production requirements, including the risks.

Be sure you choose your outsourcing development partner wisely (see Section 7.3) to make sure the vendor has a deep understanding of your goal and your project, as well as of all the potential risks.

7.2. Pros and Cons of Outsourcing Mobile App Development

As per Accelerance 2023 Global Software Outsourcing Trends and Rates Guide, recruiters cited that finding qualified developers was their biggest challenge back in 2021 and that it still remains, with an expected 22% increase in demand for software developers between 2022 and 2030. Outsourcing, with the right partner company, opens up a whole new world of resourcing options.

In order to better grasp the benefits of outsourcing your development, let's check the numbers and some factors you should pay attention to when weighing in-house and outsourcing development.

Hourly Rates

To better understand why outsourcing is profitable, you need to know the **differences between annual average salaries of software developers**— as per Accelerance 2023 Global Software Outsourcing Trends and Rates Guide, shown in Figure 7-1 are the **average hourly rates for developers** (*junior*, *senior*, or *lead*) in Latin and North America, South and Southeast Asia, and Central and Eastern Europe.

	Latin America	Central & Eastern Europe	South Asia	Southeast Asia	North America
Architect	$72 - $96	$71 - $95	$58 - $71	$47 - $70	$139 - $182
Lead Developer	$66 - $82	$68 - $82	$44 - $53	$41 - $45	$169 - $209
Senior Developer	$65 - $82	$68 - $76	$41 - $49	$34 - $41	$143 - $172
Intermediate Developer	$53 - $66	$47 - $65	$35 - $41	$27 - $34	$119 - $144
Junior Developer	$41 - $53	$35 - $53	$25 - $36	$21 - $35	$75 - $91
Business Analyst	$56 - $68	$57 - $81	$40 - $61	$31 - $47	$109 - $154
DevOps	$59 - $82	$62 - $79	$29 - $44	$35 - $62	$114 - $148
Graphic Designer	$48 - $75	$53 - $71	$38 - $43	$29 - $37	$79 - $100
Project Manager	$59 - $82	$53 - $78	$44 - $55	$37 - $60	$96 - $123
Scrum Master	$54 - $79	$61 - $74	$44 - $50	$48 - $59	$121 - $153
Junior QA (Manual)	$34 - $52	$26 - $44	$24 - $29	$18 - $28	$62 - $78
Intermediate QA (Manual)	$42 - $59	$41 - $59	$29 - $32	$22 - $32	$104 - $126
Senior QA (Manual)	$53 - $66	$47 - $61	$34 - $37	$25 - $38	$117 - $139
Junior QA (Automated)	$35 - $53	$32 - $51	$25 - $32	$22 - $29	$74 - $94
Intermediate QA (Automated)	$48 - $62	$43 - $63	$29 - $39	$25 - $35	$125 - $151
Senior QA (Automated)	$59 - $72	$54 - $74	$35 - $46	$29 - $40	$140 - $167

Figure 7-1. *Accelerance 2023 Global Software Outsourcing Trends and Rates Guide (`accelerance.com`)*

Always bear in mind that **hourly rates shift per country**, local economy standard, job position, and other relevant factors.

Overhead Costs

If you have your in-house team, the burden rate provides a clearer picture of total labor costs than the payroll costs alone. The fully burdened cost of an employee includes *payroll taxes, insurance benefits, pensions, worker's compensation, health insurance,* and so on.

According to the Bureau of Labor Statistics, the average cost of employee benefits is around **30% of an employee's fully burdened cost**.

When outsourcing, the burdened costs don't exist—it gives you an opportunity to invest saved money in the other segments of your business. Check Figure 7-2 below for comparison of in-house and outsource expenses.

In-House versus Outsourcing Cost Comparison		
In-House		**Outsourcing**
Salary	$60-84/hour	Salary	$20-45/hour
Benefits, Taxes, Overhead	$13-18/hour	Benefits, Taxes, Overhead	$10-21/hour
Operational Expenses	$10/hour	Operational Expenses & Profit (including Communications, Travel and Oversight)	$10-24/hour
Total Cost of Engagement	$83-112/hour	Total Cost of Engagement	$40-90/hour

* The total cost of engagement is a compilation of blended rates from the Accelerance Global Network.

Source: Accelerance Analysis 2022

Figure 7-2. *Accelerance 2023 Global Software Outsourcing Trends and Rates Guide, in-house vs. outsourcing comparison*

Recruitment Costs

If you need to scale up your in-house team, you would need a recruitment agency, and their fees aren't so moderate depending on the target country. In the United Kingdom or the United States, the recruitment fees rise as the salary increases. For example, the fees would **range from 10% to 30% depending on the salary range**.

However, outsourcing allows you to get similar services at a lower cost. Even better, you can hire services only for a specific task, while in-house employees are continuous cost regardless of the requirements.

Outsourcing software development gives you flexibility to manage your resources and scale them quickly, but if you want to grow your in-house team, you would need to repeat the entire HR drill, and there's always a chance not to get the desired result.

Supervisory Expense Costs

Management time is not free—for each new person you hire in-house, your managers need to spend additional time on one-on-one meetings, coaching, managing reporting, and so on. Many staff members would be involved (*managers, HR team*, etc.), and you may face a loss of productivity from both sides.

For many companies, new employee onboarding can be a disruptive activity of the week, which means you have to spend more money to get them working.

With outsourcing, you **do not have to invest in time to onboard employees**, as your software partner keeps pace with the latest technologies and trends. Thus, the work will be executed without having to nurture your outsourcing development team.

Office Space and Equipment

Office space is a cost you should be able to quantify especially if you think of growing your in-house team. Sometimes, setting up a nearshore office would be a better solution.

For example, in the United States, the price depends on the city and the location, while in the United Kingdom, the office space depends on the location, office size, and type of lease (*serviced, rented, freehold*, etc.).

In Belgrade, for example, you can rent furnished office space from $350 going up to $15,000 for the luxurious office building with all the additional facilities (*parking spots, separate offices*, etc.). Thus, standard prices range from 10e per m2 upward.

Don't forget that your in-house team would also need computers, storage, testing tools, etc., which your company must buy, so you must consider this cost as an add-on to the office space rental fees.

With outsourcing, these costs do not exist as you only pay for the service provided, in this case being the mobile app development.

Talent Pool

Since hiring in-house developers for all technologies is not practical, if you need specialized service, the best choice would be to outsource—you would have **access to a diverse talent pool** since software development companies that outsource have every type of talent on their hands.

Outsourcing provides you with unlimited access without paying anything extra.

More importantly, outsourcing development companies work across various industries, so they have more industry knowledge since they have to keep the pace with the technology updates, whereas in-house developers may be limited to a particular industry and may get the feeling that they are stuck with whatever they are doing. The Figure 7-3 below shows global software outsourcing rates.

Figure 7-3. *Accelerance 2023 Global Software Outsourcing Trends and Rates Guide, global outsourcing rates*

Communication

Considering "*remote*" communication, we're more keen on digital channels, and even if sitting close to each other, we'll communicate via chat (Slack, Microsoft Teams, Skype, etc.).

A good-quality communication can be set up through digital channels, regular sprint planning or retrospective meetings, tools that enable remote collaboration (Jira or Trello), and making stand-ups online a common practice.

When communicating remotely, always **try to over-communicate**. Maybe it sounds silly, but communicating via digital media may lack many physical cues such as body posture, tone of voice, etc. In order to avoid any misunderstandings, **video meetings** are an excellent choice to get around communication barriers.

Better Delivery Time

When you hire on-site developers, you have to pay the costs no matter their performance results, while with an outsourcing development company, you only pay upon delivery.

A competent outsourcing company will improve work accuracy within given deadlines and **deliver a desired product in less turnaround time**. Great outsourcers offer valuable consulting, identify advantages or risks, provide suggestions for better execution, and even more. Don't forget the best outsourcers always focus on establishing long-term relationships with their partners.

However, if your in-house projects aren't delivering, you can't offload those employees unless after an agreed period. If you end up dissatisfied with the in-house recruitment, bear in mind that you may not be able to change things to improve your revenue.

Quality

You need to be careful as some outsourcing companies may offer lower prices but accompanied with a good chance of not delivering the quality you desire.

To stay on the right track, **consider a reputable outsourcer** that has a demonstrated track record of high-quality work. You should do a short research on the company by checking their background, how long they operate, previous client records, customer retention rate, etc. You can also ask for code samples to verify if they deliver high-quality work as there can be huge differences in the quality of work. (See Section 7.3.)

Quality control may be more flexible when employing an in-house software development team, but if you find a great outsourcer for your partner, the benefits are endless.

Business Focus

A good business strategy would be to find a reliable outsourcing development company that can be **your long-term partner** while you can concentrate on the big picture and keep up with the technical changes and consumer expectations.

Outsourcing software development enables strategic focus that can greatly benefit your business—when not busy managing finances, you can use the time for more constructive purposes. It's also beneficial for your in-house IT team as it allows them to continue supporting other issues (*network maintenance, cyber security, end-user support,* etc.) that are critical for your everyday operations to run smoothly.

No matter what you choose, always bear in mind the risks that come along with outsourcing—as per the latest study, some of the risks you should consider are those shown in Figure 7-4.

The 15 Risk Indicators in Software Development Outsourcing

BUSINESS	MANAGEMENT	TECHNOLOGY
1 Undefined Metrics Do key internal players know what will produce a positive ROI from the software you're developing? Are business metrics and goals clearly defined for your internal team?	**6 Unrealistic Expectations** Are expectations for the outsourced software engagement understood and agreed to by all team members at both companies?	**11 Inadequate Skills** Do outsourced partner team members have the right technical experience? Are they adequately trained? How do you know?
2 Inconsistent Priorities Does everyone on your internal team know the most important aspects of your software development roadmap?	**7 Unfocused Leadership** Are the right internal people assigned to your engagement? Are they able to lead the outsourced software team to success?	**12 Undefined Operations** Do both parties understand who will handle hosting? Is the software optimized for the intended platform?
3 Few Executive Champions Do your senior executives spend sufficient time on the project? Have they abdicated responsibility for success to the outsourced partner?	**8 Unclear Milestones** How will progress on the outsourced engagement be defined, measured and understood by both parties?	**13 Ineffective Design** Is there a good fit between the business problem and the design of the software solution? Will users be successful using the software to solve or mitigate the problem?
4 Lack of Team Engagement Do your internal team members care about the success of the outsourced engagement? Are they demonstrating active involvement with the outsourced partner?	**9 Lack of Team Interactions** What procedures are in place to ensure hand offs between team members don't break down? Have time zone differences and cultural communication differences been addressed? Are meetings producing actionable items?	**14 No Quality Assurance** Are QA procedures in place and understood by both parties? Are they robust enough? Are the standards for the software clearly understood?
5 No Partnership Contract Does your outsourcing contract position each company as participants in a transaction or as partners in software development?	**10 Weak Processes** Are the roadmap and software methodologies laid out and understood? Is the lifecycle established and accepted by both companies?	**15 Technical Debt** Is there a threshold for an acceptable level of technical debt? Is there a process in place to pay it off?

Source: Accelerance Analysis 2021

Figure 7-4. *Accelerance 2023 Global Software Outsourcing Trends and Rates Guide, risk indicators in software development*

Globalization's now showing its full potential—the world is shrinking, and you can gain with it!

Don't allow yourself to dismiss the option of outsourcing software development as "*too expensive*" because of incomplete comparison of outsourcing rates and internal labor costs.

Mutual trust, respect, and teamwork—these three things are the main ingredients for a great recipe of client-developer partnership and thus a successful outsourced development.

In the following section, I will list more detailed factors to consider when choosing your mobile app development company.

7.3. Things to Consider When Choosing an Outsourcing Technical Development Partner

Outsourcing includes contracting out your mobile app development to a third-party company, in order for your business not only to reduce costs but also to find appropriate capacities at more competitive prices.

Considering the advantages, it's no surprise that 64% of IT executives say they need expertise from external partners for their digital transformation initiatives—they realized the power of outsourcing and are open to alternative talent sources such as on-demand outsourcing.

If you decide to outsource, take a look at some potential issues to prevent them on time and ensure a smooth work process flow.

#1:Whom to Choose

If you consider going down the path of outsourcing, make sure to **spend time researching** before engaging with a particular company.

It means checking the company references and the team of developers that would be assigned to your project as those can affect the quality of the delivery. If you want to speed up the process of your development, you will need a dedicated team of developers—a team stretched over multiple projects may end up unable to deliver the desired result within the time agreed.

Usually, people hand over the project once they find a reliable partner; however, if you don't want to risk your overall project, you can start small, being a "**PILOT**" project—this way, you ensure mitigating any potential risks.

#2:Communication

Since you're not physically present to overview the entire process, it's also hard to determine the pace of the process. If the time zone difference or a language barrier represents additional obstacles, it can be even more difficult to rely only on the word of the company, so be sure to spend some time on research of a potential mobile partner prior to plunging into a development adventure together.

Once you do that, **set up proper communication tools** (Slack, Jira, etc.) and make stand-up meetings (video) a regular practice to ensure clear communication between the teams.

Communication with the team and the management is a cornerstone, so make sure to lay the foundation for successful cooperation as this is the most important element.

If you're outsourcing, be extremely precise when communicating—**be specific and detailed** on what you want. Otherwise, you may face the situation of plenty re-dos in the process.

Communication is extremely important for your project to be delivered as agreed—Accelerance 2023 Global Software Outsourcing Trends and Rates Guide brings us a checklist you can use once you decide to choose your outsourcing partner. As you can see, besides technical requirements, English skills and cultural fit are very important as indicators that the communication will be transparent and clear. Some most important global outsourcing criteria is shown in Figure 7-5.

CRITERIA INCLUDE	
☐ Size of company (including ability to complete projects effectively and forced on schedule)	☐ Longevity (well-established companies that have been operating for at least five years)
☐ Technical competencies	☐ English skills
☐ Multiple technical certifications	☐ Time-zone flexibility
☐ Industry/vertical experience	☐ Cultural fit
☐ Project structure	☐ Pricing structure
☐ Viability of the region (solid infrastructure, political/ social stability and relationship with the US)	☐ Insurance (professional indemnity and public liability insurances at a level adequate for Western customers)
☐ Human Resources processes (such as recruiting, vetting, and retention of talent)	☐ Business continuity plans (ability to handle economic fluctuations or an unexpected crisis)
☐ Prior experience working with Western partners, and education or prior work positions in Western countries	☐ Compliance with legislation related to the Office of Foreign Assets Control (OFAC), anti-corruption and money-laundering, human trafficking and other legal requirements for onshore operations

Source: Accelerance Insights 2022

Figure 7-5. *Accelerance 2023 Global Software Outsourcing Trends and Rates Guide, criteria for outsourcing*

#3: Business Analysis

Prior to any action, a **proper business analysis should be made**—the sooner, the better. This can help you save time and resources later as business analysis can anticipate potential threats and risks.

The business analyst can help maintain communication among stakeholders, to interpret the client's business requirements as tasks for developers, present future development tasks to the client for better understanding, and make any adjustments on time, if needed.

#4:Technical Documentation

Prior to any outsourcing, you need to think about the parts of the process that should be developed in-house and the ones that can be outsourced.

Technical documentation (see Section 3.2) includes **defining the requirements of your mobile app** idea. These specifications are used and followed to complete the same requirements accurately.

Technical specification is a roadmap for your outsourcing development team—it's best to **be as detailed as possible**, setting major points such as idea, overall description, specific requirements, supporting information, concerns, etc.

Don't forget about **hardware and performance requirements**—you cannot expect your outsourcing team to guess what you want. If you fail to specify all details, you've created a recipe for project failure.

If you think that you cannot specify the mobile app development process, think again. You don't have to write **ALL** details, but if you standardize the procedure for your outsourcing team, it will facilitate the entire process and prevent any delays.

#5:Protect Your Intellectual Property

Your app idea, no matter how original, is **your OWN intellectual property**, and you should protect it—don't assume that your outsourcing partner will do it by default as some countries don't have such regulations at all.

First priority is an NDA (non-disclosure agreement) —make sure that all participants (*a.k.a. parties*) sign an NDA as it provides legal protection for your idea—your internal information belongs to your company alone. When creating an NDA, you have the freedom to split up the source code to independent sections, limit access to the database, or control sharing of confidential information depending on the situation.

If you don't have a signed NDA, you put your IP address to risk. Don't assume that your outsourcing vendor's IP is safe—always check properly. Additional security measures can be to check if the vendor has proper agreements with its own employees prior to commencing the work.

#6: Development Methodologies

Following the mobile app development process is highly important, but there can be some aspects that can be done improperly—for example, a developer managing the development process or a person with limited technical knowledge instead of a proper project manager.

Sometimes it happens that you don't set milestones for your outsourcing team or you impose the release deadline, causing empty promises and additional stress.

If you don't set each participant's roles clearly, they will be confused with their tasks and priorities. Use proper coding standards and **ask your engineers to document their source code**.

Keep in mind that both of your teams (*in-house and outsourcing*) must work together to accomplish the goal and don't make a strong difference between them as you risk causing lack of teamwork and communication failure.

#7: Delayed QA

QA (Quality Assurance) is a crucial part of the mobile app development process. You can cause major issues if you don't use the QA system immediately, but keep it for later. **Keeping track of issues, bugs, or defects** is essential for the development process, and lack of QA will certainly affect your overall app quality.

If you wait to start with testing until just before the release, you risk rushing the process and getting an inadequate product out to the market—in this case, your users will find bugs themselves, and thus their user experience can result in negative reviews, leading to a failure of your app.

Don't wait for automated testing to be implemented as you can find a large number of bugs leading to extensive rework and delay in releasing your app.

#8: Time Zone Differences

We live in a global marketplace, but what if you need immediate feedback and your outsourcing team is offline?

Let's face it. An outsourcing team is often located outside of your own time zone. This means that the problem cannot be resolved until tomorrow, and it may create delays within the project deadline.

Don't worry as this can be overcome easily—your outsourcing team can take the tasks during your nighttime, and you can check the output results the following day. This way, you save time and prevent any delays within the project development process.

Sometimes, it can be tricky to manage the Agile methods and Scrum with two different time zones, so be prepared to work on these challenges as well.

#9: Beware of Companies Behind Global Trends

If your app requires to be designed as per the latest trends or technologies, pay attention to the development company's policy and culture fit. If they seem outdated to you, it may be that they're behind the global trends.

Every cheap price has a good reason, so don't give in to bargains. **Choose the company that understands technological innovation**, keeps the pace with the current trends, and puts effort to follow the culture of your company or country.

There is a possibility that some companies may offer technologies that they know the best instead of the ones that fit better.

Always make sure to check if the outsourcing vendor has presented the solution that will bring the best result and save your resources.

As use of outsourcing is growing rapidly, ensuring you can mitigate the risks will bring you significant benefits like cost reduction, a chance to cooperate with experts on the project, and the possibility to find a reliable long-term outsourcing partner.

Outsourcing your app development doesn't carry more risks than other types of development—just bear in mind the potential risks you will outsource with confidence.

Key Takeaways

- Outsourcing can be a good choice in case it matches your business goals. If you have no tech development, expertise, or skills or if your in-house team is just overloaded, maybe it can be a good move to outsource a mobile app development. Some other reasons include limited timeline or budget, no internal resources, or if you cannot commit to app maintenance and support.

- Outsourcing has its advantages and disadvantages— hourly rates are certainly a plus, and there are no overhead or recruitment costs, which is another benefit. If you choose to outsource to a technical partner, you won't have to pay any office space or equipment, and the talent pool is much greater. Nowadays, remote communication is a "new normal"; thus, it does not represent such a barrier—just make sure to choose a reliable and good-quality technical partner.

- When considering which specific company to choose for your technical partner, follow a few of these simple steps:

  - Do your research and check references and/or developers, background, etc.

  - Check the time zones and methods of communication and tools (*Slack*, *Jira*, *Bitbucket*, etc.).

  - Conduct a business analysis to define the requirements as tasks for developers.

  - Manage technical documentation as detailed as possible (*hardware, performance requirements*, etc.).

  - Protect your intellectual property and always sign an NDA. Also check security protocols and development methodologies of a specific development company.

  - Check for QA and testing habits (early testing?) and if the company follows the technology trends.

CHAPTER 8

Technology Use Cases

Chapter 7 provided all the details related to outsourcing your mobile app development. Since we all work in different industries, this last chapter will give you insights into how to boost your mobile app with modern technologies for competitive advantage on the market. I will put the emphasis on examples of app features in various industries like logistics, retail, manufacturing, agriculture, and more. Each industry will bring you both specific features to implement and benefits.

8.1. How to Boost Your Mobile App

Your mobile app can handle a boost in order to perform better and to attract users with its specific features that cannot be found in other mobile apps.

There are some common practices you can do:

- *Reduce app size*: If you make your app huge in size, it will be a true nightmare for your users. If you manage for your app to consume less space on users' constrained devices, it will improve user acquisition and retention.

- *Optimize images*: Images are larger in size when compared with text, but you cannot imagine a good online experience without attractive visuals and videos.

© Maja Dakić 2023
M. Dakić, *Mobile App Development for Businesses*,
https://doi.org/10.1007/978-1-4842-9476-5_8

You can resolve this by choosing efficient file formats like JPEG and WebP formats as they are size-efficient. Your development team will advise you on the best image loading libraries (*Picasso*, *Fresco*, etc.) as they can speed up the image loading process, while other actions include image caching, using vector images, applying color filters, and more.

- *Reduce load*: These are also actions your development team will help you with like reducing server load.

- *Optimize screen size*: Build for small and medium screens, optimize for MDPI and HDPI, as well as implement adaptive UI flows.

- *App launch time*: Pay attention to your app loading time as it is crucial for user retention. For example, with iOS, try to eliminate static initializers, and as Apple recommended, use more Swift for development. For Android, use tools for launch time optimization (e.g., Apteligent) and avoid memory churns and initialization code in your app's object.

- *Limit the number of third-party sources*: Limit third-party latency sources and similar APIs for your mobile app, except for the mandatory ones.

Some other features you can consider are

- *Augmented Reality*: AR enables you to better showcase your products and triggers users to further engage with your app. Some great examples are IKEA and Sephora. AR gives users try-out experience—such real-life interaction gives users a chance to reach a conscious decision.

- *Gamification*: Gamification lets you create a story—such an approach increases customer loyalty and retention rates and helps provoke word of mouth. H&M developed such an idea for the H&M Club—the story goes: "*Become a member and get a 10% discount when you join and unlimited free delivery, earn points on all or some purchases, and get exclusive discounts.*" They went the extra mile and added some personalized features like 25% discount on the user's birthday, early access to selected collections, and so on.

- *Recommendation system*: A type of information filtering system that analyzes user behavior to showcase personalized messages or content. It's similar to experiencing top ecommerce apps like Amazon to help the app learn users' preferences and display relevant products.

There are different types of recommendation systems:

- *Collaborative filtering*: Similar to LinkedIn or Facebook where you get friend suggestions based on mutual connections or similar demographics and/or behavior. It is effective, yet it requires a reasonable amount of user data (*many users*).

- *Content-based filtering*: Based on customers' likes as each item carries certain attributes or keywords. Items are recommended if the characteristics match the user's profile. It's less effective as it's not easy to attach attributes to the items and the recommendation may turn out to be vague.

- *Hybrid model*: It's a combination of the first two types. By combining the two approaches, you can enjoy the benefits of both without having to handle drawbacks. An example is Netflix that earned many loyal users with such an approach.

  A recommendation system can bring you a certain level of trust from your users, thus making them into long-term customers, which is essential for every business, not only ecommerce.

- *Geofencing*: Your mobile app can make use of GPS, RFID (Radio Frequency Identification), Bluetooth beacons, etc. to allow your app to identify the location of the user. You can send personalized marketing messages to users based on their location like promotional offers and others. Geofencing can automatically detect which store the user is in and provide them with a map leading to specific products based on their position. Keep in mind to fully state why and how you are using the data to explain it to users especially in countries where strict data regulations apply like GDPR (General Data Protection Regulation).

- *Mobile cloud computing*: Mobile cloud computing is a combination of cloud computing and mobile computing for better user experience. A cloud engine reduces server response time, thus increasing your mobile app speed. Mobile cloud computing allows you to scale your services up or down as per the demand, traffic, or seasonal spikes. For example, while a sudden spike in traffic can slow down a website, cloud computing provides you with a greater bandwidth, power, and storage. As ecommerce business greatly depends on its customers' data, it's wise to use cloud-based structures—it can save your business from data loss and keep the data secure, backed up, and easily accessible.

- *Chatbots*: Chatbots are programs that can understand human inputs within the right context and provide outputs—a customer can ask about purchase suggestions or the payment process, raise issues, find desired products, and more with the help of a bot. Chatbots require a small investment for development and maintenance, allowing instant assistance to users. Personalization is also important—although FAQ on your website can provide some answers, chatbots can immediately answer your customers' queries and help them with personalized recommendations afterward.

- *Multiple shipping methods*: Excellent for ecommerce apps where you provide better choice in shipping methods for your consumers. For example, if a customer wants delivery only to their PO box address, then you should have that option. Allowing users to choose from various shipping options and letting them add the shipping address easily will create a positive user experience in your mobile app. Different available shipping methods are a must-have, and it would be practical for users to show the cost and estimated delivery time for each option. If you start with developing an MVP, you can start with a simple option for users to order an item in one of your stores, and once the app gains popularity, you can upgrade this feature and add new options. Another feature that is nice to have is the option to easily check the shipping status of the ordered items. It will help boost transparency and enhance the quality of interaction that customers have with your store after completing the purchase. Users like to know the details about their online purchases, so this feature will help them know exactly what is going on with their ordered items.

- *Loyalty programs*: People who decide to download your mobile app initially show a higher level of investment in your brand. Besides regular promotions and exclusive access to products, you can also provide options to collect points and win discounts through your mobile app—driving loyalty through a special loyalty program is a smart move. You can easily notify your customers about the upcoming events, exclusive discounts, and rewards if they wish so. You can also use the app to distribute promotion codes to users, motivating them to download and use the app. Such loyalty programs will improve user experience and increase sales as you'll be reminding your customers to make purchases on a regular basis.

- *Extra functionalities*: Besides the above-mentioned add-on features, there are some extra functionalities that are optional but can be added to boost your sales:

  - *Push notifications*: Send personalized messages and offers

  - *Beacons*: Personalize push notifications better per customer, offering them exclusive deals

- *Magazine*: An in-app blog about the latest industry trends

- *Store locator*: To easily find a brick-and-mortar store nearby

8.2. Technologies to Implement
Artificial Intelligence (AI)

Artificial Intelligence (AI) technologies have been increasingly exploited by different industries and companies. Let's see what type of technologies and features can be utilized for your mobile application. In Figure 8-1 below, you will see how smartphone users benefit from AI technology.

Benefits

- *Image recognition*: Retail giants such as Amazon, Target, and Macy offer image recognition with their mobile apps to increase user retention, while "*scan-to-buy*" options enable customers to shop directly from a retailer's catalogue—in-store signage increased in demand and became a standard offer today.

  Some retailers are employing image recognition allowing consumers to point their phone at any object and receive suggestions for similar products.

  The easier you make it for your customers, the more they will return and engage with your business.

- *Visual search*: Let's say you saw something you really liked, but you don't know how to find it or how it's called—visual search lets you find all those things you don't have the words to describe.

Visual search can help businesses in ecommerce **increase catalogue discovery, customer engagement, and conversion rates**. Mobile visual search is faster and more accurate than text or voice, and smartphones are the perfect devices for this technology.

Some of the well-known visual search engines are Bing Visual Search, Google Lens, Amazon Rekognition, Instagram Shopping, and Snapchat Camera Search, so try it out if it matches your mobile app and your business goals.

- *Natural Language Processing (NLP) and Understanding (NLU)*: Your first contact with NLP might involve a GPS navigation app—today, the best-known mobile app with NLP is Siri, a virtual assistant (VA) technology, followed by other VAs including Alexa, Cortana, and Google Assistant.

  NLP became common especially in **wearable and health apps**, **allowing verbal input** as this field requires hands-free communication.

  A huge potential is in data from the education portals—a user can give **verbal input to search a plethora of ebooks**, websites, videos, footages, etc. There are also improvements within **language translation** apps and mobile apps that include talk-to-type functionalities.

  On the other hand, Natural Language Understanding (NLU) converts text pieces into more formal illustrations. NLU can be applied to a different set of computer applications—from **simple tasks** like short commands issued to robots to highly complex ones such as full **comprehension of the newspaper articles**.

- *Text-to-speech (TTS) systems*: TTS is a high-fidelity speech synthesis that gives **better user experience for some groups** like people with learning disabilities or literacy difficulties, people who speak a language but cannot read it, people with visual impairment, or people that access content from mobile phones.

  Making your **digital content audible** helps the online population understand the text better, and as people are increasingly going mobile, TTS can turn any digital content into a multimedia experience that people can listen to.

  Some of the examples of text-to-speech software are as follows: besides Alexa, Amazon created a TTS system called Amazon Polly. Then there are Voice Reader Home 15, Capti Voice, and Cloud Text-to-Speech powered by WaveNet.

- *Speech-to-text (STT) systems*: If you're at a conference or a lecture, it can be quite hard to write down every word, and this is where speech recognition comes in— STT **identifies spoken language and turns it into text**.

  These systems can differ in capabilities where simple ones can recognize only a selection of words, while the most advanced ones can understand natural speech.

  Some of the best STT apps are Evernote **for Android**, Dragon Dictation, Voice Assistant, **Transcribe**, Speechnotes, and more.

- *Chatbots*: Let's mention chatbots again as they are great for specific tasks—they won't replace websites, but they work great when integrated with apps and websites to boost interaction with customers.

It's essential to engage with your customers on a regular basis, and mobile apps are the best platform for this. Some great examples of chatbots are Duolingo, Erica by Bank of America, Lemonade Maya (replacing brokers and bureaucracy), and others.

Chatbots provide more engaging **customer interaction** and **add to the quality** of your mobile app—with the intelligence support it gets from AI since it will help you increase customer conversions.

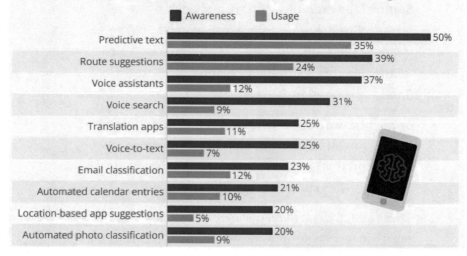

How Smartphone Users Benefit From Artificial Intelligence
Awareness and usage of smartphone applications featuring machine learning in 2017

■ Awareness   ■ Usage

	Awareness	Usage
Predictive text	50%	35%
Route suggestions	39%	24%
Voice assistants	37%	12%
Voice search	31%	9%
Translation apps	25%	11%
Voice-to-text	25%	7%
Email classification	23%	12%
Automated calendar entries	21%	10%
Location-based app suggestions	20%	5%
Automated photo classification	20%	9%

Figure 8-1. *AI benefits for smartphone users (`bosctechlabs.com`)*

The most obvious changes AI will bring are *processing speed* and *efficiency*—doing things faster and without multiple charges of your phone.

The whole point of AI is to create a more personalized and user-friendly relationship with our smartphone.

Augmented Reality (AR)

Augmented Reality (AR) is a technology that "*augments*" your reality by blending the real and digital worlds in such a way to provide a unique experience.

AR has become widespread due to a simple fact that you can experience AR using only a smartphone—it is a rather powerful add-on to any industry as it can boost engagement and create realistic-like experiences with diverse products.

According to a study from the Ohio State University, people are more prone to buy a product after "***touching***" it or after interacting with it since during the process, an emotional bond is established.

Benefits

- *Improved customer engagement*: Examples can be apps where you can virtually "*try on*" the products like Ray-Ban did with their Virtual Try-On or the IKEA Place app. Usage of AR like here actually simplifies a product trial and an overall purchase process. Sephora Virtual Artist allows consumers to plunge into an adventure of trying out different colors of lipsticks and other delicacies they offer. This is not just for fun—Sephora is actually **improving customer engagement** by keeping consumers entertained for a longer time plus increasing chances of purchase through a new way of communication. More examples are Uniqlo Magic Mirror, which enables customers to try out multiple colors and patterns of the same garment—it was followed by Adidas and Gap.

- *Interactive advertising*: An excellent example of interactive advertising is Starbucks Cup Magic, allowing customers to send/receive Valentine messages, or Motorola with Moto X's customization where people can change the color of the phone by pushing buttons. It improves user experience by creating an **interactive bond** between them and your brand. Product-based companies can show their goods with *AR-driven 360 view* and interactive experience where the customers can test their products. Service-based companies can create AR tutorials showing customers exactly what they will get for their money prior to any commitments. There are many more examples of interactive advertisement, print or not, so keep the pace!

- *Video and 3D display*: Simple old flyers or even videos won't do the trick anymore. If you want to stand out, you need to evoke a *"fascination"* effect with people— for example, a projection of a video displaying a 3D interactive AR product model will make people focus on your product with a fascination that other mediums cannot trigger. And fascination creates an emotional bond, which is good for sales.

- *Customer loyalty*: To maintain customer loyalty and enable repeat purchase, you will need to go the extra mile. The example is Audi eKurzinfo—their app converts your smartphone into a detailed user manual explaining how the parts work. It helps them identify buttons and knobs in a way hard-copy manuals never could do. Such strategies help create a trust in a brand where they will come back to buy again.

- *Geo-targeted market*: Apps using the geolocation feature can use your device camera to show nearby restaurants,

stores, etc. with important information about each—
reviews, directions, open/close time, etc. An example app
is Street Lens developed by Google, which uses geo-
targeting for enhancing your experience. Such features
in apps can be exploited to give recommendations about
the best nearby locations and the directions how to get
there or more specific goals like to find your car inside
large parking lots or garages using GPS.

Today's industries are focusing more on mobile devices because they
are ubiquitous and have all required elements for AR—screens, cameras,
processors, sensors, etc.

As tools for AR are rapidly evolving, this technology is finding its way to
various industries, and we can expect to see more use cases involving AR,
which will take the mobile app ecosystem to the next level. In Figure 8-2
below, you can see how many consumers would rather shop at retailers
that use AR technology.

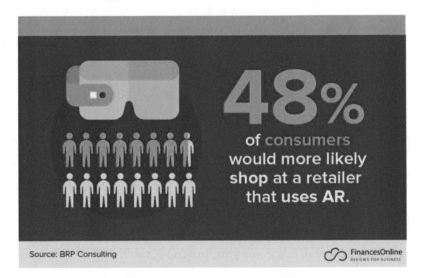

Figure 8-2. *AR in retail (financesonline.com)*

Gamification

Gamification can be a good choice if the nature of your mobile app allows—it involves applying game dynamics to a mobile app, resulting in increased traffic and users' engagement if done properly. The entire process is based on principles of simple psychology as gamified elements help trigger a sense of achievement and motivate users to use your app more.

However, be careful. Users must become familiar with the app itself prior to any engagement—only then can they get enthusiastic about the incentives your app has to offer (*collectibles and/or points*).

With gamification, people tend to spread the word about *"a great app they've tried,"* which is an extremely valuable add-on.

Benefits

- *Rewards*: Whenever we complete something, we like to receive some kind of reward in return (*material or not*). The fact also applies to mobile app users where people are more motivated if the app offers a prize for completing a certain type of task. An example of this is Habitica—a gamified task manager that helps you turn your daily routine tasks into a fun game while helping you organize your duties.

- *Quizzes*: A survey from a few years ago revealed that quizzes are shared at least 1900 times! It can increase interaction with your app users, if it meets the requirements of your app. If nothing else, users can try answering the questions for fun. Sometimes it happens that quizzes don't meet your business needs—in those cases, you can always turn to some tools to create your own compelling and engaging quizzes and others that would serve your purposes.

- *Virtual goods*: Virtual goods resemble rewards but with longer-term value. For example, you can earn points on a certain mobile app, which you can later on use for making a real purchase. Virtual goods are often used as a part of loyalty programs like with airline flyer miles, which you can later use for payment of flights, specific upgrades, etc. An example that is interesting is PocketPoints—a mobile app that rewards students for **NOT** using their phones in the classroom. Afterward, the students can redeem their points in the local stores or online retailers.

- *Badges*: No matter how old we are, receiving a medal is a great moment for us. This is called recognition, and it is an additional motivation to take on the next challenge. If done right, badges can be a powerful gamification tool to engage your users. One of the examples is an app Kobo—it offers their users these types of rewards, plus you have the ability to connect with other people with the same reading preferences.

- *Leaderboards*: People are competitive souls, and being able to see their name on the list of winners encourages a person to continue. This is great for sports apps where the app tracks people's moves turning them into *"fuel,"* and upon a finished session, a leaderboard is added, which improves the entire experience. The higher the score, the greater the motivation.

- *Progress display*: It is very important to people when they struggle to achieve their goal. Whether it is losing weight or learning a new language, progress display is an excellent way to retain users and support them throughout their journey. A great example is Duolingo—it has a set of gaming interactions that allow users to track their progress and practice their linguistic skills. Another example is the Monitor Your Weight app, which was awarded several times.

Borrowing some elements from games and adding them to your app will help you **increase user acquisition** because people talk and people love to share. It enables word of mouth, and spreading the word about your product will help you bring in new users. It can also help **increase customers' engagement**, resulting in more retention. Once the users realize the potential of your gamified mobile app, it will be a good reason to **share it with their friends**.

Gamification is revolving around the user—gamified elements **increase "stickiness" of your app**, so the result is increased user retention. If you enable an "adventure" with your game elements for your users, you will definitely have **returning customers** who truly enjoy your app.

Provide triggers for your users (notifications, badges, etc.), and it will result in **developing a powerful relationship with your app** and brand in general as per Nir Eyal, the author of *Hooked: How to Build Habit-Forming Products*. Figure 8-3 below shows the key gamification trends.

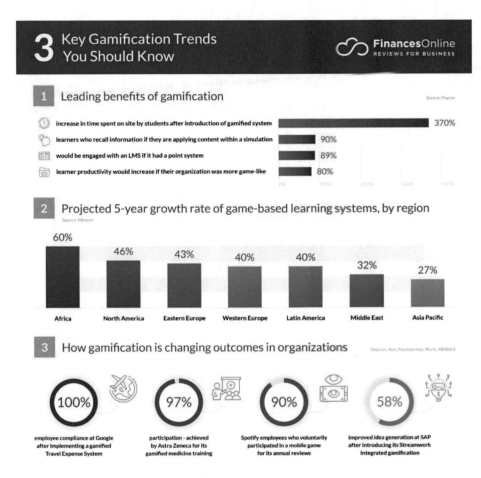

Figure 8-3. *Key gamification trends (financesonline.com)*

And today's marketing and sales are ***all about relationships***.

Bear in mind that gamification is **NOT a makeover tool**—if your app is not working properly, if it's broken, or if the gamification process inside would be pointless, there's no use in trying to gamify it.

Internet of Things (IoT)

Internet of Things (IoT) is a network of devices, sensors, etc. linked via network connectivity. It enables automated collection of consumer data, and since smartphones are widely accessible today, they are a perfect tool for IoT technology.

Benefits

- For example, **wearables** are an integral part of IoT solutions—with Bluetooth or Wi-Fi, you can connect wristwatches or wristbands to your phones, enabling data exchange between the two devices.

- **Healthcare** has also benefited greatly due to IoT solutions—medical devices connected to sensors can obtain health data from patients, which is then further transferred to a mobile app. The same data can later be accessed by doctors or family members in case of emergency. Other use cases in medicine cover clinical or chronic disease monitoring, assisted living, preventive care, etc.

- **Home automation** has been taken to a whole new level. Home appliances like bulbs, heating systems, locks, etc. can now be controlled remotely via a mobile device. IoT solutions can ensure security and also reduce energy consumption. Smart cities use technologies like IoT to improve issues like traffic management or water distribution and many other applications.

- Internet of Things is widely used in **agriculture** today— IoT-based sensible farming uses sensors to monitor field crops (*light, temperature, humidity,* etc.) where farmers can remotely monitor the conditions using their mobile devices. Other uses are precision farming, livestock monitoring, agricultural drones, and smart greenhouses.

- The **retail industry** is rapidly evolving with IoT solutions—RFID inventory tracking chips, digital signage, infrared customer counters, etc. obtain data that can be transferred to mobile apps. Predictive maintenance equipment can help reduce operational costs, while smart transportation and stores along with demand-based warehouses can help with efficiency increase.

- Some future trends of IoT are related to **self-driving cars**/vehicles, routers equipped with more security, and **smart grid** and energy solutions.

IoT enables businesses to execute required operations **more efficiently and at less cost**. Collecting relevant data with help of social media, video surveillance, or mobile Internet can help the businesses **understand consumers' preferences better**. If applicable, IoT solutions can help companies **monitor the most productive hours**, for example, hence scheduling meetings or certain tasks during those hours for more efficiency.

IoT technology helps users in performing transactions via mobile card readers and similar. Users can keep track of their transactions and such data, making the entire experience seamless.

Such a technology can help you cut down costs and reach more data-driven decisions. The data insights can be further analyzed for research purposes, just keep an eye on the key IoT trends as shown in Figure 8-4.

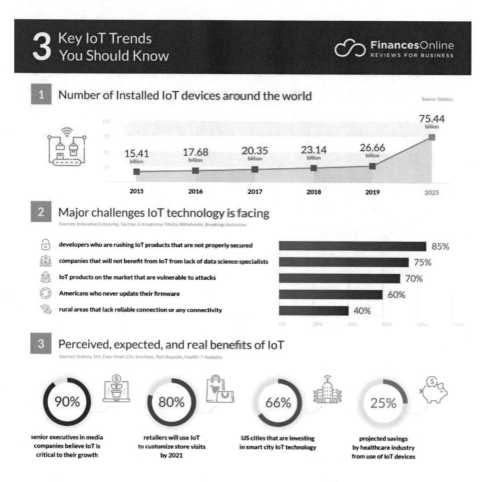

Figure 8-4. *Key IoT trends (financesonline.com)*

Beacon Technology

Beacons are tiny transmitters allowing communication with other devices through Bluetooth connection. The right combination of a beacon device with your mobile app helps you expand your customer base, accomplish inviting product display, and create a clear mapping.

Benefits

- Beacon technology is an excellent choice for retail and similar businesses as they can **send notifications on special offers** when a device enters the vicinity of a store within a few meters. You can add **cookies that help track customers' preferences** and interests and send targeted ads for maximizing conversion rates.

- Payments are an extremely important part in the user experience journey. You can **incorporate beacons into payments** in Apple and Android payment apps.

- Beacons enable **easier detection and prevention of fraudulent activity** like identity fraud, data phishing attacks, etc. with help of Machine Learning and Big Data technologies. Major devices with Google and Apple Pay are able to link via Bluetooth as well as Wi-Fi to perform the payments.

- Retail companies can **send offers to customers** when they are near a product or a certain shop or offer collectibles only for them if they visit certain parts of your store and so on. Companies can also provide **detailed maps of a shop** or a mall with facilities and parking information.

- Real estate companies can notify prospective clients when they drive past a house available on the market or give property information in open houses. With beacons, agents can gain insight into a customer's property buying experience and obtain details like when the buyer viewed the house information and others.

- The healthcare sector can offer **a view map with all** the facilities, elevators, or guides while detecting your current position. Beacon technology can also help **promote any event taking** place or **search the institution** (e.g., *hospital*) by department, facility title, specialist, and much more.

- Education institutions can also utilize beacon technology and provide **guided campus tours to new students** and even reach a higher level of students' safety by notifications about the students' location. Bookstores can **provide information of the costs or discounts** on certain books.

- Travel and hospitality companies can use beacons to **expedite security checks** at airports or subways, provide **keyless entry to hotel rooms**, offer discounts at their restaurants and clubs, **notify customers on the events** nearby, etc.

- Logistics and fleet management companies can **track assets** more easily with help of beacon technology. Warehouses can identify the assets and create a map of each through huge locations. The same can be applied to parking lots as well. **Location detection** of cargo on the move helps employees load and unload shipments much easier under closed spaces.

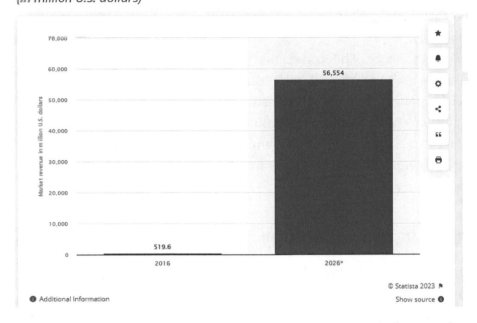

Beacons technology market value worldwide in 2016 and 2026
(in million U.S. dollars)

Figure 8-5. Beacon technology market value worldwide (Statista)

Retail and similar industries require stable management, and with beacons, a retail store can **notify users about the latest offers**, discounts, personalized promotions, and similar details. Beacons can **improve operations** of warehouse monitoring, easy navigation, inventory management, the security system, and more.

Beacons can be used **for user experience** in a wider perspective. For example, an energy drink used beacon technology to gather data on the audience at a music event. The data was used to formulate an algorithm that could indicate the impact of the product on different customers. This particular test was not performed on a mobile app, yet it showed the magnitude on how you can combine and integrate technologies and devices for more valuable insights.

Integration of a mobile app and beacons can **redefine personalized services**. Custom software development can greatly aid businesses identify their customers' preferences and promote their products and services adequately.

A great feature of beacons is that they contribute to reliability of this technology, it supports both mobile platforms (*iOS and Android*), giving you the opportunity to reach a vast number of users.

Beacon technology can contribute to many industries like hospitality and tourism, sports, event management, security services, or navigation tracking. Beacon technology can simplify life for your users if applied and used properly.

Blockchain Technology

Ever since its introduction, blockchain technology has opened up a world of fresh and amazing opportunities in the IT sector.

In 2018, everyone heard about the buzzing word "cryptocurrency" and mostly saw the use of blockchain technology in creating "smart contracts" also. But in reality, blockchain is more useful than one can imagine.

For instance, with the proper utilization of blockchain, it is possible to **build decentralized mobile applications**.

"*Decentralized mobile apps*" or Dapps are basically applications that are not owned by anyone, but also impossible to shut down, nor do they have any downtime.

Blockchain's secure architecture makes this technology suitable for a wide range of enterprise mobile apps. Any business using a mobile app to record or share transactional data can benefit from blockchain.

Benefits

- Supply chain management can easily **track a product history and process from manufacturing to sales**, while end users can use a mobile app to **access transaction details** like quantities, shipment notifications, warehousing specifications, and similar.

- Real estate can also benefit from this technology—mortgage companies can use it to streamline the purchase process and **ensure documents are accurate and valid**.

- Healthcare companies can **process insurance claims, share patient records, or manage medical trials** with the help of blockchain.

- Government organizations can provide **access to public records, payment of property taxes, or voting** to individuals from their mobile devices.

- One of the major reasons blockchain is considered to be revolutionary is the **security of data**. It provides the most advanced cryptography, which can be a great benefit for mobile app development companies. Offering superior security for a mobile app will be a benefit to the **fintech or stock market**. Blockchain provides **easy access to information and transparency**, which is also beneficial.

- It offers a **high degree of transparency**, and since stored in more than one location, it is more secure and more accessible when required. It is quite unlikely that a single event will affect multiple locations; thus, it is perfect for financial applications or any dealing with banking, **smart contracting**, or storing academic records.

In simple words, blockchain is predicted to contribute more in the mobile app market by nurturing the place for decentralized mobile apps, as shown in Figure 8-6 below, just in the same manner bitcoin blockchain did for money.

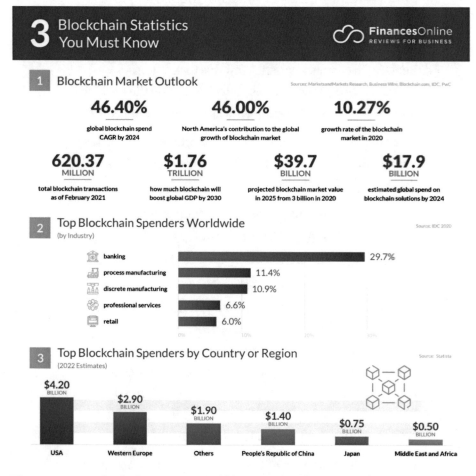

Figure 8-6. *Blockchain trends (*`financesonline.com`*)*

5G Technology

4G LTE has delivered huge benefits to customers — streaming, high-definition videos, fast Internet browsing, reliable video conferencing, and online gaming.

Now the mobile applications are edging toward 5G technology. In terms of mobile apps, it means a great boost to your **app load speed** and **faster mobile Internet**. But that's just some of the benefits. Some others include latency cut to near zero and maximized connection density.

5G has the power to greatly expand how data is transferred and enable a wide range of new applications that will go beyond the smartphone. Figure 8-7 below shows forecasted number of mobile 5G connections globally from 2021 to 2025.

Benefits

- Industry applications will improve customer experiences, increase revenue opportunities, or **reduce total costs**.

- Healthcare 5G use cases will enable doctors and patients to **stay connected**, while retail can use it to **manage inventory and stocking in real time**.

- Smart farms will use more data and less chemicals. As 5G makes it easier to **scale networks for IoT devices**, health monitoring will be enabled, resulting in **more accurate data** and **disease prevention with livestock**.

- Manufacturing companies will use 5G to enable predictive maintenance, helping with cost control and **minimizing downtime** as well as **analyzing industrial processes** with a higher degree of precision. Traditional Quality Assurance processes can be improved with sensor technology and AI.

- Logistics and shipping require **keeping track of inventory**, and it may be expensive and complex. 5G offers better infrastructure communication—**fleet monitoring and navigation** will become easier to scale. It can also be combined with Augmented Reality for the system that would identify and **flag potential hazards** without distracting the driver.

Forecast number of mobile 5G connections worldwide from 2021 to 2025 (in billions)

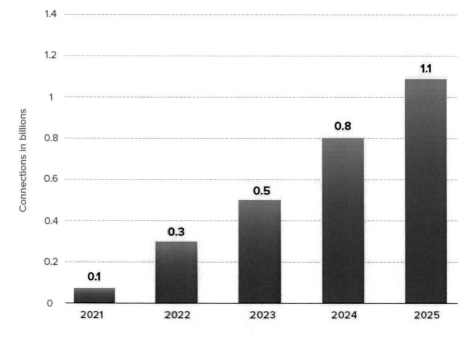

Figure 8-7. *Impact of 5G on mobile apps (appinventiv.com)*

8.3. The Best Mobile App Features per Different Industries

In this section, we will focus on different industries and how you can exploit diverse features for your mobile app to help your business become more efficient and your employees more productive.

Let's dive in.

Transportation and Logistics

The transportation industry is always on the go—their nature of work is "*mobile.*"

Smartphones with several built-in technologies (*high-resolution cameras, scanners, GPS capabilities, memory power, RFID, Wi-Fi, Bluetooth,* and more) that can integrate with other third-party apps can help transportation companies run a successful and efficient organization with the help of mobile applications.

Features

- *Offline support*: Be prepared for the eventual absence of connectivity, especially in transportation that takes place on the road. If you include offline support in your app, you'll enable automatic upload of information, ensuring your employees can complete tasks in the required timeframe.

- *Driver and vehicle tracking*: Locating vehicles/drivers/ cargo is highly important in the transportation industry. Technologies such as *GPS, location-based services (LBS),* and *telematics* enable tracking moving vehicles with real-time updated data, history, and communication. You can monitor the activities of your vehicles on Google Maps or other map services to track the route and sync it with your main system.

- *Shipment tracking*: This feature allows you to log carrier and delivery information. Transportation companies require a logistics management app allowing employees to attach photos, documents, and even barcodes, thus simplifying the data collection process.

- *Driver/job log*: Provide a daily log of activities—recording the mileage traveled, number of pickups and deliveries, total hours of work done, etc. Your staff can record such information by mobile forms in real time without too much data entry. It enables a transparent work process with inputs on/off duty, sleeper berth, any remarks, etc. With GPS-enabled mobile apps, the entire process is updated by a real-time interface with map display capabilities. Instant notifications can deliver messages about changes or updates within the routes or tasks.

- *Payroll management*: A mobile app can record the login and log-out inputs, job hours, and data entries. GPS location stamps ease calculations regarding working and overtime hours—you can automate the entire payroll and expenses with help of a mobile app and avoid unnecessary discrepancies or errors.

- *Common features*: Usually, transportation mobile app development can have three modules:

  - *Customer panel*: User registration/authentication, profile creation, selecting a vehicle, schedule booking, driver contact, tracking shipment, getting a fare estimate, canceling a reservation, etc.

- *Driver panel*: Driver registration/authentication, shipper/freight details, managing requests, GPS, payment, etc.

- *Admin panel*: Dashboard, shipper/driver/ dispatcher management, fleet and payment management, etc.

If you'd like to give your users a better user experience, add some **additional** features like *maps, booking systems, price display*, and others. You can go beyond and include **extra** features like *in-app chat, driver safety, multilingual driver support, real-time analytics,* etc. if you wish to offer even more.

With a mobile app, you can **better manage your fleet**—since traffic is one of the major reasons deliveries are late, transportation companies need to be aware of the traffic situation at all times. A mobile app is able to deliver such information and **provide actual data updates about the traffic situation in real time**, which aids your employees who are on the road.

Tracing cargo is simplified with usage of QR code or RFID or NFC technology. **QR code** is the easiest way as you just need to scan the code for each item using your smartphone—the other technique, **RFID** (*Radio Frequency Identification*), uses the frequency or the radio waves for scanning the goods. With RFID, you have active and passive tags (*tags are fixed to a chip or an antenna*) where active tags have tracking capability of around 100 meters, while passive tags have only 25 meters. NFC or Near-Field Communication technology is based on the same technique as RFID, but the difference is in the distance. NFC tags must be placed in very close proximity with the scanner, so it cannot scan all goods.

A mobile app will help reduce paperwork to a minimum with digital forms and easy access to documents. The data is easily entered into the app and then submitted further instead of the good old "*snail way.*"

Being able to complete an **online booking** is a great asset for your transportation or freight company as it's entered into the mobile app and easily synced with your main system.

No more last-mile problems as all you need to do is to scan the good's ID and enter the details such as time of delivery, location, and quantity. Monitoring inputs and outputs by your delivery staff is simplified, allowing them to update information in the app by sending delivery alerts.

A **cashless system** is another benefit since online payment systems can be implemented in tracking and delivery apps to facilitate the entire process. You can choose the most suitable payment system as per your users' preferences as there are different types of payment.

Such an approach will help efficiency, since per FinancesOnline.com (Figure 8-8), there are 29 billion miles truckers usually drive partially or completely empty as in the following.

Figure 8-8. Number of miles driven with empty trucks (financesonline.com)

The mobile app for the transportation industry doesn't cost as much as not having one utilizing a mobile app can be a great benefit not only to your company and employees who can carry out their duties more easily but also to your customers as you can build trust, which will lead to boost of your company's credibility.

Ecommerce and Retail

Although a large portion of sales is made via a mobile app, only a few retailers actually offer a mobile app!

Considering such an opportunity at the market, any ecommerce business wishing to increase their sales should seriously think about building a mobile app.

When you're an ecommerce, you must create a great customer experience for your buyers as it is critical for your success.

Features

- *Security*: With an ecommerce app, you ask a lot of details from your customers like bank account details, credit card info, address, and so on. A poorly secured app can easily be breached, leaving personal information and financial data unprotected. This is the reason you should always provide a high level of security in an app to **keep their information safe**.

- *Multiple payment methods*: If you wish to play smarter, ensure that your payment method covers credit cards, debit cards, net banking, and ewallets being at the top. During the process, always keep in mind the new GDPR for mobile apps as every app is obliged to communicate which data of the user is collected, why, and what it will be used for. If your app doesn't comply with the regulations, you can face fines.

- *Quick login and checkout*: If you do not make your login/checkout process quick, you will definitely lose customers. A good idea is to make social media login via Gmail, Facebook, etc. so that customers can easily log in without bothersome inputs. Here are some examples of how you can ensure a streamlined service:

  - The button **"PAY"** or **"CHECKOUT"** must be in a thumb-friendly zone.

  - Allow the users to modify their order.

  - Use autofill fields.

  - Add a social "SHARE" button for users to share your products or services online.

- *Consistent and simple navigation*: Keep your mobile app consistent—consistency can be

  - *Visual consistency*: Buttons, fonts, and color schemes should look identical.

  - *Functional consistency*: Interactive elements (e.g., *navigation elements*) should operate the same way on different screens.

  - *External consistency*: All your products (e.g., *a website and both Android and iOS apps*) should share similar design patterns.

  For example, if your **"Pay Now"** button is green on one page, then it should be green on all other pages as well.

Consistency makes your app easy to use—it eliminates confusion, helps prioritize content, and evokes a positive emotional response with users. The best is to use standard elements like the *tab bar for iOS* or *navigation drawer for Android*.

- *Eye-catching CART button*: The cart button should be always visible where users can add a product without taking them to the cart page, so that they can continue shopping. Product screens should always have a visible and prominent button "***Add to Cart***" or "***Buy Now***," allowing users to easily add or remove the items to or from the cart.

- *One-hand input*: A thumb-friendly zone is a space on the screen that a user can easily reach with their thumb while holding a phone in the same hand.

  Which buttons should be placed in the thumb-friendly zone?

  - Add to cart

  - Proceed button that leads from cart to checkout

  - Pay button at the payment screen

  You can also use the "***Three-Tap Rule***"—not more than three taps for a user to get any of the products they want to buy. Organizing your products in categories will help here, for example:

  - Categories

  - Sub-categories

  - Products

You can also use tags to arrange products into specific campaigns like *"Xmas Sale," "Valentine's Gifts,"* etc. However you decide to proceed, the search bar is essential as it helps users get directly to the products they want. If you want to go the extra mile, you can implement *smart search*—as a user types in the first letters, a number of possible suggestions should be displayed to choose from.

- *Favorites and WISH LIST*: Customers like to browse or pick the best items before they actually make a purchase. Providing an "***Add to favorite***" or "***Add to wish list***" option lets users gather their selection in one place before they decide to buy. Once they decide, customers can revisit their collected lists and decide which one will be the one as per their taste.

- *Auto-suggestion*: Auto-suggestion predicts common search queries and helps customers find products more easily. If you implement app analytics, it will provide you with insights for user behavior like session time, click-through rate, and more. Such data will help you understand buying patterns and provide better recommendations based on their interests, all amounting to higher revenue streams.

- *Prompt customer service*: Facilitating the interaction between customers and representatives is a must-have for any ecommerce mobile app. Providing a communication channel will allow your customers to easily get in touch. Tell your developers to implement such features in your ecommerce app as it will be more likeable by the customers and ensure more downloads, meaning more revenue.

These can help you get an app that really makes a difference in the retailing business and make you successful in your ecommerce journey.

The ecommerce mobile app development process is full of challenges because the process needs to be quick, intuitive, and transparent and it should encourage customers to complete the purchase.

Another way to boost your mobile app is to build your brand. If you want to increase the visibility of your ecommerce brand, then focusing on ecommerce SEO is critical. Proper SEO can provide you not only with the higher ranking but also a strong brand recognition.

Your brand needs to stand out as it's important that shoppers recognize your brand and choose your ecommerce mobile app for their next shopping destination. As per Twilio Segment (Figure 8-9), the future lies in personalized experience for users.

Figure 8-9. *The State of Personalization 2021, statistics on personalized shopping experience (segment.com)*

Manufacturing

With recent advances in IoT and digitization, the entire concept of manufacturing has taken a new leap. The modern technologies help increase productivity and profitability by streamlining complex manufacturing processes at a better pace.

In order to provide the best service and customer experience, while keeping the costs low, many manufacturing, consumer goods, and supply companies are turning toward Agile or Lean manufacturing as per the survey from Foley & Lardner (Figure 8-10).

Figure 8-10. *Global Supply Chain Disruption and Future Strategies (Foley & Lardner)*

Features

- *Real-time data collection*: Increased data collection will help your business prevent release of improper products, avoid injuries, increase efficiency, and more. **DO NOT focus on the amount** of data, but on the quality of data—it must be meaningful to provide you with insights. Try to identify the worst-performing stages in the production or storage process and then adjust and use the analytics to determine your facility's shortcomings.

- *Material and cost tracking*: Staff can record quantities of materials installed through the day and assign them. You can also add options of adding images or videos for a visual record of progress. The barcodes and scans help check the order quality and status and track the product location and delivery status. With manufacturing apps, you can also succeed in cancelation management and input real-time data on changes in CRM or ERP.

- *Time tracking*: Tracking the working hours of the entire team can help assign value to the hours, plus it can help predict labor cost for a project. Communication is improved, helping cross-communication between different departments. In case of any latent issue, an immediate call for assistance helps mitigate downtime, and necessary measures can be taken before the matter escalates. Furthermore, diagnostic capabilities guarantee dealing with any problem that may occur remotely.

- *Planning*: This feature can facilitate defining staff availability for certain tasks and help with production planning—it delivers reports and data on the dashboard where you can get insights into daily, weekly, or monthly production outputs. Predictive analytics is already in use by some consumer goods companies for maintenance activities, resulting in possible maintenance cost reduction from 10% to 40%. Companies can deploy sensors to collect data and use it for analysis (*or comparative analysis*) and determine the optimal time for a certain action (*replacement of*

machine parts, product processing stages, etc.). Such
precision predictions based on thorough analysis can
increase your product quality and lower inventory or
other costs.

- *Analytics and reports*: Analytics will provide an
  overview of your KPIs. You can create and test different
  production schedules to find the best-performing
  production window. You can also generate reports
  showcasing the past and current information on
  how your team or business performs. For example,
  if you produce and distribute polymer solutions (*or
  any other product*), you can adjust your warehouse
  process to analyze sensor data and deliver productivity
  increases. Usage of sensors can significantly reduce
  the time necessary for employees to complete the tasks
  (*scanning the labels, monitoring the storage facility,*
  etc.) and improve product quality control. Quicker
  inputs and more efficient communication reduce
  administrative workload.

- *Inventory management and control*: You can better
  manage products in your stock as it helps you categorize
  products by type, location, serial number, etc. and prevent
  overstocking or understocking. Inventory management
  features will help you process the products even before
  they arrive at your location. Inventory barcoding
  will improve data entry errors, automate inventory
  operations, and enable paperless documentation.

- *Supply chain management*: This feature is vital
  when it comes to procurement. It will streamline the
  interaction with your suppliers, display the cooperation

history, and analyze the supplier performance and contribution to your business model. If related to logistics, you can also manage your logistics suppliers— track rates, routes, contracts, and transactions. Apply analytics solutions including Big Data for warehouse management and data inputs from barcodes, RFID, GPS, etc. These can obtain traffic sensor data, road network, and vehicle data in real time, enabling logistics teams to optimize transportation or delivery processes. Moreover, they can react to unforeseen events (*accidents, blockage*) more effectively. Supply chain optimization software can generally help manufacturers connect the entire manufacturing value chain, from procurement to the final production and delivery.

- *Work and order management*: Order processing includes sales order processing, order management, order fulfilment, billing, etc. You can also create, review, and edit orders as well as deal with work requests (*maintenance work and others*). The system places the request, and depending on the type, the request gets assigned and scheduled for processing.

- *Internet of Things (IoT)*: Some of the benefits of IoT technology in manufacturing are cost reduction, increased efficiency, improved safety, and product innovation. Most companies can make more informed decisions based on real-time information, and coupled with other tech innovations, IoT technology can help manufacturing companies drive more efficient short- or long-term goals. IoT adoption has increased significantly over the past years as manufacturers are realizing its potential and value.

- *ERP system*: ERP systems automate and optimize the company's processes using real-time information. This helps reduce operational costs and prevent any bottlenecks through the operational process. ERP systems provide businesses with real-time access to enterprise data, enabling efficient communication from any part of the world. ERP systems provide quicker communication with vendors or suppliers across the globe while supporting drop ship purchase orders, saving extra expenses and labor. Coupled with forecasting and predictive analytics, ERP systems can help you not only improve operational efficiency but also build a better consumer-friendly brand.

- *Augmented Reality (AR) and Virtual Reality (VR)*: A good example is Walmart, which opened another "test store" in October 2020 for the purpose of implementing AR technology for inventory control. Their application helps employees with inventory control—employees hold up a handheld device, which highlights the boxes ready to go to the sales floor, improving the process so they do not have to scan each individual box. This is a great example of AR used for a more streamlined workflow. There are many more examples of AR/VR use cases, where manufacturers and consumer goods companies offer a complete customer-driven experience, thus increasing their online presence and building a stronger brand.

- *3D printing*: Prototyping with 3D printing is much quicker, allowing designers to fine-tune and test the products quickly. 3D printing made it possible to produce prototypes much quicker than with traditional manufacturing methods, like CNC. It speeds up the process of designing concepts and making changes with 3D prototypes—you can produce them overnight, and they will be ready for testing the next day. 3D printing enables companies to produce complex features, which lead to innovative products, optimized for durability and/or strength. Customization is another benefit of 3D printing because it does not require expensive tooling changes for individual specifications. As data is transferred to the 3D printer, there is no need for other tools other than the printer itself. Zero tooling means printing a variety of designs at no extra production cost.

- *Alerts*: Notifications and alerts are very effective as these prevent waste, optimize the financial processes, and deal with customer expectations.

- *Visual manuals*: Adopting mobile apps reduces the repeated, manual work and eliminates paper-based manuals. The interactive, AR-based instruction via a mobile app guides the employee on how to use the tool at the assembly line. No detached theory and instructions can be updated in real time. The employee works productively and makes fewer mistakes.

With a mobile app or a digitized platform, you will have no more situations when the *"left hand doesn't know what the right hand is doing."* You will **improve quality checks and data accuracy** and prevent chaos at your facility. The apps for manufacturing help **build digital simulations**, cutting down the expenses and to-market time.

Using the manufacturing apps, you get a **birds-eye view of the process** and production. The analytics and dashboards help visualize and analyze information in real time, as well as share it with relevant stakeholders or management. Mobile apps enhance the safety and quality regulation checks and compliance with the security regulations in general.

Wastage of material is also decreased when streamlined procedures are followed for production. This is owing to the accuracy of the product obtained in terms of dimensions and finishing. Errors in production are minimized, and so does the time consumption of each process. Therefore, production goals are attained at a better pace and improved accuracy.

Manufacturing industries like the die casting industry have immensely been facilitated by digitization. Real-time predictive analysis is carried out at each step of the process with the help of the supplied sensors. The sensors are installed within a process cell and **record data to look out for anomalies**, unsatisfactory performance, and any unwanted circumstances that can lead to a decreased efficiency. **Overall forecasting of productivity** and profitability trends is attained by the real-time analysis using sensors.

In addition to improved productivity, **energy consumption is also reduced** by technological means. A green environment is achieved by monitoring and adjusting processes in an energy-intensive industry.

Integrating modern technologies into manufacturing processes leads to increased productivity and, thus, increased profit. Adopting these technologies also helps in attaining better accuracy of a product due to standardized procedures.

The popularity of modern technologies is not surprising owing to the benefits they offer. With a significant decrease in error, increased efficiencies, and less downtime, resources are better utilized in other integral areas of the business to promote its growth and development.

Thanks to the use of this technology, the companies can also design and test new machine parts with less time and costs involved.

Consumer companies should turn to digital transformation and then can hope to reap greater benefits from digital tools.

Implementing digital solutions will leverage the benefits to the company, and in the long run, it will start a new era of manufacturing efficiency.

Supply Chain and Warehousing

The supply chain industry today cannot be imagined without technology—a Warehouse Management System (WMS) is a digital solution helping companies streamline their warehouse activities (Figure 8-11).

Such systems enable companies to maximize their space utilization by coordinating resource usage and material flow. A Warehouse Management System (WMS) can be integrated with other software solutions and improve your business operations to be more efficient.

By getting insights into which products are sold often, you can find other ways to optimize the way you organize your warehouse. You can also track materials entering your warehouse or rearrange the goods so that your best-selling products can be next to the loading dock and accessed easily.

Features

- *Inventory management*: A critical feature including inventory visibility, forecasting, purchasing history, tracking/analysis, and accounting. If you handle specialized types of products, you can benefit from inventory tools like goods tracking and FIFO/LIFO protocols. Make sure that your WMS software offers these features as well: *barcode scanning, cross-docking, cycle counting, inventory reordering, de-kitting, slotting methods, task interleaving, physical inventory count*, etc.

Figure 8-11. *Inventory management techniques (Pinterest)*

- *Cartonization*: This feature is based on the number and size of cartons you have—you can choose standalone apps or modules that are part of ERP systems. This is best to use in warehouses involving multiple distribution operations. It helps analyze the best ways to pack and arrange cartons, thus minimizing labor costs. With this feature, you can run your distribution operations efficiently while reducing overall shipping costs. Besides this feature, pay attention to your WMS app to include the following as well: *container loading, packing workbench, container splitting, container management*, etc. This will greatly help you run your warehouse efficiently and with minimal waste or errors.

- *Automation*: This includes technologies like robotics, AI, and Machine Learning, which can drastically increase efficiency and speed. Robots or automated tools can find and transport your goods without requiring employees' help. These technologies enable accuracy and safer operations from order fulfilment to faster deployment and picking accuracy. No matter the features your WMS can provide, check for the following features as well: *pick-to-light, automated storage and retrieval, maintenance and inspection*, etc.

- *Labor management*: Essential to keep employees on task and discover processes that waste valuable resources. Your staff can maintain online attendance using QR or pin codes for time tracking (tracking hours, paid time off, overtime, etc.). Some other features can include *labor allocation, warehouse safety control, labor cost optimization, employee engagement*, and more.

- *Putaway*: Proper putaway reduces the chances of misplaced items, speeds up the picking process, and leads pickers to the exact location where the item is stored. There are four types of putaway methods according to the *product type, SKUs, purchase order*, and *storage location*. You should strive for the system creation that supports different types of putaway, like the example in Figure 8-12 below.

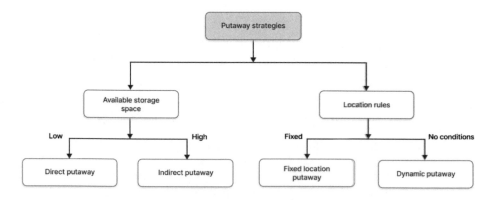

Figure 8-12. *Putaway strategies (mindinventory.com)*

- *Reports and analytics*: When developing your own
  software solution or app, try to aggregate business
  intelligence from warehouse operations. Real-time
  tracking is essential as it lets you view your inventory
  levels and know when you're low on certain products
  or if you have a surplus of certain products. Collecting
  high-quality data will help decision makers change key
  business processes and reach smarter decisions related
  to the strategy. Language, tax, and multi-currency
  features are also important for businesses that operate
  on an international level. Keep an eye on these helpful
  features such as *inventory analytics, performance
  metrics, procurement analytics, discrepancy reports,
  total landed costs*, etc.

- *Billing*: Billing management tracks and captures
  metrics like costs and billable services across multiple
  levels. It includes cost data across activities like
  inbound/outbound logistics, receiving, distribution,
  and warehousing. Some helpful features include
  *order history, multichannel ordering, wholesale orders,
  activity-based billing*, and *order life cycle management*.

- *Shipping*: One of the core functions—if it includes a TMS (*transportation management system*), you can optimize shipments, handle planning, and strengthen execution to improve efficiency. Efficient shipping management will boost customer satisfaction, reduce costs, and provide real-time visibility. Your system should support multimodal and intermodal transportation if your business requires such an approach. When building your product, always strive for integration of the TMS and WMS as you can handle multiple tasks simultaneously including labor scheduling, load building, and goods palletization. Some great features also include *freight procurement, picking and putaway, packing and dispatch, IoT fleet monitoring, goods arrival*, and more.

- *Returns management*: Managing returned products can be a lengthy process, and it is integral to maintain a healthy supply chain. Some companies utilize services of a third-party logistics provider to handle product returns, but the downside can be the up-front cost. If you decide to build your own application, include this module as well as you will be able to handle fulfilment processes as well as returns. Features that can help here are *refund management, return processing and management*, and *return status tracking in real time*.

The WMS has the ability to analyze the **best usage of your storage space** as per tasks and material aspects, thus optimizing your warehouse flow. Such an approach also lessens potential costs, resulting from excessive material movement and retrieval. Digital solutions will help maintain product rotations (FIFO, LIFO, FEFO, HIFO, LIFO) no matter the rotation rule required. Considering the best locations to put your products can also **reduce your operating expenses**.

Automatic update and managing product stock in real time is one of the benefits—it minimizes chances of over-selling and prevents entry of redundant results. Warehousing applications, if used with scanning, RFID, etc., ensure visibility at the location and reduce the situations where inventory can become lost or misplaced within the warehouse. If you integrate ERP, you can provide precise details on how some products perform, thus getting certain forecasting features. With such information at hand, you can make reliable decisions for the company to mitigate any losses.

You can use labor forecasting , allowing the WMS to assign daily tasks and efficiently outline schedules and also optimize traveling time within the warehouse. Scanning items at warehouse entry can eliminate the need to double-check the work, thus saving time and quickening the entire process. The result is **labor, equipment, and space efficiency**, which are optimized by an appropriate work assignment.

Going mobile can assist transition from paper to electronic logging, plus it can greatly **automate internal work responsibilities**. There are many levels of automation—from automated packing, robotics, analytics-driven movements, and more. The WMS helps such strategies by contributing basic elements to record and communicate activities. Sensors, barcodes, voice, and automated carousels can increase output if integrated to a WMS by monitoring packing activity. Implementation of robotics and automated conveyors can streamline your warehouse operations and reduce impediments.

Warehouse workforce can achieve **fast and accurate shipments** by reducing nonproductive activities. This can also help your internal or external partners, allowing them to improve their own operations as well.

Your managers can select zones or batches, thus picking and packing products more effectively. Additionally, customers can **receive early notifications** on shipments and the way the products are sent—such options enable quicker customer order cycle time. A good warehouse solution should also have a proper validation system—it ensures that the correct items are shipped to your customers as too many incorrect shippings can be a real profit killer. Furthermore, barcode scanners prevent mistyping the numbers, which greatly reduces errors.

Understanding WMS analytics abilities requires to watch the core metrics that can help you see a clear picture of your business. One of the examples is the total landed cost for each product, which can provide you with an insight into what drives your revenue. Another important metric to follow is a completed inventory optimization as this data allows you to confirm what stock you have, where to place it in your supply chain, and, generally, how to optimize your inventory budget. Restock analytics enables you to **integrate your orders across multiple levels** (wholesalers, retail partners, etc.) Procurement analysis within a WMS will help you determine vendor costs and quality along with the ability to track their "*historical*" performance. Such performance metrics should track the entire process, from receiving to timeliness of your order completion.

Installing mobile PCs in service vehicles can **improve performance** when using GPS for accurately tracking the vehicle's location. The PCs can help the driver plan the most efficient route and even **provide insight into traffic conditions** or detours to suggest faster routes and prevent traffic delays. Using a mobile PC to record mileage or fuel purchases helps improve accuracy since the driver is less likely to forget. That means **better cost analysis**, including capture of gas taxes. Keeping close track of mileage can help with scheduling fleet maintenance as well, so vehicles will be better maintained and less apt to break down.

Recycling packing materials and reusable containers are great ways to reduce environmental impact and run a greener operation. Using mobile PCs helps you track the dwell time, location, and condition of reusable packaging materials—enabling you to plan replacement cycles more effectively.

No matter if your warehouse is small or large, a WMS will help you increase your profitability and mitigate errors.

That is the very reason you should get started with an advanced Warehouse Management System today, but be careful and consider which choices are important for your own business.

Agriculture

Agricultural companies and farmers across the globe are exploring sustainable methods of increasing productivity to deal with the growing demands and unforeseen events, like pandemic situations.

Today, agriculture is entering the "*data and connectivity*" revolution. Data standards, software solutions, smart irrigation, drones, Internet of Things (IoT), etc. are all the technologies that made their way into the agriculture industry.

AgriTech is applying technology in agriculture for improving crops and efficiency. The IoT in Agriculture (IoTAg) represents a specific use of technology where agricultural operations become linked.

Nowadays, there are technologies like AI, advanced analytics, sensors, and other emerging technologies that can help improve efficiency of precision irrigation, increase crop yields, and build sustainability for crop cultivation.

However, if you do not have a strong connectivity infrastructure, this cannot be possible. If connectivity is implemented successfully in agriculture, the precision farming market could grow at around 15% CAGR from 2019 to 2025 as compared with 2018 (Figure 8-13).

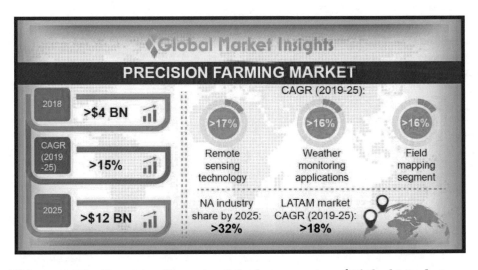

Figure 8-13. *Precision Farming Market overview (Global Market Insights)*

Despite this, agriculture still remains less digitized when compared with many other industries worldwide. To address such challenges, agriculture must adopt a digital transformation that should be supported by connectivity.

In recent years, many farmers have started to consult data about essential variables like soil or crops/livestock condition and weather, but only a few had access to advanced analytics tools that would help them turn such data into actionable insights. In less-developed regions, the majority of farmwork is still manual, with almost no connectivity.

Current IoT technologies are able to support simpler cases, such as monitoring of crops/livestock, but in order to achieve full connectivity in agriculture, the industry must fully utilize digital applications. Digital applications include high bandwidth, high resiliency, low latency, and support for a number of devices offered by frontier connectivity technologies like 5G, LPWAN, or LEO satellites. Figure 8-14 below shows the connectivity spectrum and value proposition.

Exhibit 1

Over the next decade, existing connectivity technologies will advance and totally new ones will emerge.

Connectivity spectrum and value proposition

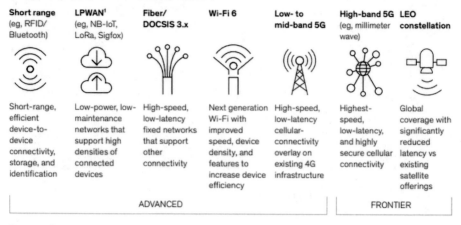

Short range (eg, RFID/ Bluetooth)	LPWAN[1] (eg, NB-IoT, LoRa, Sigfox)	Fiber/ DOCSIS 3.x	Wi-Fi 6	Low- to mid-band 5G	High-band 5G (eg, millimeter wave)	LEO constellation
Short-range, efficient device-to-device connectivity, storage, and identification	Low-power, low-maintenance networks that support high densities of connected devices	High-speed, low-latency fixed networks that support other connectivity	Next generation Wi-Fi with improved speed, device density, and features to increase device efficiency	High-speed, low-latency cellular-connectivity overlay on existing 4G infrastructure	Highest-speed, low-latency, and highly secure cellular connectivity	Global coverage with significantly reduced latency vs existing satellite offerings
			ADVANCED			FRONTIER

[1] Low-power wide-area network.

Figure 8-14. *Connectivity spectrum and value proposition (mckinsey.com)*

However, connectivity coverage is expanding almost everywhere, and the solution is to develop more effective digital tools for the industry.

Features

- *Crop and livestock monitoring*: If farming companies integrate weather data, including irrigation details, nutrient analysis, and more, it can boost yields, enabling them to predict and identify deficiencies more accurately. For example, if sensors monitoring soil conditions can communicate via LPWAN (see Figure 8-12), they can guide sprinklers and adjust watering or nutrient dosing.

IoT sensors can provide images from remote land areas, helping farmers with early warnings on potential diseases or pests. Farmers can improve crop revenue if monitoring crops for quality characteristics like fruit color, size, etc., thus optimizing the entire harvesting process.

It is similar for livestock—preventing disease outbreaks and spotting early warnings are crucial in livestock management. Chips, body sensors, and already popular ear-tag technology allow farmers to monitor livestock's heat and pulse among other indicators, detecting early signs of illnesses and preventing herd infection. Ear-tag can also trace location, allowing farming companies to trace their livestock in real time.

Ecological responsibility is important for every industry, and implementing environmental sensors can automate adjustments in ventilation or heating in barns, thus improving living conditions of livestock.

IoT networks are still being developed as they cannot support bandwidth and connection issues; however, 5G and Narrowband Internet of Things (NB-IoT) are good candidates to resolve the problems.

- *Pest management*: Up to recently, most farms used visual signs for monitoring pests.

Although it was a common practice, it was inefficient and expensive, and in such conditions, farmers lacked the ability to identify the early warnings and react to an outbreak in a timely manner.

Pest management can include the following: *collecting and accurately interpreting data on pests' activity for more efficient treatment, integrating biosecurity tracking for rapid response across infected areas, the ability to share data with the relevant institutions to enable faster risk mitigation, connection of devices to report specific pest levels,* etc.

All these actions automate monitoring and data collection for farming companies to take more precise countermeasures.

The ability to automate and remotely monitor pests helps farmers maintain good health of their farms.

- *Farm and land management*: This includes identifying and preventing any diseases, application of pesticides and fertilizers, etc. Smartphone applications enable farmers to manage their resources efficiently, eventually increasing productivity. Farmers can record any part of their land data anywhere from their phones. No need for paper-based records, reports, etc. as you can easily record data and manage your land via a digital farm journal or logbook. If speech or recognition technologies are integrated, these processes can gather precise geographical data for further analysis.

- *Imaging and drones (UAVs)*: Satellite imaging, smart drones, and unmanned aerial vehicles (UAVs) assist farmers to collect images and recognize changes to soil/crops, assess irrigation, or spray crops.

  Agriculture has already been using drones with crop spraying, but the new generation of drones can survey crops/livestock over vast areas and send real-time data to other connected devices. With the addition of computer vision, drones are able to analyze field conditions and notify on any necessary interventions like fertilizing, spraying pesticides, etc. where crops need them the most. Drones can also plant seeds in remote or inaccessible areas, reducing the costs of equipment and manpower.

With inputs from imaging, farmers can conduct crop forecasting and improve their production management. Integrated mapping can help identify issues and improve yields and time spent on certain agricultural processes.

For livestock, it can be a valuable tool to deliver information on stock conditions, preventing disease outbreaks.

- *Autonomous farming machinery*: Implementation of smart autonomous machinery allows farmers to operate different equipment simultaneously, without human assistance. Such automation reduces time and costs where more precise GPS controls (*paired with sensors*) could advance the usage of smart machinery.

Autonomous machines are more efficient and precise than human-operated ones, and using them can help generate fuel savings and higher crop yields.

Modern farming companies complete most processes with the help of a computer or a mobile app. It allows them to access the data on the go, communicate with other key people in the supply chain, and provide them with a chance to place an order at any time.

Such an approach leads to higher customer satisfaction as consumers can access information and conduct transactions directly online while ensuring that the products will arrive fresh from the farm.

These faster solutions give farming companies a competitive edge in the world of revenue and business.

- *Smart irrigation*: As per EU report from 2019, approximately 70% of total volume of water usage is used in agriculture irrigation. A certain percentage of that is lost whether due to land runoff or inefficient usage methods.

  Smart irrigation offers a solution—IoT platforms that closely monitors and adjusts water utilization on the farms. Platform dashboard combines various data like timing, reducing waste, and soil analysis, enabling farmers to adjust their irrigation requirements.

  Implementing smart irrigation lowers the chances of human errors with the automated systems such as smart valves.

  Smart irrigation can reduce water wastage and improve the quality of crop growth through precision agricultural practices.

- *Building and equipment management*: The advancement in IoT technologies along with chips and sensors to monitor and measure certain levels of silos or warehouses can automate ordering, reduce inventory costs, and more.

These solutions can improve *"shelf life"* of products and reduce losses by monitoring and automatically optimizing storage conditions. Such monitoring conditions and usage of equipment can also reduce energy consumption.

Predictive maintenance systems paired with computer vision or sensors can curb repair costs and extend machinery/equipment life at the same time.

- *Weather climate monitoring*: Climate changes and extreme weather conditions create further uncertainty for farmers. That is where technology comes to help with weather predictions for farmers to manage their crops and farms more efficiently.

  For example, if the farmers know that a blizzard is coming, they can pick a crop a day early to prevent any losses.

  The ability to manipulate inputs enables the farmers to better control their crops. For example, if rainfall increases, they can adjust their irrigation systems for less water to balance wet conditions.

Mobile technologies enable brightness analysis, which helps estimate the amount of light plants receive as well as radiation levels based on real-time GPS data.

To recap, some of the must-have features when developing farming apps (according to your own needs) should include *satellite field monitoring, field mapping, fertilizer application, crop maps, weather precipitation with alerts for excessive weather conditions, crop rotation data and productivity, vegetation indices, zoning as per productivity, advanced reporting with comparisons of real-time and archived data, irrigation needs,* and more.

Agricultural companies today strive to make farm running sustainable—farmers seek ways to lower inputs and moderate resource consumption to least harm the environment.

Farm management mobile solutions immensely contribute to precision and sustainability in agriculture. All these technologies helping agriculture can assist in increasing sustainability that the industry needs to thrive in the future.

Although agriculture has begun its technological revolution, the industry is yet to overcome challenges of deploying advanced connectivity.

The sustainability in agriculture depends on technological transformation, and if you embrace it, you can position your business to thrive in an AgriTech-driven future.

Hospitality and Tourism

The meaning of "*business as usual*" within the hotel industry has quickly evolved. Guests nowadays demand more personalized options so that accommodation can meet their requirements.

Some of the trends in this industry lead to improvements and savings for the hospitality sector, while others change how hotel owners plan their management structure and workforce requirements. The hotel industry has begun to implement technology to improve guest experience, streamline their business operations, manage post-COVID protocols , and improve the overall communication between employees and guests.

With technology today, consumers are able to do their own research on destinations, accommodation facilities, schedules, or the money needed for a tour. These are available on the Internet, and it has become essential for budget and decision making.

Technology provides the opportunities, tools, and solutions that hospitality needs to create memorable experiences and lead to positive growth in the industry. As per Finances Online, 81% of travelers want greater digital customer experience from hotel brands (Figure 8-15).

Figure 8-15. *Statistics on digital customer experience in hospitality (financesonline.com)*

Features

There are a lot of travel management tools on the market, so what must-have features should you develop for your custom mobile app?

- *Booking*: After choosing the destination, users will look for their travel tickets and accommodation online. If you integrate a booking system in your tourist app allowing users to compare prices or get reminders about any hotel deals or discounts, it will greatly improve user experience. Make it intuitive and easy to use for your users with clear guidance and visible buttons. You can collaborate with various hotels or flight companies to provide exclusive offers to your users.

- *Geo-tracking services*: The integration of a GPS location service is an important feature in travel application development. Such services can detect users' location and quickly provide the nearest results. This feature enables you to provide various kinds of services a tourist can avail on a trip.

- *Weather forecasting*: You should be prepared in case users book flights and end up in a plan change due to weather changes. To prevent such situations, develop travel mobile applications with real-time weather forecast updates. While creating their travel itineraries, users can see the upcoming weather predictions and plan their trip accordingly.

- *In-app language translation*: This is one of the tricky features to implement, but keep in mind that in most cases, tourists are not familiar with the local language of the places they visit. Including such a feature can boost user experience although it may be on a costly side. Users would be able to look up the word or scan texts for visual translation or voice translation.

- *Currency and time converter*: These are essential travel mobile app features. Users will have no headaches when converting their currency to the local one, as they will already know the currency exchange rates. This feature can also track the current and past fluctuations of the currency rates. Another valuable feature is the time converter due to crossing time zones. It will clear any confusion among users as they will be able to check the correct clock time for different time zones across the world.

- *Location-based emergency services*: This feature helps tourist users to contact emergency services no matter the time and place. While developing the app, you can include the phone number and services based on the locations as it will allow users to get a nearby service.

- *Cab service integration*: Every travel app user requires transport service when moving from their destination to the hotels or famous tourist places they would like to visit. You can cooperate with local cab services and integrate their services and offer your users such services via the mobile app.

- *Digital wallet*: In most cases, users do not like to carry cash with them, or they do not want to go through the exchange hassle. Digital wallet facilitates digital payments and ensures secure transactions. Users can shop and make their payments for reservations or hotels via digital modes of payment. Provide your users with a rich experience as it is not only time saving but also very secure. Security is the crucial question in the digital world of online transactions, so pay attention to use the latest encryption technology to prevent any unpleasant situations.

- *Customer support*: Travel management solutions like any of the available tools out there should make things easier, not more difficult. It's why having customer support that's inclusive of the cost of the software is essential. Having to pay extra for any support that's needed can often increase your overall spending, making it less cost-effective as a result. As consumers, 54% say that they have higher customer service expectations according to Microsoft. That means that your expectations should be no different. When developing a travel management tool, it should include support without you having to spend any extra dollars. That way, you can confidently budget for your business, knowing there are no hidden fees or charges that you'll face.

- *Loyalty programs*: A lot of airlines and accommodation companies will offer loyalty points or rewards schemes to help save you money and upgrade your client's or employee's experience. Never underestimate the benefits that loyalty schemes and points can bring. A lot of businesses will miss out on these for the sake of it lengthening the booking process. However, with the right management tool, it doesn't need to be complicated. There are lots of benefits that come with loyalty points, and it can open up to new opportunities for your employees or, alternatively, for impressing your clients.

- *Travel itinerary generator*: This is one of the most demanding features in the travel industry. This feature helps users create a complete travel plan by just adding the location they want to visit. You can add existing tourist attractions or landmarks to generate a tour plan for users. Such a complex algorithm may sound difficult, but with the help of professional mobile app developers, it can be integrated.

- *Social messaging/review*: Social media integration plays a major role in application development. Real-time social media will let your users interact with friends and contacts by sharing their experiences. In case you do not want social feed or messaging services, you can rely on a review system, allowing users to review a place and share their experience with other travelers. It creates awareness and helps improve hospitality services.

In case you wish to track your internal travel expenses within your business, some features you can find beneficial may be the following:

- *Customizable travel policies*: For any business, travel can vary from conference events to long-haul trips to meet overseas clients. An essential feature to look out for is the ability to customize your travel policies. Depending on your criteria, your travel policies can be adapted to suit the needs and requirements of your business. For example, you might have a differentiation between what C-Suite employees get for their expenses vs. what your low-level managers get. There may be certain limits to budgets available when it comes to each of the departments within the organization. This is a useful feature because it helps keep everyone on the same page, avoiding any overspending that could contribute to financial issues.

- *Travel spend analytics*: Reporting and analytics can be handy when it comes to business travel. It can be useful to have the data available so you can make necessary changes to improve efficiency and save money. With travel spend reporting, you'll be able to track the spend by department or individually, and you can see the amount of travel spent in relation to a campaign, client, or event in particular. Data of any kind can be helpful for a business to understand how they're spending their money on business travel and what similarities or problem areas need addressing. You can also make comparisons between your expenditures whether that's between two quarters or years.

- *Data encryption and security*: It's safe to say that security and how data is handled within a business is crucial. It's not just your business data that is at risk but also any customer or client data you hold too. Forty-five percent of Americans have had their personal information compromised by a data breach in the last 5 years, so it's certainly a concern. When it comes to the travel management tool itself, you want a service that's going to protect your data with the right encryptions and level of security. For security features, a lot of consumers are looking for two-step authentication and, in the case of mobile apps, facial recognition and pin codes for extra protection. In a time where data breaches are rife, it's a key feature to look out for.

- *Easy-to-use booking system*: Not all businesses will have account managers or roles within the organization that oversee the booking of travel. You may have a number of employees all needing to use the booking system, and so with that in mind, it needs to be simple to navigate, with an easy-to-use interface. A great user experience is also going to keep your employees happy. You want a system that everyone's going to love using and that won't cause more complications and stress. It's worthwhile to have management systems that you can try out, perhaps selecting a group of regular travelers that can try out the platforms before

committing to one fully. With this initial research
and trialing in place, you'll find the right fit for your
business.

- *AI learning travel habits*: Machine Learning technology
  is becoming a lot more popular, just like automation
  has implemented itself in many areas of business.
  Having a travel management system that has AI
  technology could be useful when it comes to learning
  the company's travel habits. With this technology, it can
  quicken the booking process, which makes it easier for
  your employees to book travel. Artificial Intelligence is
  something that 86% of CEOs are saying will become the
  mainstream technology in office beyond 2021.

- *Expense tools for seamless integration*: Managing your
  travel expenses is good to keep within your company's
  budget and your internal departments' individual
  budgets. Having a management tool that integrates
  seamlessly with your expenses can save a lot of admin
  on your employees' part. You may find a system that
  offers its own expense system that you might find useful
  to transfer over to. However, if you are happy with your
  current expense tool, then look for an external API that
  you can integrate easily. Tracking expenses is definitely
  important as a business. It helps improve cash flow and
  will also allow your business travel to continue without
  any financial bumps in the road.

Today's hospitality businesses are faced with many demands, and
they must meet those needs and requirements. Customers a.k.a. guests
want their experience to be quick and hassle-free—they want a seamless,

tech-driven, and contactless experience in the hotel industry. Technology has added a boost as people are able to **access information about the locations** they want to visit and get more insight into additional activities that can be done.

Introducing automation will help the hospitality business to lower the **time-consuming** and repetitive tasks, allowing companies to be **more productive** on a day-to-day basis. For example, hotels can automatically send notifications (or emails) to their guests offering coupons or special promotions, hence gathering customer feedback.

Technology has become an important cornerstone in the modern hospitality industry since many customers expect streamlined services.

That is the very reason more and more hospitality businesses adopt technology to **improve customer experience** and keep their business running smoothly.

Hotels can create their own apps where guests can find useful information such as nearby venues, restaurants, sightseeing sites, and more. Having a mobile app can allow hotel staff to connect with the guest via messages (*SMS, Viber, WhatsApp*, etc.), send them personalized offers or promotions, and much more.

Another good choice can be **chatbots** powered by Artificial Intelligence (AI) that can help hotel staff to keep up with the customer's demands and take off certain burdens from their plate.

Chatbots can carry out many tasks like responding to FAQs, making reservations, ordering food, or processing payment—chatbots offer timely service that makes customers happy and willing to return to your hotel. Hospitality places (*hotels, motels*, etc.) that already utilize chatbots have reported benefits like increase in direct bookings, streamlined check-in/checkout service, and 24-hour reception.

Technology has greatly affected the way of communication—today, many hotels use communication platforms to **enable cross-department communication** in order to respond to the guests' requests more efficiently.

Many hotels have systems that automatically save guests' preferences and notes (*their preferences during their last stay, extra pillows or not,* etc.), so in case the same guests return, the hotel staff can accommodate them adequately. Such a **personalized approach** (Figure 8-16) is necessary as it makes the experience much better for your guests.

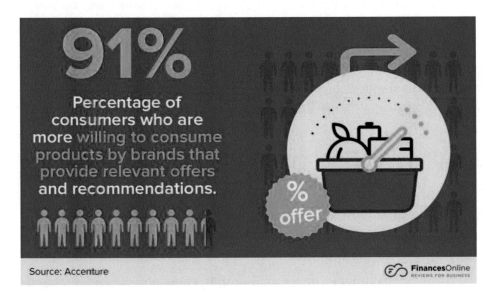

Figure 8-16. *Statistics on relevant offers in hospitality* (*financesonline.com*)

Another strategy can be **social listening**—it is a strategy including monitoring digital comments or statements in order to understand what customers say about your brand. Social listening enables companies to determine customer sentiment and **collect feedback on the customers' preferences**. There are many social listening tools for you to choose and implement this strategy successfully— "*word of mouth*" in online society is still the most valuable type of recommendation since it comes from real people.

Hotel management companies need to embrace new technological ideas if they wish to stay relevant and operate efficiently.

People that travel always like to stay in touch with their family or friends, and that is where technology opens up a world of opportunities that the hospitality industry can take advantage of.

If brands take this opportunity, it can make them really stand out, leading to greater growth within the hospitality industry.

A travel management tool can provide a lot of assistance for your business when booking travel both domestic and international.

Whatever size your business is, there are numerous benefits that can come from investing in this software.

Banking and Finances

Speed and convenience are the two main features customers expect from any service today. In order to better understand customer needs and offer high-quality service, many businesses launch their own apps, and banking institutions are no exception.

Providing customers with a mobile app is a new normal for banks and financial facilities nowadays if they wish to keep pace with the dynamic trends of the banking industry (Figure 8-17).

Although each financial institution has its own policies and ways of operating, most of the desired features within a banking mobile app are common for each financial facility.

Features

- *Advanced security and fraud alerts*: Mobile banking requires strong security features and not just signing in with a PIN or a password but rather multi-factor authentication and biometrics. Besides being secure, the process must be fast and easy. Although multi-factor authentication and biometrics are the most common, they are also "hackable." To boost your app's security, you can enable PIN and password encryption and hashing, limit the number of login attempts, store PINs and passwords on a server of the source code, use two-factor authentication with SMS for outside app payments, and more.

- *CORE banking features*: A CORE banking system is a centralized platform enabling banks to quickly execute key activities like transactions, updating user accounts or financial records, customer relationship management (CRM), and others. Many banks adopted this system as it can handle large volumes of transactions without interruption in functioning of the banking products.

- *QR code payments*: QR technology has quickly spread among diverse industries including the banking industry. Customers can directly purchase any products they like contact-free, which was extremely valuable during the recent pandemic. Banks integrate QR code scanning technology into their apps, allowing more freedom to their customers with their preferable payment options.

- *Bill payments*: One of the basic features enabling users to pay any bill just by tapping a few buttons. If you upgrade it with some other features, you can boost user experience. For example, a banking app can integrate automatic bill payment to avoid any payment issues, notifications on activities that occur on the bank account, payment history tracking for spending habit control, and much more.

- *Mobile check deposits*: The fintech industry has introduced portable scanners based on OCR (*Optical Character Recognition*) technology—it helps with mobile check deposits. With a mobile device, users can scan their checks and send the documents with a digital image and recognized text to their financial institution. The deposit data goes straight to the user's account, and users do not have to come to a branch to perform a simple task.

- *Peer-to-peer (P2P) payments*: A convenient way to transfer money to someone else's account via a mobile app. This feature enables users to split up a bill in a restaurant or pay for any services used. There are many payment systems such as PayPal, Venmo, Apple Pay, and many more that make money transfers quick and easy. The recent P2P method enables payments with cryptocurrencies based on blockchain—it transfers funds between bank accounts from different parts of the world at much lower cost.

- *ATM locator*: If users need to find the nearest ATM or a bank branch quickly, the branch locator within their mobile app will get handy. These features can also provide additional information like the working hours and others, thus enhancing the customer experience with the bank brand.

- *Chatbots*: Smart AI bots have been used by banks for some time now as they bring a more personalized approach while increasing service efficiency. Using chatbots, users do not feel overwhelmed with repetitive tasks—bots provide faster service obtaining more details from the users.

- *Personalized money management insights*: Today's technologies like Artificial Intelligence can turn simple services into an add-on for your business. Based on bank statistics, this feature can provide money management tips like the most profitable loan schemes based on users' income, where to invest money, etc. Users can use these insights to track everyday spending habits or check personalized reports.

- *Voice assistants*: Several banks are already offering AI-powered customer service. Users are serviced by virtual assistance, making it easier to get immediate help for diverse banking tasks. Some examples are Erica of Bank of America, which helps with everyday banking and others. U.S. Bank Smart Assistant helps users monitor their accounts, analyze spending, and manage transactions. Another example is Capital One Eno—which helps monitor transactions to prevent fraud by providing virtual credit card numbers for shopping online and alerts people on spending habits.

- *Check balance without logging*: Some banks make it easier for their users to check their bank account without having to log into their account. Examples of this are Wells Fargo FastLook, enabling users to see their bank account balance via one swipe, while another example, Citi Mobile Snapshot, provides a quick overview of your bank or credit card summary. There are more examples like Discover Bank Quick View and Bank of the West Quick Balance. Thus, think about this kind of feature if you wish to attract and retain more users.

Banks and financial institutions can **learn more about their customers** and better plan their marketing campaigns with a mobile app, as it **reduces the cost of provided services**.

Mobile banking is **more secure** than online web banking due to multiple layers of authentication and protection. As clients tend to handle more transactions via mobile phones, the result may be an **increase of your bank revenue** generated by mobile.

Paperless benefits to mobile banking not only help protect the environment but also **reduce postage costs** for banks.

Banking apps **reduce human errors** and let your clients manage their own finances in a smarter way while you **have better visibility** of bank processes and **address service issues instantly**.

Mobile provides **push and in-app notifications**, which significantly improve the communication. Those notifications are personalized alerts notifying users about certain actions—these can **improve customer relations** with your brand if used properly.

If banks want to learn more about their customers' habits and preferences, the mobile is the right way to go. Mobile banking apps enable banks to collect feedback, thus **improving the overall customer experience**.

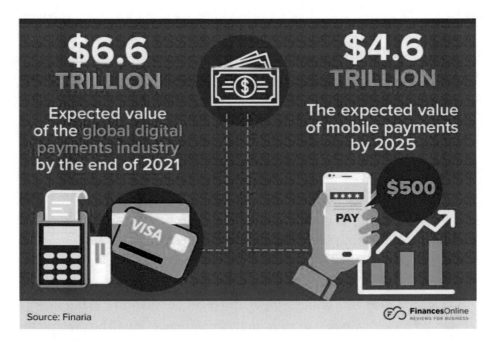

Figure 8-17. *Expected value of global digital and mobile payment (financesonline.com)*

Banks are going digital to take advantage of technological innovations, becoming stronger and more trustworthy. Today, the most competitive banks offer their clients mobile banking—the ability to complete the financial transactions via their smartphones or tablets.

In order to keep up with growing demands of clients, both digital and legacy banks must continue to adapt to mobile market trends.

BONUS: How to Promote Your Mobile Banking

If you want to motivate your banking mobile app adoption, explore the hurdles standing in customers' way. If you wish for your adoption to be effective, try to implement both online and in-branch strategies.

Let's see some of the best practices to promote your mobile banking application.

Offers and Incentives

Think about what is in it for the customers.

People usually need a slight push, so think about the benefits of giving your mobile app a try.

You should try to figure out what to offer in order to meet the requirements of your customers—such a strategy can result in success when promoting your banking mobile app.

Adjust It for Everyone

Do not forget about older people or people with physical disabilities— carefully choose a plan that includes all demographic groups, and you may be surprised.

If you want to attract both younger and older generations, make sure that your offers are valuable to your targeted audience. It will be difficult to attract or retain people if the app is slow or complicated—the whole point is convenience and ease of use, so make sure your app delivers exactly those features.

Empower Your Frontline

A great chance to promote your mobile banking app is when the clients visit your banking branch—you can walk them through how to complete their transactions via mobile.

That means that your frontline staff must be familiar with your mobile app. Your staff that interacts with your customers regularly must be able to use your app and help customers with any issues that customers may have.

If you want to cover all angles, you can offer help to people to download your app or set it up physically in your bank, while online you could provide a tutorial on your website.

Onboarding users and showing them the simplicity of your mobile banking app are the best way to drive them to use your app.

Create a Resource Center

One of the major obstacles to adopting your banking mobile app is the confidence when using your mobile app. If clients do not believe they can complete their transactions correctly and securely, they will not use it.

You can overcome this issue by providing product simulations on your website. Such an approach will properly onboard your users and give them a chance to educate themselves on how to use your app without any difficulties.

Any mobile app needs an onboarding section, so providing various forms like tutorials, step-by-step guidelines, or a FAQ section or chat will surely help in educating people and supporting the adoption.

Run an Interactive Marketing Campaign

Interactive campaigns are a great way to promote your mobile banking app. You can raise awareness, educate your clients, and incentivize mobile app adoption all within a single experience.

Interactive campaigns create engaging experiences that encourage people to stick around—you can also combine experiences (e.g., games) with awards that customers will care about.

Engaging techniques will give your customers a reason to engage with your app in the long run, building their usage habits and getting insights into their preferences.

A Single-Feature Emphasis

The biggest mistake of many marketers is to try to explain **ALL** benefits at once. Highlighting specific features at a time will allow customers to focus only on one feature and more easily process the information.

If you send marketing emails promoting your banking mobile app, always highlight only the most important details to engage users to keep reading.

Step-by-step guidelines and checklists will help with this approach, but remember to stay clear of heavy text in your emails or newsletter.

Social Media for Promotion

Today's consumers want to be able to manage their own accounts, spendings, or savings, and that is the reason financial institutions focus a lot on mobile technology.

A new approach would be to promote mobile banking as a lifestyle itself—such an approach will create a better sense of integration between the bank's products and their mobile apps.

However, be careful with social media and ads so as not to trigger a counter-effect. Step into the users' shoes and give them a good reason to download your new app—once you perceive things this way, consider adding it to your strategy.

If you want to differentiate your mobile app from your competitors', your marketing team should convey the value proposition of your mobile app into the messaging that will support the lifestyle of your customers.

Mobile banking is definitely the future of the banking industry.

If you wish to increase adoption, try to figure out the reasons your clients hesitate and help them with the onboarding—only if you offer them unique value will they try your mobile app.

Customers today are bound to their smartphones, and they expect their banks to be at their pocket's reach. If you combine useful features with high-security standards, it will enable you to retain both new and existing customers.

Key Takeaways

- If you want your mobile app to perform better, you can boost it by several good practices like optimizing images, reducing app size and server load, and third-party sources. Apart from these, you can also boost your mobile app by implementing some of the modern technologies like *Augmented Reality*, *geofencing*, *chatbots*, *gamification*, and more as it will surely improve the user experience and increase stickiness of your mobile app.

- There are many modern technologies you can integrate with your mobile app for better results like the following:

  Artificial Intelligence: With features like image recognition, visual search, chatbots, and much more, AI can help make the business operations automated and easier for your workforce. It can also increase customer engagement and conversion rates.

  Augmented Reality: Helps increase "stickiness" of your app, meaning increased customer retention with interactive advertising, 3D display, geo-targeted campaigns, and more.

  Gamification: A great way to engage your users through rewards, points, quizzes, or virtual boards. It can help increase user acquisition and engagement, triggering a powerful relationship with your mobile app.

IoT: This technology is applicable in many industries from healthcare, agriculture, and retail to home automation. It enables you to run your business more efficiently at less cost, while with the insight from the gathered data, you can understand your users' preferences better.

Beacons: Tiny transmitters that can help with geo-targeted campaigns to track customers' preferences, send notifications, or help customers navigate the stores with a detailed map of a shop, warehouse, etc.

Blockchain: Blockchain does not have to be used only in finances. This technology ensures easy access to information and transparency since information is stored in more than one location. It also helps with smart contracting and secure sharing of the important data.

5G technology: This technology enables increase in app load speed and faster mobile Internet. It can help reduce total costs for your business or scale it quickly for any IoT devices you may have. Keeping track of your assets, monitoring overall business operations, and efficiency are simplified with 5G.

- Different industries require a bit different features in order to fully serve the business operations within the specific industry branch. Most of the mobile applications have similar features, but when it comes to particular business tasks, features start to differentiate. For example, here are some features you should have per specific industry:

Transportation: Offline support, real-time tracking (fleet, cargo, drivers, etc.), job log, payroll management, etc., while some additional features may include booking systems, maps, in-app chat, multi-lingual driver support, and more.

mCommerce: Features include a high level of security, multiple payment methods, quick login and checkout, visible CART button, auto-suggestion, and customer support.

Manufacturing: With smart manufacturing today, features can greatly differ. Some features can include real-time data collection, tracking of materials/costs/time, analytics and reporting, supply chain management, ERP systems, alerts, and more.

Supply chain: Features include inventory management, automation, labor management, putaway, billing, shipping, returns management, etc., as these can help with the best usage of your resources and facilities.

Agriculture: Depending on the nature of your business, features can include crop/livestock monitoring, farm/land management, autonomous machinery and drones, smart irrigation, and weather monitoring.

Hospitality: The hospitality industry needs to invest into technology for better business results. Features you may add to your mobile app include booking, geo-tracking services, currency/time converter, digital wallet, loyalty programs, and a review/rating system. If you wish to track your internal travel expenses, keep in mind additional features like customizable travel policies, spend analytics, AI learning travel habits, and similar.

Banking: The banking industry deals with sensitive information like finance or personal data; thus, those apps have to be highly secured. Some features you should consider are advanced security and fraud alerts, CORE banking features, QR code and bill payments, chatbots or voice assistants, peer-to-peer payments, as well as personalized money management insights.

Index

A

A.C.A.F. customer loop, 206
Access to a diverse talent pool, 281
Accounting/finance
    FreshBooks, 23
    Gusto, 24
    QuickBooks, 23
    Wave, 23
Action cohorts, 263, 264
Agile methods, 291
Agriculture, 346, 350
    agricultural companies, 354
    AgriTech, 346
    building and equipment
        management, 352
    climate changes, 353
    crop and livestock
        monitoring, 348
    digital transformation, 347
    ear-tag technology, 349
    ecological responsibility, 349
    farm and land
        management, 350
    farm management, 354
    IoT networks, 349
    IoT sensors, 349
    IoT technologies, 347
    smart irrigation, 352
    sustainability, 354
Airbnb app, 184
Alpha testing, 54
Analytics, 20, 25, 55, 60, 137, 187,
    219, 228, 334, 342
App development
    activities, 53
    app idea, 51
    beta testing, 54
    feature set, 52
    launching, 54
    maintenance, 55
    mobile app, 56
    wireframing, 53, 84
App development partner, 56
    budget, 45
    companies, 48
    cost-effectiveness, 48
    developers, 45
    innovative approach, 47
    requirements, 44, 45
    social media, 46
    support, 47
    websites, 47

© Maja Dakić 2023
M. Dakić, *Mobile App Development for Businesses*,
https://doi.org/10.1007/978-1-4842-9476-5

V

Printed in the United States
by Baker & Taylor Publisher Services